JOHN KREMER, AIDAN MORAN,
GRAHAM WALKER and CATHY CRAIG

Key Concepts in
Sport Psychology

Los Angeles | London | New Delhi
Singapore | Washington DC

© John Kremer, Aidan Moran, Graham Walker and Cathy Craig 2012

First published 2012

SAGE Publications Ltd
1 Oliver's Yard
55 City Road
London EC1Y 1SP

SAGE Publications Inc.
2455 Teller Road
Thousand Oaks, California 91320

SAGE Publications India Pvt Ltd
B 1/I 1 Mohan Cooperative Industrial Area
Mathura Road, Post Bag 7
New Delhi 110 044

SAGE Publications Asia-Pacific Pte Ltd
33 Pekin Street #02–01
Far East Square
Singapore 048763

Library of Congress Control Number: 2011920516

British Library Cataloguing in Publication data

A catalogue record for this book is available from the British Library

ISBN 978-1-84920-051-6
ISBN 978-1-84920-052-3 (pbk)

Typeset by C&M Digitals (P) Ltd, Chennai, India
Printed in India at Replika Press Pvt Ltd
Printed on paper from sustainable resources

Dedication

To our parents, who first kindled our passion for sport.

Contents

About the Authors

John Kremer is a half-time Reader in Psychology at Queen's University Belfast, where he has lectured since 1980. He combines his academic interest in sport and exercise psychology with practical work with numerous sports, including several national and international teams and individual athletes. His list of publications include *Pure Sport* (2008), *Sport Psychology: Contemporary Themes* (2006), *Psychology in Sport* (1994) and *Young People's Involvement in Sport* (1997).

Aidan Moran is a Professor of Cognitive Psychology and Director of the Psychology Research Laboratory in University College, Dublin. A Fulbright Scholar and Editor-in-Chief of the *International Review of Sport and Exercise Psychology*, he has published extensively on mental imagery and attentional processes in athletes. A former psychologist to the Irish Olympic squad, he has advised many of Ireland's leading athletes and teams.

Graham Walker is a practising educational psychologist who combines his professional work in this field with a longstanding interest in applied sport psychology. Graham has worked with a range of teams and individuals, both amateur and professional, in a diverse range of sports including soccer, golf, tennis, rugby and equestrian sports. He is also a part-time lecturer, at undergraduate and graduate level in applied sport psychology at the University of Ulster.

Cathy Craig is a Professor in Perception and Action Psychology at the School of Psychology, Queen's University Belfast and is director of the Perception Action Research Lab (www.qub.ac.uk/parl). She publishes extensively on motor timing, perception/action and decision making in sport. Much of her work involves using innovative technologies, such as immersive, interactive virtual reality to understand how perceptual based information influences the timing of action.

Foreword

Since the earliest days of competitive sport there has been a concern with how the mental and physical combine to determine sporting performance. In other words, how psychological skills can be harnessed to ensure that performance and wellness is enhanced in both the short and longer term, and for the benefit of all those involved in the wide world of sport. Many centuries later this work has now coalesced into the discipline of sport psychology, a discipline that integrates expertise and diverse contributions from a wide range of backgrounds, both academic and professional, from psychology and sport science, in the pursuit of sporting excellence.

This collection has been brought together to give insight into the current state of play across sport psychology. Divided into seven sections that reflect recognisable fields within sport psychology, the 37 chapters, when read either separately or collectively, should provide the reader with a thorough overview of key issues that currently engage those who work in the field. Furthermore, for those who work with teams and athletes directly it is hoped that the contributions will help give you a grasp of what sport psychology can contribute to your sport, your team, or your athletes.

Our aim was to give an insight into both practical and theoretical considerations but to present the material in a style that was accessible to the novice and expert alike. Each chapter gives insight into how the field has developed, what are the major priority areas today, and what are key findings that can help inform both theory and practice.

While any list of key concepts can be challenged as being incomplete or skewed, we have endeavoured to bring together contemporary international literature under titles that are each discrete, easily recognisable and, in combination, we hope provide coverage of the many fields and perspectives that define modern day sport psychology. We hope you enjoy this collection; we have certainly enjoyed putting it together.

In producing this book we would like to thank in particular Dr Gareth Watson for his contribution to the five chapters that make up Section 6. His help was much valued and appreciated by us all.

John, Aidan, Graham and Cathy

1

Introducing Sport Psychology

1.1: The History of Sport Psychology

Definition: The chronology of key events in the development of sport psychology from its earliest roots through to the present day.

Contrary to popular opinion, sport psychology is not a new phenomenon (Kremer and Moran, 2008). From the time of the Ancient Greeks there is strong evidence to show that preparation for sporting competition has been willing to acknowledge the mental alongside the physical. Indeed, the standard four-day procedure followed by Greek athletes in the build-up to their games (known as the tetrad) incorporated specific time set aside for psychological skills training, including concentration (Day 2) and relaxation (Day 4).

Given the importance that commentators, both paid and unpaid, routinely attach to 'the mind' in athletic performance, it should come as no surprise to learn that the world of sport has long recognised that success will depend on 'total preparation' involving the mind as well as the body. However, despite this tacit acceptance, sport psychology had to wait several centuries before finally being afforded due recognition as an academic enterprise in its own right (Green and Benjamin, 2009), and even today there is still resistance from traditionalists who resent the interference of 'shrinks' in what they see as their unsullied world of sport.

From ancient roots it took until the early 20th century to see the coming-together of the subdiscipline from diverse sources – but not before a number of false trails had been laid. While there had been some interest in sporting personalities, play, motor learning, reaction times and transfer of training around the turn of the 19th century, the individual who is now generally credited with carrying out the earliest systematic sport psychology research is Norman Triplett.

Born in Illinois in 1861, Triplett was awarded his baccalaureate degree by Illinois College (Jacksonville) at the age of 28, followed by his Masters two years later in 1898, and finally his PhD from Clark University in 1900. Although his interests were wide ranging (his PhD was on the topic of conjuring deceptions), it is his Masters' thesis that has become his lasting legacy not only to sport psychology but also another subdiscipline, social psychology. His dissertation was based on archival and experimental investigations of what he coined 'dynamogism' (now known as social facilitation, or the improvement in performance in the presence of others – see **5.25**). The archival research considered recorded cycling times either alone, paced or in competition, while his experimental work involved children winding silk line onto a fishing reel so as to pull a flag around a track. A keen sportsperson (he was one of the first US athletes to run the 100 yards in under 10 seconds) and active supporter of all forms of sport, in 1901 he became Head of the Department of Child Study at Kansas State Normal School (KSNS) where he continued to work until his retirement in 1931, all the while extending his fulsome support to all forms of sporting activity within the college (Davis et al., 1995).

While Triplett had made some important observations, his academic legacy was not strong and until the 1930s evidence of sport psychology activity in the western world was sparse. In contrast, from the late 19th century onwards in eastern European universities there had been more concerted efforts to establish sport psychology as a scientific discipline. The world's first dedicated sport psychology laboratory opening in 1920 at the Deutsche Sporthochschule (German Sport University) in Berlin under Dr Carl Diem, a person who played a positive and significant role in the development of European sport, a role later overshadowed by his involvement as chief organiser of the infamous 1936 Berlin Olympics (later referred to as Hitler's Games).

In the former USSR, from the 1920s onwards both Avksenty Cezarevich (A.C.) Puni (1898–1986) and Piotr (Peter) Roudik played key roles in the establishment of sport psychology (see Ryba et al., 2005). Professor Puni opened a sport psychology laboratory at the Institute of Physical Culture in Leningrad in the 1920s and had a wide ranging interest in both pure and applied sport psychology. At around the same time Roudik established the first Soviet sport psychology laboratory in Moscow (1925), where he focused his attention not on competitive sport but the psychophysiology of motor behaviour. These endeavours reflected in longstanding interests in the psychology of sport that stretched throughout the 20th century in eastern Europe.

It was in that decade that the person now generally regarded as the founding father of contemporary western sport psychology began to carve out his career at the University of Illinois. Born in 1893, Coleman Griffith was a lecturer in educational psychology at the University of Illinois when, with the help of his Dean and mentor Professor George Huff, he turned his sights towards sport psychology. Following his introduction of taught courses in sport psychology from 1923, in 1925 he set up the Athletic Research Laboratory and worked frenetically, writing more than 20 sport psychology articles and two books up until 1931. Sadly, the entire enterprise within the University then came apart for reasons now obscure but perhaps related to the Great Depression, or perhaps because the college's head football coach, the legendary and highly influential Robert Zuppke, failed to see any benefit accruing to his team from all this academic research (Green, 2003).

Disillusioned, Griffith then turned his attention back towards educational psychology, only once returning to sport psychology in 1937 when he was asked to work with the Chicago Cubs Baseball Club by the club's owner, Philip Wrigley. Griffith worked more or less closely with management for three years but the relationship eventually petered out. The Cubs' manager, Charlie Grimm, referred to Griffith as the 'headshrinker', and would have nothing to do with his work (Gould and Pick, 1995) despite the considerable investment that the club had made in recording equipment and the huge investment that Griffith himself made in time, effort and report writing, including detailed analysis of every players' performances, a very early forerunner of what is now so influential in most professional sports, notational analysis or the systematic recording and analysis of performance.

The years following Griffith were fallow for most of sport psychology in the West, apart from a continuation of the longstanding interest in motor learning and motor control on both sides of the Atlantic. In eastern Europe the early work involving competitive sport continued to be studied in European universities, such as Leipzig, often in conjunction with applied research, for example involving the mental preparation of Soviet cosmonauts. By 1960, sport psychologists were routinely working with elite Eastern Bloc athletes, and from the 1970s onwards Olympic competitors from countries including the USSR, East Germany, Hungary and Czechoslovakia used sport psychologists to help with self-regulation, mental practice and imagery (Roberts and Kimiecik, 1989).

It was around this time that sport science began to truly emerge (Massengale and Swanson, 1997) as coaches considered how various disciplines, including psychology, could help improve performance. Ahead of its time, the Brazilian soccer team that won the World Cup in Sweden in 1958 had brought along not only a nutritionist and a dentist but also a psychologist, Prof. Joao Carvalhaes. Carvalhaes conducted various tests on the players to determine their mental toughness, including asking them to sketch pictures of men. From such tests he concluded that the 17-year-old Pelé was, 'obviously infantile. He lacks fighting spirit. He is too young to feel aggression and react in an adequate fashion.' Fortunately the team coach Feola trusted his instincts. According to Pelé's autobiography, 'He just nodded gravely at the psychologist, saying: "You may be right. The thing is, you don't know anything about football. If Pelé's knee is ready, he plays." Which he did' (Pelé, 1977).

Prominent among European practitioners at this time was Dr Miroslav Vanek (Vanek and Cratty, 1970). As well as working directly with athletes, and including the Czechoslovakian team that travelled to the Olympic Games in Mexico in 1968, along with Ferrucio Antonelli, he was instrumental in helping found a pioneering body specifically constituted to further the advancement of sport psychology. This was the International Society of Sport Psychology (ISSP), and its first congress was held in Rome in 1965.

Over the next ten years a succession of other organisations sprang up on either side of the Atlantic including the North American Society for the Psychology of Sport and Activity (NASPSA, 1969), the Fédération Européenne de Psychologie de Sport et des Activités Corporelles (FEPSAC, 1969) and the Association for the Advancement of Applied Sport Psychology (AAASP, 1986) (see **1.4**). However, the driving force behind all these initiatives came not from within psychology but from physical education and sport science, and the major 'players' within sport psychology all came from these disciplines. Indeed, the first body to regulate the practice of sport psychologists in the UK was not the British Psychological Society but the British Association of Sport and Exercise Sciences (BASES, first founded in 1984), and it was not until the late 1980s that the parent discipline of psychology slowly began to take greater interest in sport psychology. For example, the American Psychological Association (APA) formed a separate division in 1987

(Division 47: Exercise and Sport Psychology), and it was in 1993 that the British Psychological Society (BPS) first set in motion the long procedure that eventually led to the creation of a separate BPS division 'Sport and Exercise Psychology' in 2004. Nowadays the discipline's governing bodies are increasingly concerned with regulating the use of the term 'sport psychologist'. For example, in the UK only those who are chartered through the BPS have the right to describe themselves by this title, and currently there are around 200 individuals who are either chartered or are in the process of becoming chartered.

The history of sport psychology has been divided, chequered and tortuous, and it continues to make its mark to this day. Those who did not graduate as psychologists feel disenfranchised now that the parent discipline has attempted to exert greater control, while across sport psychology there continues to be tension between those who 'do' or practice sport psychology, and those who teach or research. Despite these tensions, the subdiscipline continues to grow and flourish.

REFERENCES

Davis, S.F., Becker, A.H. and Huss, M.T. (1995) Norman Triplett and the dawning of sport psychology. *The Sport Psychologist*, 9, 366–375.

Gould, D. and Pick, S. (1995) Sport psychology: The Griffith era, 1920–1940. *The Sport Psychologist*, 9, 391–405.

Green, C.D. (2003) Psychology strikes out: Coleman R. Griffith and the Chicago Cubs. *History of Psychology*, 6, 267–283.

Green, C.D. and Benjamin, L.T. (eds) (2009) *Psychology Gets in the Game: Sport, Mind, and Behavior, 1880–1960*. Nebraska: University of Nebraska Press.

Kremer, J. and Moran, A. (2008) Swifter, higher, stronger: The history of sport psychology. *The Psychologist*, 21 (8), 748–750.

Massengale, J.D. and Swanson, R.A. (eds) (1997) *The History of Exercise and Sport Sciences*. Champaign, IL: Human Kinetics.

Pelé, with Fish, R.L. (1977) *My Life and the Beautiful Game: The Autobiography of Pelé*. New York: Doubleday.

Roberts, G.C. and Kimiecik, J.C. (1989) Sport psychology in the German Democratic Republic: An interview with Dr Gerard Konzag. *The Sport Psychologist*, 3, 72–77.

Ryba, T., Stambulova, N. and Wrisberg, C. (2005) The Russian origins of sport psychology: A translation of an early work of A.C. Puni. *Journal of Applied Sport Psychology*, 17, 157–169.

Vanek, M. and Cratty, B.J. (1970) *Psychology and the Superior Athlete*. New York: Macmillan.

1.2: Practising Sport Psychology

> **Definition:** The translation of sport psychology theory into practice through appropriate professional interventions with athletes and teams.

In the first instance, how does someone become a practising sport psychologist? On the one hand, the trite answer would be 'it is not difficult as anyone who voices an opinion on sport performance by definition becomes a naïve sport psychologist'. These views may not be informed, solicited or even welcomed, but if they have an effect on an athlete's thoughts, feelings or performance, either positively or negatively, then unwittingly that person will already have practised as a sport psychologist. However, that type of spontaneous intervention is quite different from one that has been grounded in the necessary skills, experience and knowledge to make a positive and long-lasting impact for the good of the athlete or team. Good sport psychologists try to sort the wheat from the chaff in terms of helping the psychological work in harmony with the physical in improving sport performance and athlete wellness (Andersen, 2000, 2005).

To ensure that the goods on offer are not damaged, psychology's governing bodies have worked hard to establish strict criteria and regulations governing the use of the title 'sport psychologist'. To become accredited as a sport psychologist in the UK, at the time of writing, you can follow one of two routes. The body that oversees the governance of professional psychology across the UK, the British Psychological Society (BPS), normally requires a first degree in psychology (or a closely related discipline) which qualifies the person for Graduate Basis for Chartered Member (GBC), followed by an approved higher degree related to Sport and Exercise Psychology, followed in turn by a lengthy period of supervised experience. In contrast, the British Association of Sport and Exercise Sciences

(BASES) requires a first degree in either psychology or sport science, followed by a higher degree in the other discipline, together with a period of supervised experience, and there are moves to try to harmonise the two systems.

Today there are a growing number of accredited sport psychologists working across the globe, and the number seems set to continue to rise for the foreseeable future (Lidor and Bar-Eli, 2001). However, operating outside the bounds of these professional bodies, there are a great many self-styled 'sport consultants' who often have no formal training in psychology but who adopt the role of sport psychologist or mental coach. When choosing a sport psychologist, the watch-words for any athlete must be *caveat emptor* (buyer beware) for, as with any profession, the potential to harm as well as help is ever present. Many sportspeople have had difficult experiences with sport consultants whose advice may have been given with the best of intentions but which has lacked the psychological know-how to ensure good quality control.

Having first established the credentials to be able to work with teams and athletes, a great many ways to practice then present themselves. Typically sport psychologists operate in at least three ways: as basic researchers (investigating the science of sport psychology but not necessarily working with athletes or teams); as educational sport psychologists (teaching and educating athletes and coaches); and as clinical sport psychologists (counselling or supporting individual athletes with problems). In reality, many sport psychologists will fulfil all three roles at some stage in their careers, but the primary focus of this chapter will be on those who work directly with sportspeople and teams, in either educational or clinical roles, or a combination of the two.

The distinction between the educational and clinical role can be blurred but was neatly characterised by Rainer Martens (1987) as the difference in the direction of travel of the intervention: either from abnormal to normal (clinical), or from normal to 'supernormal' (educational). That is, clinical sport psychologists will tend to use their clinical training to help address psychopathologies, including emotional, behavioural and personality disorders, while educational sport psychologists will aspire to enhance 'normal' sports' performance through appropriate interventions with both athletes and their coaches. When these two worlds come together, ethical problems can arise. In particular, an intervention may reveal an underlying clinical condition that would go beyond the professional competence of the practitioner, raising serious ethical and professional considerations (see **1.3**).

The work of a clinical sport psychologist is likely to vary depending on the 'practice philosophy' that he or she brings to the intervention (Stainback et al., 2007). This is likely to incorporate personal beliefs and values along with a theoretical paradigm that has been acquired through appropriate training which then reflects in a model of practice and ultimately in particular types of intervention that are used. Given the wide range of perspectives that can underpin clinical psychology, it is not surprising that the types of intervention can vary considerably, including psychodynamic (Freudian), humanist (Rogerian), cognitive-behavioural (CBT) and systems or family therapy. While very different in approach, all rely on a good relationship between client and therapist, and are primarily underpinned by a medical model of intervention.

Educational sport psychologists often are first confronted with 'problems' (e.g. confidence, concentration, stress), but these issues are not typically pathological but instead they are obstacles that stand in the way of optimal performance. Furthermore, while one specific concern may trigger the engagement with a sport psychologist, it rarely remains the dominant issue over time as performance enhancement in more general terms is addressed through a wider array of interventions.

The practice model underpinning a clinical intervention is probably best characterised as medical, aimed at 'curing' or healing the athlete, but over recent years it has become apparent that this model is less effective in helping athletes to truly grow and mature. Instead, it is argued that the goal of the sport psychologist may be different, to carefully nurture independence and self-reliance to a point where the athlete is equipped with the right skills and techniques to be able to self-regulate performance as and when required. That is not to say that there may still be the need to seek out occasional advice and support but this need is likely to diminish, not grow, over time if the intervention has been successful.

In addition, according to Kremer and Scully (1998), the best person to help this process may not be the sport psychologist but rather the person who on a daily basis works most closely with the team or athlete, the coach or manager. This opens the possibility of an alternative model where the coach or manager becomes the primary point of contact but supported in this role by the sport psychologist. This has advantages in many ways, not least because it avoids the player or team potentially being caught in the crossfire between different messages, and at the same time it ensures that the 'naïve psychology' that may have informed the coach's previous interactions has now been cross referenced and balanced by input from sport psychology. In this way the sport psychologist becomes an integral part of the support team used by the coach or manager but is not centre-stage. Indeed, most coach development programmes now include significant elements devoted to sport psychology, and this model then becomes the natural progression.

Robin Vealey (2007) has suggested that apart from distinguishing between educational and clinical approaches, it is also useful to categorise interventions as being either programme-centred (i.e. pre-planned sequence of activities) or athlete-centred (i.e. an interactive, needs-based approach), and also whether the intervention is concerned primarily with performance enhancement or with personal development. The suggestion is that the most successful are not narrowly confined but succeed in addressing not only immediate performance concerns but also broader lifestyle issues, and are tailored to the needs of individual athletes.

Beyond this point the model of intervention will vary depending on the perspective of the sport psychologist and the context. According to Vealey (2007), these include the following models:

- systems for individual, team, organisational and family interventions;
- self-regulatory or cognitive-behavioural models;
- behavioural management models;
- educational mental skills models;
- developmental models;
- sport-specific mental skills models;
- clinical intervention models;
- perceptual training models.

Whichever model is adopted it is likely to follow a particular strategy. Over the years a number of staged practice strategies have been suggested, but all are broadly similar in approach. Among the most popular is Morris and Thomas's (2003) seven-phase model or strategy. The first stage is *orientation*, where the purpose of the intervention is clarified, objectives identified, and commitment determined in relation to performance enhancement. Once the task is identified, the sport psychologist then conducts an *analysis* of the particular sport, followed by an individual/team *assessment* that is completed to develop a profile of strengths and weaknesses. This profile can be based on a number of quantitative and qualitative techniques including psychological tests and inventories, interviews, observations of the athlete performing (via videos, diaries and/or performance statistics) and talking to coaches and significant others about the athlete. The fourth stage is *conceptualisation* through a profile analysis, where the personal characteristics of the athlete are placed in the context of his or her sport. The fifth stage is *psychological skills training*, involving practical skills relating to e.g. imagery, goal setting, cognitive techniques, stress management, attention/ concentration skills, thought stopping and building self-confidence. These skills are then *practised* in the sixth stage before being implemented within competition. The seventh and final stage in this process is *evaluation*, and this considers evidence of performance enhancement, improved personal adjustment and adherence to the psychological skills training programme.

In essence, the seven steps describe the process of action research and while it may appear overly prescriptive, as a general framework for describing the stages that comprise a systematic intervention it is valuable. Beyond this, however, there is a widespread agreement that the cornerstone of a successful intervention must be establishing and developing a trusting relationship with the athlete. This is not to imply that the relationship is equivalent to that between a counsellor and client. Instead, counselling skills may be brought to bear at certain occasions during the intervention but at others times the relationship may be fundamentally different, for example when testing an athlete or instructing in the use of mental skills.

To many athletes and coaches, professional sport psychologists are still viewed with a degree of suspicion, perhaps because of previous negative experiences or stereotypical images of 'The Motivator' type characters, as falsely portrayed in the media. For most practising sport psychologists nothing could be further from the truth, but these stereotypes can be difficult to dispel. However, as the subdiscipline continues to mature and the profession regulates the work of those who describe themselves as sport psychologists, so it is to be hoped that the image will change to reflect reality more closely.

REFERENCES

Andersen, M.B. (ed.) (2000) *Doing Sport Psychology*. Champaign, IL: Human Kinetics.

Andersen, M.B. (ed.) (2005) *Sport Psychology in Practice*. Champaign, IL: Human Kinetics.

Kremer, J. and Scully, D. (1998) What sport psychologists often don't do: On empowerment and independence. In Steinberg, H., Cockerill, I. and Dewey, A. (eds) *What Sport Psychologists Do*. Leicester: BPS Books. pp.75–88.

Lidor, R. and Bar-Eli, M. (eds) (2001) *Sport Psychology: Linking Theory and Practice*. Morgantown, WV: Fitness Information Technology.

Martens, R. (1987) *Coaches Guide to Sport Psychology*. Champaign, IL: Human Kinetics.

Morris, T. and Thomas, P. (2003) Approaches to applied sport psychology. In Morris, T. and Summers, J. (eds) *Sport Psychology: Theory, Applications and Issues*. 2nd ed. Brisbane: Jacaranda Wiley. pp. 215–252.

Stainback, R.D., Moncier, J.C. III and Taylor, R.E. (2007) Sport psychology: A clinician's perspective. In Tenenbaum, G. and Eklund, R.C. (eds) *Handbook of Sport Psychology*. 3rd edn. Hoboken, NJ: Wiley. pp. 310–331.

Vealey, R. (2007) Mental skills training in sport. *Handbook of Sport Psychology*. 3rd edn. Hoboken, NJ: Wiley. pp. 287–309.

1.3: Ethical Issues

> **Definition:** A code of moral and professional principles and associated procedures to ensure that practising sport psychologists act responsibly at all times and in accordance with the profession's primary values and ethical standards.

In keeping with other branches of applied psychology, sport psychologists must adhere to professional principles and codes of conduct in relation to their work and engagement with clients. The codes attached to each international professional body may vary but all are governed by similar principles. As one example, the American Psychological Association (APA) recently (July 2010) revised their ethical principles and code of conduct. The revised guide includes the following five general principles, along with 10 standards:

- *Principle A: Beneficence and Non-maleficence* – Psychologists strive to benefit those with whom they work and take care to do no harm.
- *Principle B: Fidelity and Responsibility* – Psychologists establish relationships of trust with those with whom they work.

- *Principle C: Integrity* – Psychologists seek to promote accuracy, honesty, and truthfulness in the science, teaching, and practice of psychology.
- *Principle D: Justice* – Psychologists recognize that fairness and justice entitle all persons to access to and benefit from the contributions of psychology and to equal quality in the processes, procedures, and services being conducted by psychologists.
- *Principle E: Respect for People's Rights and Dignity* – Psychologists respect the dignity and worth of all people, and the rights of individuals to privacy, confidentiality, and self-determination.

While it would be expected that any professional sport psychologist would have little difficulty in adhering to these principles, the special nature of sport psychology interventions do present real and significant challenges that must be addressed in order to balance effective practice with ethical good practice (Sachs, 1993; Moore, 2003; Andersen, 2005). Unfortunately, history would suggest that many previous interventions may not have achieved this balance.

In a survey of 508 professional and student members of the Association for the Advancement of Applied Sport Psychology (AAASP), Petitpas et al. (1994) asked respondents to indicate their engagement with, or aware-ness of, the existence of 47 different behaviours, 24 of which were deemed to be ethically controversial (e.g. 'Including athlete testimonials in advertising', 'Using profanity in your professional work', 'Serving concurrently as coach and sport psychologist for a team', 'Being sexually attracted to a client'). In a further open-ended question, participants were asked to describe ethically challenging or troubling incidents that they or a colleague had faced in the last two years. Of the 89 incidents mentioned, 78 referred either to General Standards (e.g. providing services without training, engaging in dual role relationships, failing to make referrals), or to Confidentiality (e.g. coaches who want information on athletes, responding to coaches who abuse their athletes). While acknowledging the real difficulties faced by practitioners out in the field, the authors nevertheless concluded that many reported practices could correspond to violations of APA Ethical Standards, and hence recom-mended that all applied sport psychologists should routinely be trained in ethical considerations and how to deal with ethical dilemmas.

A follow-up, on-line survey of AAASP members was issued subsequent to the publication of the AAASP ethics code in 1992 (Etzel et al., 2004). This survey found fewer examples of controversial behaviour but more differences within the sample (e.g. men v. women; professionals v. students;

certified v. non-certified consultants; PE v. psychology background), suggesting on the one hand that awareness of ethical issues had been raised since the earlier survey, but on the other hand flagging that there were now worrying inconsistencies in knowledge/awareness/practice across the membership.

As to what makes sport psychology so unique within the discipline, there a number of issues that warrant close attention relating to the consultant/athlete relationship (Kremer, 2003), and these will be discussed later. While being unique in certain ways, applied sport psychology is not exceptional in others, including the need to base the intervention on a good personal relationship with the athlete or team. In common with other client/consultant relationships, by its nature, it will be characterised by a power imbalance and hence has the potential to become abusive.

In order to begin to operate according to clear ethical standards there is a need to identify a sovereign regulating body, and this can present immediate problems given the fractured history of sport psychology (see 1.1 and 1.4). Within the UK, some practising sport psychologists would regard themselves primarily as sport scientists but with a specialism in psychology and so align themselves with the British Association of Sport and Exercise Sciences (BASES). Others would see themselves as psychologists but with a specialism in sport, and be chartered as sport psychologists under the aegis of the British Psychological Society (BPS) and hence are bound professionally by its ethical code (Kremer, 2003).

This can obviously lead to confusion and divided loyalties as to which professional standards apply. In the US this issue has been avoided as all those who work as sport psychologists, including the broad church of sport counsellors, therapists and consultants, have agreed to adopt the American Psychological Association's (2010) revised Ethical Standards. This includes those members of the North American Society for the Psychology of Sport and Physical Activity (NASPSPA) and AAASP who may not belong to the APA, nor necessarily be trained or qualified as psychologists.

Within the UK and Ireland, the picture is rather murkier as potentially three separate bodies (BASES, BPS and the Psychological Society of Ireland [PSI]) can claim to govern the work of sport psychologists and each currently operates according to separate codes of conduct. The BPS most recently updated its code in August 2009 to coincide with the date from which regulation of activities of UK applied psychologists fell under the governance of the Health Professions Council (HPC).

All practising sport psychologists should be guided by the code of ethical conduct as agreed by the professional body or bodies to which he or she belongs, and should regularly keep up-to-date through a working model of reflexive practice (Moore, 2003; Anderson et al., 2004). While it is unlikely that the guidance offered from each body will be contradictory, from a practical, ethical and legal standpoint where there are differences then common sense would dictate that the more rigorous code should be adhered to.

Having established a set of guiding principles for practice, a number of authors have gone on to describe the special ethical characteristics attaching to a sport psychology intervention (Biddle et al., 1992; Sachs, 1993; Moore, 2003; Andersen, 2005; Pope and Vasquez, 2011), and these are summarised below.

Confidentiality and Allegiance – In the first place many interventions are set up not by the client (the athlete) but by a third party (e.g. the coach, manager or parent), immediately creating the possibility of divided loyalties with regard to confidentiality. This dilemma is familiar to many applied sport psychologists and can undermine the personal relationship with the athlete unless handled carefully. The 2009 BPS Code states that psychologists should 'Restrict the scope of disclosure to that which is consistent with professional purposes, the specifics of the initiating request or event, and (so far as required by the law) the specifics of the client's authorisation.' (p. 11). From the first meeting it is important to establish ground-rules with the athlete, followed by an open and honest discussion of the nature of the relationship, and including the rules of confidentiality, with all those involved (see Andersen et al., 2001).

Competency – This can become problematic where an intervention opens up issues which are beyond the professional expertise of the sport psychologist. This could include the need for: a) other sport science specialisms (e.g. biomechanics, physiology); b) knowledge of the sport or c) psychological competence. In relation to the first two areas then common sense must prevail in establishing the extent of 'knowledge and expertise boundaries', and being disciplined not to move beyond that point. In relation to the third area, Heyman and Andersen (1998) suggest the following three criteria should be used to establish when the issues are of a clinical nature and deserving of a referral: how long a problem has existed, its severity and its relationship with other life events; unusual emotional reactions (e.g. depression and anger); lack of efficacy of traditional performance enhancement interventions.

While the list of issues which have the potential to become problematic is considerable, any of the following may warrant a specialist intervention: eating disorders; drug and alcohol abuse; psycho-pathology/personality disorders; anger and aggression control; identity issues and sense of self; sexuality and sexual orientation; relationship issues.

To help deal with such situations quickly and effectively it is useful to have an established network of contacts, although recent research would suggest that many sport psychologists are disturbingly reluctant to pass clients on (Gayman and Crossman, 2006). For those applied sport psychologists who are trained in counselling and/ or clinical psychology the boundaries of competence will be broader, but even here there may be particular issues which arise which are beyond their experience and once more a referral network that is readily to hand is likely to be useful.

Dependancy, Attachment and Abuse – Any one-to-one counselling relationship has the potential to be problematic, especially when the athlete comes to depend overly on the person providing him or her with specialist or expert knowledge. To counter this danger, the fundamental goal of the intervention should be clear from the start. The sport psychologist is not setting out to foster long-term dependency but rather to empower and equip the athlete with a set of skills and knowledge so that he or she can become independent and in control of future life events (Kremer and Scully, 1998). These matters aside, where a relationship begins to become unprofessional or dysfunctional then the onus falls on the sport psychologist to take whatever steps are necessary to remedy the situation, including terminating the relationship if necessary.

Use of Psychometric Tests – The use of psychometric tests in applied sport psychology has attracted some attention over the years. Lay people can often place uncritical faith in results obtained from such tests, reinforcing the need to use tests sensibly and ethically. Where tests are employed, it is important that the measures are appropriate, that their psychometric properties are robust, that they are used for the purpose and population for which they were designed, and that they are not used to inform selection procedures. Interpretation of the results and subsequent feedback must be appropriate and written consent should be obtained for the release of any data.

Drugs, Cheating and Illegality – When a sport psychologist becomes aware that a client is using drugs or any illegal means to enhance performance, does this create an ethical dilemma? The answer should be 'no', because it would be difficult to imagine how any meaningful intervention could continue in such circumstances.

REFERENCES

Anderson, A.G., Knowles, Z. and Gilbourne, D. (2004) Reflective practice for applied sport psychologists: A review of concepts, models, practical implications and thoughts on dissemination. *The Sport Psychologist*, 18, 188–201.

Andersen, M.B. (2005) 'Yeah I work with Beckham': Issues of confidentiality, privacy and privilege in sport psychology service delivery. *Sport and Exercise Psychology Review*, 1, 5–13.

Andersen, M.B., Van Raalte, J.L. and Brewer, B.W. (2001) Sport psychology service delivery: Staying ethical while keeping loose. *Professional Psychology: Research and Practice*, 32 (1), 12–18.

Biddle, S., Bull, S. and Seheult, C. (1992) Ethical and professional issues in contemporary British sport psychology. *The Sport Psychologist*, 6, 66–76.

Etzel, E., Watson, J. and Zizzi, S. (2004) A web-based survey of AAASP members' ethical beliefs and behaviors in the new millennium. *Journal of Applied Sport Psychology*, 16 (3), 236–250.

Gayman, A.M. and Crossman, J. (2006) Referral practices: Are sport psychology consultants out of their league? *Athletic Insight: The Online Journal of Sport Psychology*, 8 (1), 47–59.

Heyman, S.R. and Andersen, M.B. (1998) When to offer athletes for counseling or psychotherapy. In Williams, J.M. (ed.) *Applied Sport Psychology*. Mountain View, CA: Mayfield Publishing. 359–371.

Kremer, J. (2003) Ethical considerations in sport psychology. In Lavallee, D. and Cockerill, I. (eds) *Counselling in Sport and Exercise Contexts*. Leicester: BPS Books. 18–26.

Kremer, J. and Scully, D. (1998) What sport psychologists often don't do: On empowerment and independence. In Steinberg, H., Cockerill, I. and Dewey, A. (eds) *What Sport Psychologists Do*. Leicester: BPS Books. 75–88.

Moore, Z.E. (2003) Ethical dilemmas in sport psychology: Discussion and recommendations for practice. *Professional Psychology: Research and Practice*, 34, 601–610.

Petitpas, A.J., Brewer, B.W., Rivera, P.M. and Van Raalte, J.L. (1994) Ethical beliefs and behaviors in applied sport psychology: The AAASP Ethics Survey. *Journal of Applied Sport Psychology*, 6, 135–151.

Pope, K.S. and Vasquez, M.J.T. (2011) *Ethics in Psychotherapy and Counseling: A Practical Guide*. 4th edn. Hoboken, NJ: Wiley.

Sachs, M. (1993) Professional ethics in sport psychology. In Singer, R., Murphey, M. and Tennant, L.K. (eds) *Handbook of Research on Sport Psychology*. New York: Macmillan. 921–932.

1.4: Organisations, Sources and Resources

> **Definition:** Organisations, sources and resources devoted to the science and practice of sport and exercise psychology

Sport psychology can be defined as the application of psychological theory and methods to the understanding and enhancement of athletic performance (Kremer and Moran, 2008). As the history of this discipline is well documented (see **1.1**), it is sufficient to note here that empirical research on mental aspects of athletic performance is at least as old as psychology itself. Unfortunately, despite this research tradition of over a century (Green and Benjamin, 2009), the field of sport psychology is difficult to define precisely. This imprecision is due, in part, to the 'twin-track' nature of the discipline. To explain, sport psychology is not only a growing field of mainstream psychology but is also a key component of the sport sciences. Not surprisingly, therefore, sport psychology organisations may be found both in psychology and in sport science. Against this background, here is an alphabetical list of the main contemporary sport psychology organisations and their respective mission statements, along with key publication resources for members (where such information is available).

AMERICAN PSYCHOLOGICAL ASSOCIATION (APA)

APA Division 47 (Exercise and Sport Psychology, founded in 1986) seeks to further the clinical, educational and scientific foundations of exercise and sport psychology. Applied service interests include: promoting best practices in mental training techniques; ethical considerations in sport psychology service provision; practitioner self-care; and clinical issues. Areas of scientific inquiry include: motivation to persist and achieve; psychological considerations in sport injury and rehabilitation; counselling techniques with athletes; assessing talent; exercise adherence and well-being; self-perceptions related to achieving; expertise in sport; youth sport; and performance enhancement and self-regulation techniques. Among its resources are an official newsletter (*Div47 News*) which is published three times a year (Spring, Fall and Summer) and convention .

ASSOCIATION FOR APPLIED SPORT PSYCHOLOGY (AASP)

AASP (founded in 1986) aims to promote the science and practice of sport and exercise psychology. It advocates the application of psychological principles that have been supported by research in sport and exercise. It is an interdisciplinary organisation, drawing from the fields of exercise and sport sciences as well as psychology. AASP provides opportunities to share information-related theory development, research and the provision of psychological service to consumers. Among its resources are:

- Journal of Applied Sport Psychology
- Journal of Sport Psychology in Action
- AASP Newsletter
- Member Directory
- Position Statements

BRITISH ASSOCIATION OF SPORT AND EXERCISE SCIENCES (BASES)

BASES offer a number of interest groups, one of which is the Sport Psychology Interest Group (SPIG) whose objective is to promote the progression of evidence-based practice, support innovative research and establish stronger communication links between sport scientists with an interest in the field of sport psychology. In particular, SPIG aims to:

- promote sport psychology as a field within sport science in relation to both research and applied practice;
- establish a network of sport psychology researchers and practitioners in the UK with a common interest in the psychological aspects of sport performance;
- provide a forum for members to develop and discuss theories of best practice when working with athletes;
- provide an opportunity for collaboration between researcher and practitioners as a means of furthering knowledge in our field;

- establish effective working relationships with key organisations and associations such as the British Psychological Society (BPS) and the Association for Applied Sport Psychology (AASP);
- contribute to continuing professional development of members.

BRITISH PSYCHOLOGICAL SOCIETY (BPS)

The BPS Division of Sport and Exercise Psychology (DSEP, established in 2004) represents the interests of psychologists working in sport and exercise settings and aims to further the development of sport and exercise psychology. It draws its membership from a broad range of psychologists including those working in academic settings and professional practice. The Division was formed in 2004 in response to the increase in academic status and public recognition of sport and exercise psychology and ensures that members who practise and offer services within sport and exercise psychology are qualified and trained according to the Charter, Statutes and Rules of The British Psychological Society. Among its resources are:

- DESP journal – *Sport and Exercise Psychology Review*.
- *How to become a Chartered Sport and Exercise Psychologist* – For students of psychology, there are four steps to becoming a Chartered Sport and Exercise Psychologist. First, one has to obtain a BPS-accredited undergraduate qualification in Psychology (i.e. by having a recognised undergraduate degree or a recognised graduate conversion course in this subject). Second, one has to obtain a BPS-accredited master's degree in Sport and Exercise Psychology (or pass the Society's Stage 1 qualification. Third, one must obtain either the BPS's own Stage 2 Qualification in Sport and Exercise Psychology or a Society-accredited Stage 2 Qualification in Sport and Exercise Psychology. Fourth, one can apply for Registration as a Chartered Sport and Exercise Psychologist.

EUROPEAN NETWORK OF YOUNG SPECIALISTS IN SPORT PSYCHOLOGY (ENYSSP)

ENYSSP is an international organisation concerned with the promotion and dissemination of knowledge in the field of sport and exercise psychology in the areas of research, education and applied work.

FÉDÉRATION EUROPÉENNE DE PSYCHOLOGIE DES SPORTS ET DES ACTIVITÉS CORPORELLES (FEPSAC; EUROPEAN FEDERATION OF SPORT PSYCHOLOGY)

FEPSAC consists of 24 group members (associations of sport psychology) and a small number of individual members. It aims to promote scientific, educational and professional work in sport psychology.

INTERNATIONAL SOCIETY OF SPORT PSYCHOLOGY (ISSP)

ISSP (founded in 1965) is a worldwide organisation devoted to promoting research, practice, and development in the discipline of sport psychology. Its members are those whose research interests focus on some aspects of sport psychology. The Society aims to:

- encourage and promote the study of human behaviour within sport, physical activity, and health settings;
- facilitate the sharing of knowledge through a newsletter, meetings and a quadrennial World Congress;
- improve the quality of research and professional practice in sport psychology.

NORTH AMERICAN SOCIETY FOR PSYCHOLOGY OF SPORT AND PHYSICAL ACTIVITY (NASPSPA)

NASPSPA is a multidisciplinary association of scholars from the behavioural sciences and related professions. The Society aims to:

- develop and advance the scientific study of human behaviour when individuals are engaged in sport and physical activity;
- facilitate the dissemination of information;
- improve the quality of research and teaching in the psychology of sport, motor development, and motor learning and control.

LISTSERV INFORMATION (A BULLETIN BOARD ON SPORT PSYCHOLOGY)

If you would like to learn more about sport and exercise psychology using the Internet, you can subscribe to an electronic bulletin board called SPORTPSY that is devoted to sport and exercise psychology. SPORTPSY can be found at http://listserv.temple.edu/.

The purpose of this list is to post issues, questions and findings concerning research in sport and exercise psychology as well as related professional practice issues in this field.

To join SPORTPSY, go to http://listserv.temple.edu/archives/sportpsy. html and select 'Join or leave the list' which will take you to a secure page or send a message to listserv@listserv.temple.edu with nothing in the subject heading and only the following in the text: SUB SPORTPSY [your name].

REFERENCES

Green, C.D. and Benjamin, L.T., Jr. (2009) *Psychology Gets in the Game: Sport, Mind and Behaviour, 1880–1960*. Lincoln, NE: University of Nebraska Press.

Kremer, J. and Moran, A. (2008) *Pure Sport: Practical Sport Psychology*. Hove: Routledge.

1.4: organisations, sources and resources

2

Anxiety and Stress

2.5: Anxiety and Arousal

> **Definitions:** 'Arousal' is a form of diffuse or undifferentiated bodily energy which primes us for emergency action. 'Anxiety' may be defined as negatively interpreted arousal – an emotional state characterised by worry, feelings of apprehension and bodily tension that tends to occur in the absence of real or obvious danger.

Most athletes know from personal experience that if they wish to perform consistently well in competition, they must learn to control their arousal levels effectively. For example, tennis champion Rafael Nadal revealed that 'the important thing is for me to have the calm. It is what is needed to play my best' (cited in Flatman, 2010, p. 14). However, for Christine Ohuruogu, Britain's 2008 Olympic gold medallist in the 400m sprint, some anxiety before a race is essential because 'you need some level of pre-race nerves to get the adrenaline going but it is crucial to keep it under control' (cited in the *Guardian*, 2009, p. 35). These quotations raise two key questions for sport psychology researchers. First, what exactly is arousal and how does it differ from anxiety? Second, what is the relationship between arousal, anxiety and athletic performance?

In psychology, the term 'arousal' refers to a form of diffuse or undifferentiated bodily energy which primes us for emergency action. According to Gould et al. (2002), it is a 'general physiological and psychological activation of the organism which varies on a continuum from deep sleep to intense excitement' (p. 227). Physiologically, feelings of arousal are mediated by the sympathetic nervous system. In particular, when we become aroused, our brain's reticular activating system triggers the release of biochemical substances like epinephrine and norepinephrine into the bloodstream so that our body is energised for action. Although arousal involves *undifferentiated* bodily energy, anxiety is an emotional label for a particular type of arousal experience. In short, anxiety may be defined as *negatively interpreted* arousal – an emotional state characterised by worry, feelings of apprehension and bodily tension that tends to occur in the absence of real or obvious danger. This proposition raises the question of individual differences in arousal interpretation.

It has long been known that athletes differ from each other in how they perceive and interpret their arousal states. For example, a low level of arousal may be experienced either as a relaxed state of readiness or as an undesirable 'flat' or sluggish feeling. Conversely, symptoms of high arousal such as a rapid heartbeat and a feeling of 'butterflies' in one's stomach may be perceived as pleasant excitement by one athlete but as uncomfortable anxiety by another performer. To illustrate the former interpretation, consider Tiger Woods' view that 'the challenge is hitting good golf shots when you have to ... to do it when the nerves are fluttering, the heart pounding, the palms sweating ... that's the *thrill*' (cited in Davies, 2001, p. 26). Taken together, these observations suggest that it is not the *amount* of arousal that affects performance but the way in which such arousal is *interpreted*. Exploring this idea empirically, Jones and Swain (1992) showed that somatic symptoms of anxiety can have either a *facilitative* or a *debilitative* effect on sport performance depending on how the athlete perceives them. Interestingly, in a recent review, Thomas et al. (2009) claimed that athletes who perceive arousal symptoms as facilitative tend to perform better, have higher levels of self-confidence, use more effective coping strategies and display more resilience than do counterparts who perceive such symptoms as debilitative of performance. Unfortunately, there is a semantic problem at the heart of research on 'directional' anxiety effects. Specifically, as 'anxiety' is usually defined as negatively interpreted arousal, it makes little sense to talk of facilitative *anxiety*. Instead, it is more accurate to refer to facilitative *arousal*.

Three main theories in sport psychology have guided research on the relationship between arousal, anxiety and athletic performance since the 1990s: 'Catastrophe theory' (e.g. Hardy et al. 2007); the 'conscious processing' (or reinvestment) hypothesis (Masters and Maxwell, 2008); and 'attentional control theory' (Eysenck et al. 2007). These theories may be summarised briefly as follows.

To begin with, catastrophe theory (e.g. Hardy, 1990; Hardy et al., 2007) distinguishes between cognitive anxiety and physiological arousal. Furthermore, it postulates that when cognitive anxiety is high, increases in arousal tend to improve performance up to a certain point beyond which further increases may produce a swift, dramatic and discontinuous (hence the term 'catastrophic') decline in performance rather than a slow or gradual deterioration. The cornerstone of catastrophe theory is the assumption that arousal may have different effects on athletic performance depending on the prevailing level of cognitive anxiety in the performer. Specifically, when an athlete experiences high cognitive anxiety, the arousal-performance curve should follow a different path under conditions of *increasing* versus *decreasing* arousal. This hypothesis was supported, in part, by Vickers and Williams (2007) who discovered that high level of cognitive anxiety combined with a high level of physiological arousal sometimes led to 'choking under pressure' (see **2.8**) among biathlon performers – but not when these athletes were able to pay attention to task-relevant information. Unfortunately, the complex three-dimensional nature of catastrophe theory has made it difficult to test.

The second theory of the relationship between arousal, anxiety and athletic performance is the conscious processing (or reinvestment) hypothesis (Masters, 1992). This theory has generated a considerable amount of research in sport psychology (see review by Masters and Maxwell, 2008) – especially with regard to the relationship between conscious attention and skilled performance under anxiety-provoking conditions. It was spawned, in part, by an attempt to explain the well-known 'paralysis-by-analysis' phenomenon (see **2.8**) whereby skilled performance tends to deteriorate whenever people try to exert conscious control over movements that had previously been under automatic control. According to Masters (1992), when athletes experience increases in their anxiety levels, they attempt to ensure task success by reverting to a mode of conscious control that is associated mainly with an *early* stage of motor learning (i.e. one that relies on explicit rules and that typically results in slow and effortful movements). This temporary regression is held to involve a 'reinvestment' of cognitive processes in perceptual-motor control. So, the conscious processing hypothesis postulates that anxiety exerts a debilitating influence on performance by increasing a participant's self-consciousness of his or her movements. If this conscious processing theory is correct, then anxiety should have *differential* effects on skilled performance depending on how the skill had been acquired originally (i.e. whether it had been learned explicitly or implicitly). In an effort to test this prediction using the skill of golf putting, Masters devised an intriguing experimental paradigm in which participants who acquired the skill of golf putting using *explicit* knowledge subsequently experienced impaired performance when tested under conditions of high anxiety. Two conditions were crucial to the experiment. In the explicit condition, participants were instructed to read coaching manuals on golf putting. Conversely, in the implicit condition, participants were given no instructions but had to putt golf balls while performing a secondary task which had been designed to prevent them from thinking about the instructions on putting. Results suggested that the implicit learning group showed no deterioration in performance under stress in contrast to the golfers in the explicit learning condition. Masters interpreted this result as indicating that the skills of athletes with a small pool of explicit knowledge were *less* likely to fail than were those of performers with relatively larger amounts of explicit knowledge. To summarise, the conscious processing hypothesis predicts that athletes whose cognitive anxiety increases will tend to revert to conscious control of normally automatic skills. This prediction has been corroborated reliably. For example, Wilson et al. (2007) found that people's performance deteriorates when pressure manipulations require them to consciously attend to their movements.

Finally, attentional control theory (ACT) (Eysenck et al., 2007) postulates that cognitive anxiety (or worrying) depletes the resources of working memory and diverts the performer's attention from task-relevant to task-irrelevant information. According to Wood and Wilson (2010), ACT proposes that attentional control depends on the interaction between two systems – a top-down, goal-driven system that is influenced by the performer's current goals and a bottom-up, stimulus driven system that is influenced by salient information. ACT also suggests that anxiety increases the influence of stimulus-driven attentional system at the expense of the goal-driven system. In a test of this latter prediction, Wilson et al. (2009) used eye-tracking technology to analyse the visual search behaviour of soccer players as they prepared to take penalties in five-a-side matches (where there is a smaller distance between the goal-posts than in eleven-a-side matches) under various conditions of anxiety. Results corroborated a prediction of ACT by indicating that when anxious, the penalty takers displayed an attentional bias towards a salient and threatening stimulus (the goalkeeper) rather than to the ideal target for their kick (just inside the goal-post).

In summary, two general conclusions have emerged from research in this field (Moran, 2011). First, anxiety and arousal are best regarded as multidimensional constructs which do not have simple linear relationships with athletic performance. Second, increases in physiological arousal and cognitive state anxiety do not inevitably lead to a deterioration in athletic performance. More precisely, the effects of arousal and anxiety on sport performance depend crucially on the way in which the performer appraises them cognitively.

REFERENCES

Davies, D. (2001) Relaxed Woods identifies the major pressure points. The *Guardian*, 6 April, p. 26.

Eysenck, M.W., Derakshan, N., Santos, R. and Calvo, M.G. (2007) Anxiety and cognitive performance: Attentional control theory. *Emotion*, 7, 336–353.

Flatman, B. (2010) Holding court. *The Sunday Times*, 4 July, p. 14 (Sport).

Gould, D., Greenleaf, C. and Krane, V. (2002) Arousal-anxiety and sport. In Horn, T.S. (ed.) *Advances in Sport Psychology*. 2nd edn. Champaign, IL: Human Kinetics. 207–241.

Guardian, The (2009) *The Guardian and Observer guides to keeping fit with Britain's medal winners*. January, p. 35.

Hardy, L. (1990) A catastrophe model of anxiety and performance. In Jones, G. and Hardy, L. (eds), *Stress and Performance in Sport*. Chichester: John Wiley, pp. 81–106.

Hardy, L., Beattie, S. and Woodman, T. (2007) Anxiety-induced performance catastrophes: Investigating effort required as an asymmetry factor. *British Journal of Psychology*, 98, 15–31.

Jones, G. and Swain, A.B.J. (1992) Intensity and direction as dimensions of competitive state anxiety and relationships with competitiveness. *Perceptual and Motor Skills*, 74, 467–472.

Masters, R.S.W. (1992) Knowledge, 'knerves', and know-how: The role of explicit versus implicit knowledge in the breakdown of a complex motor skill under pressure. *British Journal of Psychology*, 83, 343–358.

Masters, R.S.W. and Maxwell, J.P. (2008) The theory of reinvestment. *International Review of Sport and Exercise Psychology*, 2, 160–183.

Moran, A.P. (2011) *Sport and Exercise Psychology*. 2nd edn. London: Routledge.

Thomas, O., Mellalieu, S.D. and Hanton, S. (2009) Stress management in applied sport psychology. In Mellalieu, S.D. and Hanton, S. (eds) *Advances in Applied Sport Psychology*. London: Routledge. 124–161.

Vickers, J.N. and Williams, A.M. (2007) Performing under pressure: The effects of physiological arousal, cognitive anxiety and gaze control in biathlon. *Journal of Motor Behaviour*, 39, 381–394.

Wilson, M. Smith, N. C., and Holmes, P. S. (2007) The role of effort in influencing the effect of anxiety on performance: Testing the conflicting predictions of processing efficiency theory and the conscious processing hypothesis. *British Journal of Psychology*, 98, 411–428.

Wilson, M.R., Wood, G., and Vine, S.J. (2009) Anxiety, attentional control, and performance impairment in penalty kicks. *Journal of Sport & Exercise Psychology*, 31, 761–775.

Wood, G. and Wilson, M.R. (2010) A moving goalkeeper distracts penalty takers and impairs shooting accuracy. *Journal of Sports Sciences*, 28, 937–946.

2.6: Measuring Stress and Anxiety

Competitive sport, especially at the elite level, is a stressful experience for many athletes. For example, Rebecca Adlington, the first British woman to win two gold medals at the Olympics for swimming, admitted that she had to lie down on the floor before her races in the 2008 Games in Beijing in order to avoid 'standing up and being sick, because I was more nervous than I've ever been in my life' (cited in Moss et al., 2008). In view of such experiences, stress and anxiety have attracted considerable research interest in sport psychology (e.g. see reviews by Hanton et al., 2008; Thomas et al., 2009). Before we address measurement issues, however, we need to define key terms.

Although the terms 'stress' and 'anxiety' are used interchangeably in everyday life, psychologists do not regard them as synonymous. To explain, psychologists (e.g. Lazarus, 1966) believe that stress is a broader construct than anxiety. Specifically, it refers to a pattern of physiological, behavioural, emotional and cognitive responses to real or imagined stimuli that are perceived as endangering us or harming our well-being in some way (Martin et al., 2009). Put simply, stress occurs whenever we perceive that the demands of a given situation threaten to tax or exceed our coping resources (see **2.9**). The key proposition here is that cognitive appraisal (or how a person interprets a situation) is central to the experience of stress. 'Stressors' are the environmental demands (e.g. competing for one's country in the Olympic Games) that people face in pressure situations. In sport, these demands include competitive (e.g. the pressure of performance expectations), organisational (e.g. logistical) and personal (e.g. family issues) stressors (Fletcher et al., 2006). Finally, 'anxiety' is a negative emotional response to stressors – an emotional state characterised by worry, feelings of apprehension and bodily tension that tends to occur in the absence of real or obvious danger. Since the seminal research of Spielberger (1966), psychologists have distinguished between anxiety as a mood state ('state' anxiety) and anxiety as a personality characteristic ('trait' anxiety). For example, a basketball player may feel anxious in the dressing-room before an important match but may become calmer once the competitive action begins. On the other hand, a player who scores highly on trait anxiety may feel pessimistic before and during the match.

As we explained elsewhere (see **2.5**), anxiety is widely regarded as a tri-dimensional construct comprising cognitive, somatic and behavioural components. *Cognitive* anxiety involves worrying or having negative expectations about oneself or about an impending situation or performance. For example, Martinent and Ferrand (2007) found that competitive athletes worried a lot about poor performances, especially the possibility of making mistakes. *Somatic* anxiety refers to the physical manifestations of the stress response which include neuroendocrine secretions (e.g. of cortisol – the 'stress hormone'), increased perspiration, a pounding heart, rapid shallow breathing, clammy hands and a feeling of 'butterflies' in one's stomach. Recently, Strahler et al. (2010) used the 'cortisol awakening response' (CAR) to investigate anticipatory anxiety among athletes one week before an important competition. Surprisingly, their results indicated that although these athletes reported experiencing a significant rise in somatic anxiety as the day of a competition loomed, there was no significant increase in CAR activity. This finding suggests that neuroendocrine indices of athletes' somatic anxiety do not always correspond with these performers' subjective experience. Finally, *behavioural* anxiety refers to the way in which nervousness affects people's posture, movement and actions. For example, Pijpers et al. (2003) found that, as predicted, the bodily movements of highly anxious climbers were jerkier and displaced more from their centre of gravity than were those of less anxious counterparts.

Historically, sport psychology researchers have used psychometric scales rather than psychophysiological instruments or behavioural indices to measure anxiety processes in athletes. This preference is attributable mainly to the simplicity, brevity and administrative convenience of self-report measures. Among the most popular psychometric measures of anxiety are the Sport Competition Anxiety Test (SCAT; Martens, 1977), the Sport Anxiety Scale (SAS; Smith et al., 1990) and its successor the Sport Anxiety Scale-2 (SAS-2; Smith et al., 2006), and the Competitive State Anxiety Inventory-2 (CSAI-2; Martens et al., 1990). These scales, which are concerned more with the measurement of anxiety *intensity* in athletes rather than how anxiety is interpreted by them, can be described as follows.

First, the SCAT is a ten-item unidimensional trait anxiety inventory (i.e. it assumes that trait anxiety has only a single dimension). Parallel versions of this test are available for children (aged 10–14 years) and for adults (of 15 years and above). Typical items include 'When I compete I worry about making mistakes' and 'Before I compete I get a queasy feeling in my stomach'. Respondents are required to indicate their agreement with each item by selecting their preferred answer from the three categories of 'hardly ever', 'sometimes' and 'often'. Reverse scoring is used on certain items (e.g. 'Before I compete I feel calm') and overall test scores can range from 10 to 30. Unfortunately, although the SCAT appears to be quite reliable, it has limited utility because it does not distinguish between or measure adequately individual differences in cognitive and somatic anxiety.

Next, the SAS-2, which is a revised (15-item) version of the SAS, is a multidimensional instrument that purports to measure individual differences in somatic anxiety, worry and concentration disruption in children and adults. It contains 15 items that load onto *three sub-scales*, each comprising five items: somatic anxiety (e.g. 'my body feels tense'), worry (e.g. 'I worry that I will not play well') and concentration disruption (e.g. 'It is hard to concentrate on the game'). According to Smith et al. (2006), the SAS-2 not only correlates highly ($r = 0.90$) with its predecessor, the SAS – a sign of convergent validity – but also has strong reliability. For example, sub-scale reliabilities were estimated at 0.84 (for somatic anxiety), 0.89 (for worry) and 0.84 (for concentration disruption). In summary, the SAS-2 appears to be a reliable and valid measure of multidimensional anxiety in children and adults.

Third, the CSAI-2 is a popular test of cognitive and somatic anxiety in athletes. It comprises 27 items which are divided into *three sub-scales*, each containing nine items: cognitive anxiety (e.g. 'I am concerned about losing'), somatic anxiety (e.g. 'I feel nervous') and self-confidence (e.g. 'I am confident I can meet the challenge'). Respondents are required to rate the intensity of their anxiety experiences prior to competition on a four-point Likert scale (with 1 = 'not at all' and 4 = 'very much so'). Doubts about the psychometric adequacy of the CSAI-2 were raised by Lane et al. (1999). For example, these authors pointed out that being 'concerned' about an impending athletic event does not necessarily mean that the performer is actually worrying about it. Thus items such as 'I am concerned about this competition' may not be valid indices of cognitive anxiety but may instead reflect the importance that the performer attaches to the event. Based on such arguments, and on a confirmatory factor analysis of the test, Lane et al. (1999) urged researchers to be cautious when interpreting data obtained from the CSAI-2. In response to some of these issues, the Revised Competitive State Anxiety Inventory (CSAI-2R) was developed by Cox et al. (2003). This 17-item scale purports to measure the intensity components of cognitive anxiety (five items), somatic anxiety (seven items) and self-confidence (five items). Unfortunately, according to Uphill (2008), the construct validity of this revised measure is also questionable.

Earlier, we mentioned the importance of cognitive appraisal processes in anxiety. In an effort to take account of such individual differences in athletes' perception of the personal meaning of anxiety symptoms, Jones and Swain (1992) recommended that a 'directional' measure of anxiety should be appended to scales such as the CSAI-2. Using this new measure of anxiety (which these authors called the CSAI-2(d)), respondents are required first to complete the CSAI-2 in order to elicit the *intensity* with which they experience the 27 symptoms listed in this test. Next, they are asked to rate anxiety *direction* by evaluating the degree to which the experienced intensity of each symptom is either *facilitative* or *debilitative* of their athletic performance. A seven-item Likert response scale is used, with values ranging from −3 (indicating 'very negative') to +3 (indicating 'very positive'). To illustrate, an athlete might respond with a maximum '4' to the statement 'I am concerned about losing' but might then rate this concern with a +3 on the interpretation scale. Through these scores, the performer is indicating that he or she feels that this concern about losing is likely to have a facilitative effect on his or her forthcoming performance. With this modification, CSAI-2(d) scores can vary between −27 and +27. The discriminative value of the CSAI-2(d) was supported in a study by Jones et al. (1993) which showed that high-performance gymnasts reported their cognitive anxiety symptoms as being more facilitative of, and less debilitating to, their performance than did low-performance counterparts – even though there were no significant differences between these groups in CSAI-2 anxiety sub-scale intensity scores.

REFERENCES

Cox, R.H., Martens, M.P. and Russell, W.D. (2003) Measuring anxiety in athletes: The revised Competitive State Anxiety Inventory-2. *Journal of Sport and Exercise Psychology*, 25, 519–533.

Fletcher, D., Hanton, S. and Mellalieu, S.D. (2006) An organizational stress review: Conceptual and theoretical issues in competitive sport. In Hanton, S. and Mellalieu, S.D. (eds) *Literature Reviews in Sport Psychology*. New York: Nova Science. pp. 321–373.

Hanton, S., Neil, R. and Mellalieu, S.D. (2008) Recent developments in competitive anxiety direction and competition stress research. *International Review of Sport and Exercise Psychology*, 1, 45–57.

Jones, J.G. and Swain, A.B.J. (1992) Intensity and direction as dimensions of competitive state anxiety and relationships with competitiveness. *Perceptual and Motor Skills*, 74, 467–472.

Jones, J.G., Swain, A. and Hardy, L. (1993) Intensity and direction dimensions of competitive state anxiety and relationships with performance. *Journal of Sports Sciences*, 11, 525–532.

Lane, A.M., Sewell, D.F., Terry, P.C., Bartram, D. and Nesti, M.S. (1999) Confirmatory factor analysis of the Competitive State Anxiety Inventory-2. *Journal of Sports Sciences*, 17, 505–512.

Lazarus, R.S. (1966) *Psychological Stress and the Coping Process*. New York: McGraw-Hill.

Martens, R. (1977) *Sport Competition Anxiety Test*. Champaign, IL: Human Kinetics.

Martens, R., Burton, D., Vealey, R.S., Bump, L.A. and Smith, D.E. (1990) Development and validation of the Competitive State Anxiety Inventory-2 (CSAI-2). In Martens, R., Vealey, R.S. and Burton, D. (eds) *Competitive Anxiety in Sport*. Champaign, IL: Human Kinetics. 117–190.

Martin, G.N., Carlson, N.R. and Buskist, W. (2009) *Psychology*. 4th edn. Harlow: Pearson Education.

Martinent, G. and Ferrand, C. (2007) A cluster analysis of precompetitive anxiety: Relationship with perfectionism and trait anxiety. *Personality and Individual Differences*, 43, 1676–1686.

Moss, S., Cochrane, K. and Burnton, S. (2008) Baffled by Beijing. *The Guardian* (g2 magazine), 19 August. Retrieved from www.guardian.co.uk/sport/2008/aug/19/britisholympicteam.olympics2008 on 25 October 2010.

Pijpers, J.R., Oudejans, R.R.D., Holsheimer, F. and Bakker, F.C. (2003) Anxiety-performance relationships in climbing: A process-oriented approach. *Psychology of Sport and Exercise*, 4, 283–304.

Smith, R.E., Smoll, F.L. and Schutz, R.W. (1990) Measurement and correlates of sport-specific cognitive and somatic trait anxiety: The Sport Anxiety Scale. *Anxiety Research*, 2, 263–280.

Smith, R.E., Smoll, F.L., Cumming, S.P. and Grossbard, J.R. (2006) Measurement of multidimensional sport performance anxiety in children and adults: The Sport Anxiety Scale-2. *Journal of Sport and Exercise Psychology*, 28, 479–501.

Spielberger, C.S. (1966) Theory and research on anxiety. In Spielberger, C.S. (ed.) *Anxiety and Behaviour*. New York: Academic Press. pp. 3–20.

Strahler, K., Ehrlenspiel, F., Heene, M. and Brand, R. (2010) Competitive anxiety and cortisol awakening response in the week leading up to a competition. *Psychology of Sport and Exercise*, 11, 148–154.

Thomas, O., Mellalieu, S.D. and Hanton, S. (2009) Stress management in applied sport psychology. In Mellalieu, S.D. and Hanton, S. (eds) *Advances in Applied Sport Psychology*. London: Routledge. pp. 124–161.

Uphill, M. (2008) Anxiety in sport: Should we be worried or excited? In Lane, A. (ed.) *Sport and Exercise Psychology*. London: Hodder Education. pp. 35–51.

2.7: Pre-performance Routines

> **Definition:** A pre-performance routine is a preferred sequence of task-relevant thoughts and actions which athletes engage in systematically prior to their performance of specific sport skills.

Sport is a highly ritualised activity. For example, golfers tend to 'waggle' their clubs a consistent number of times before striking the ball and tennis players like to bounce the ball a standard number of times before serving. These preferred action sequences are called 'pre-performance routines' (PPRs) and involve task-relevant thoughts and actions which athletes engage in systematically prior to their performance of specific sport skills (Moran, 1996). Usually, PPRs are evident prior to the execution of self-paced actions (i.e. those that are carried out largely at one's own speed and without interference from other people) such as serving in tennis, free-throwing in basketball, putting in golf or place-kicking in American football or rugby. Such routines are used extensively by athletes, and recommended by coaches and psychologists, as a form of mental preparation both to improve focusing skills (see **4.19**) and to enhance competitive performance. In short, according to Singer (2002), the purpose of a PPR is to 'put oneself in an optimal state immediately prior to execution, and to remain that way during the act' (p. 6).

Three main types of routines are evident among sports performers. First, *pre-event* routines are preferred sequences of actions that athletes habitually engage in prior to a competitive event. Included here are preferences for what to do on the night before, and on the morning of, the competition itself. Second, as mentioned above, *pre-performance* routines are characteristic sequences of thoughts and actions which athletes adhere to immediately preceding skill execution. Third, *post-mistake routines* are action sequences which athletes use in an effort to forget about setbacks, mistakes or missed opportunities so that they can re-focus on the task at hand. For example, a golfer may 'shadow' the correct swing of a shot that had led to an error. Of these three types of routines, PPRs have attracted the greatest amount of research attention in sport psychology (see Cotterill, 2010, for a comprehensive review of studies on this topic). Typically, the efficacy of PPRs has been investigated using a research design in which the performance of a control group is compared with that of an experimental group that has been taught and has practiced a designated pre-performance routine. Cotterill (2010) has summarised the results of 27 studies on PPRs using this experimental method. Although the findings from these studies are rather inconsistent, there is some evidence that routines facilitate performance. For example, Crews and Boutcher (1986) compared the performances of two groups of golfers – those who had been given an eight-week training programme of swing practice only and those who had participated in a 'practice-plus-routine' programme for the same duration. Results revealed that the more proficient golfers benefited more from using routines than did the less skilled players.

Research on the efficacy of pre-performance routines raises at least three key practical and theoretical questions. First, are athletes consistent in their implementation of a given PPR in different competitive situations? Second, can athletes' PPRs be distinguished validly from superstitious rituals? Third, what theoretical mechanisms underlie the effects of PPRs? Let us now consider each of these questions in turn.

To begin with, some studies have challenged the assumption that routines are always unwavering when executed by top-class athletes. For example, Jackson and Baker (2001) analysed the pre-kick routine of the prolific former British and Irish Lions rugby kicker, Neil Jenkins, who is Wales' highest-ever points scorer and who was the first player to score over 1,000 points in international matches. As expected, Jenkins reported using a variety of concentration techniques (see **4.17**) as part of his pre-kick routine. However, what surprised Jackson and Baker was the discovery that Jenkins *varied* the timing of his pre-strike behaviour depending on the difficulty of the kick that he faced. This finding shows that routines are not as rigid or stereotyped as was originally believed. In a further investigation of this phenomenon, Jackson (2003) analysed over 500 goal-kicking attempts in the 1999 rugby World Cup. He found that players spent on average about 10 seconds in quiet contemplation before a typical kick. But they took several seconds longer when there was a narrow angle between the ball and the posts. In other words, they varied the duration of their pre-kick routine in accordance with the perceived difficulty of the task. More recently, Lonsdale and Tam (2008) examined the consistency of the pre-performance routines of a sample of elite National Basketball Association (NBA) players by analysing their 'free throw' shooting behaviour from televised match footage. Results showed that, contrary to expectations, the *temporal* consistency of the basketball players' pre-performance routines was not associated with accurate skill execution. However, there was evidence that the *behavioural* consistency of these routines *was* related to proficient performance. Specifically, Lonsdale and Tam found that the basketball players were more successful when they adhered to their dominant behavioural sequence prior to their free throws.

Turning to a second key issue in relevant scientific literature, are pre-performance routines merely superstitious rituals in disguise? It is well known that athletes are notoriously superstitious – perhaps because of the capricious nature of sport itself. Thus Rafael Nadal apparently must have two water bottles beside the court, perfectly aligned and with the labels facing the baseline, and Tiger Woods usually wears a 'lucky' red shirt on the last day of a golf tournament. At first glance, such superstitions (i.e. beliefs that, despite scientific evidence to the contrary, certain actions are causally related to certain outcomes; see Vyse, 1997) may be distinguished from PPR on the basis of two criteria: control and purpose. First, the essence of superstitious behaviour is the belief that one's fate is governed by factors that lie *outside* one's control. But the value of a routine is that it allows the player to exert complete control over his or her preparation. Thus athletes can shorten their pre-performance routines in adverse circumstances (e.g. if the time of a competition is brought forward unexpectedly). Unfortunately, the converse is true for superstitions. They tend to grow longer over time as performers 'chain together' more and more illogical links between their behaviour and the desired outcome. The second criterion which helps us to distinguish between routines and rituals concerns the technical role of each behavioural step followed. Specifically, whereas each part of a PPR usually has a rational basis, the components of a superstitious ritual are invariably spurious in nature and randomly associated. Despite these neat conceptual distinctions, however, the boundaries between PPRs and superstitions in sport are often rather fuzzy. For example, consider how Serena Williams explained her defeat at the 2007 French Open tennis championship: 'I didn't tie my laces right and I didn't bounce the ball five times and I didn't bring my shower sandals to the court with me ... I just knew fate, it wasn't going to happen' (cited in Hyde, 2009, p. 3). Interestingly, several studies have explored the impact of ritualised behaviour on athletic performance. For example, using a sample of basketball players, Foster et al. (2006) evaluated the effect of removing superstitious behaviour (e.g. kissing the tape covering a wedding ring on the shooter's hand) and introducing a pre-performance routine (of bouncing the ball, taking a deep breath, visualising the perfect shot and then using a cue word before executing the skill) before free-throw skill execution. Contrary to expectation, there was very little difference between the players' performance following either superstitious behaviour or a pre-performance routine – perhaps because many of the basketballers had been using superstitious behaviour for years prior to the study, whereas the routine was only a recent addition to their mental preparation repertoire. Similarly, Schippers and Van Lange (2006) analysed the psychological benefits of superstitious rituals among elite athletes. Based on an examination of the circumstances in which such rituals are displayed before games, these investigators concluded that superstitious behaviour was most likely to occur when games were perceived as especially important. In addition, these researchers reported that players with an *external* locus of control tended to display *more* superstitious rituals than those with an internal locus of control. More recently, evidence has emerged to suggest that despite their irrational origins, superstitions can sometimes be helpful to performers. Thus Damisch et al. (2010) conducted a series of experiments which appear to highlight some benefits of superstitions to motor and cognitive task performance. Specifically, they showed that playing with a ball described as 'lucky' seemed to improve participants' putting accuracy and that the presence of a personal charm enhances participants' performance on memory and anagram tests. In an effort to explain these results, Damisch et al.

postulated that good-luck superstitions may have increased participants' self-efficacy (or belief in their own ability to succeed on the tasks in question) which, in turn, may have improved their performance.

Finally, what theoretical mechanisms underlie the effects of pre-performance routines in enhancing performance? Although few studies have addressed this question empirically, it is plausible that they work because they consume working memory resources and hence prevent athletes from engaging in 'reinvestment' (Masters and Maxwell, 2008) – or devoting too much attention to the mechanics of one's automatic skills (see **2.8**). In other words, pre-performance routines may help to suppress the type of inappropriate conscious control that athletes tend to regress to in pressure situations. In this regard, an important challenge for applied sport psychologists is to help athletes to attain an appropriate level of conscious control over their actions before skill execution. Another reason why routines may enhance performance is that they encourage athletes to focus only on task-relevant information (Moran, 1996). Augmenting such arguments, empirical evidence to support the value of routines comes from case studies. For example, Cotterill et al. (2010) conducted in-depth interviews with a sample of amateur international golfers in an effort to understand the nature and perceived benefits of their use of PPRs. Results showed that these golfers used routines for attentional purposes such as attempting to 'switch on and off' (p. 55) and 'staying in the present and not dwelling on the past or engaging in fortune telling' (p. 55).

REFERENCES

Cotterill, S. (2010) Pre-performance routines in sport: Current understanding and future directions. *International Review of Sport and Exercise Psychology*, 3, 132–153.

Cotterill, S., Sanders, R. and Collins, D. (2010) Developing effective pre-performance routines in golf: Why don't we ask the golfer? *Journal of Applied Sport Psychology*, 22 (1), 51–64.

Crews, D.J. and Boutcher, S.H. (1986) Effects of structured preshot behaviours on beginning golf performance. *Perceptual and Motor Skills*, 62, 291–294.

Damisch, L., Stoberock, B. and Mussweiler, T. (2010) Keep your fingers crossed! How superstition improves performance. *Psychological Science*, 21, 1014–1020.

Foster, D.J., Weigand, D.A. and Baines, D. (2006) The effect of removing superstitious behaviour and introducing a pre-performance routine on basketball free-throw performance. *Journal of Applied Sport Psychology*, 18, 167–171.

Hyde, M. (2009) Obsessive? Compulsive? Order of the day at SW19. The *Guardian* (Sport), 1 July, pp. 2–3.

Jackson, R.C. (2003) Pre-performance routine consistency: Temporal analysis of goal kicking in the Rugby Union World Cup. *Journal of Sports Sciences*, 21, 803–814.

Jackson, R.C. and Baker, J.S. (2001) Routines, rituals, and rugby: Case study of a world class goal kicker. *The Sport Psychologist*, 15, 48–65.

Lonsdale, C. and Tam, J.T.M. (2008) On the temporal and behavioural consistency of pre-performance routines: An intra-individual analysis of elite basketball players' free throw shooting accuracy. *Journal of Sports Sciences*, 26, 259–266.

Masters, R.S.W. and Maxwell, J.P. (2008) The theory of reinvestment. *International Review of Sport and Exercise Psychology*, 2, 160–183.

Moran, A.P. (1996) *The Psychology of Concentration in Sport Performers: A Cognitive Analysis*. Hove: Psychology Press.

Schippers, M.C. and Van Lange, P.A. (2006) The psychological benefits of superstitious rituals in top sport: A study among top sportspersons. *Journal of Applied Social Psychology*, 36, 2532–2553.

Singer, R.N. (2002) Pre-performance state, routines, and automaticity: What does it take to realize expertise in self-paced tasks? *Journal of Sport and Exercise Psychology*, 24, 359–375.

Vyse, S. (1997) *Believing in Magic: The Psychology of Superstition*. New York: Oxford University Press.

2.8: Choking Under Pressure

anxiety and stress

> **Definition:** 'Choking under pressure' is a phenomenon in which an athlete's normally expert level of performance deteriorates suddenly and significantly under conditions of perceived pressure.

At first glance, the term 'choking under pressure' is easy to define. Specifically, it refers to a phenomenon in which athletic performance deteriorates suddenly as a result of anxiety. On closer inspection, however, this definition has two main problems. To begin with, as Hill et al. (2010) pointed out, we must be sure that for any sub-optimal performance to be regarded as an example of 'choking' in sport, and not just a random lapse, the athlete in question was *capable* of performing better than he or she did, was *motivated* sufficiently to succeed, and that he or she perceived the sport situation as being *important*. Second, Gucciardi and Dimmock (2008) have argued that the deterioration in performance that characterises choking should be *significant* – not trivial. And so, choking is probably best defined as a phenomenon in which an athlete's normally expert level of performance deteriorates suddenly and significantly under conditions of perceived pressure. Two other features of choking are notable. First, as the term 'anxiety' is derived from the Latin word *angere* which means 'to choke', it is clear that choking and anxiety in sport are inextricably linked. In addition, choking is an intriguing mental state because it reflects a motivational paradox. Specifically, the more effort the 'choker' exerts on his or her performance, the more it appears to deteriorate. In short, choking is paradoxical because it occurs when anxious people try *too* hard to perform well. Not surprisingly, this phenomenon has attracted considerable attention from psychologists – ranging from coverage in popular science (e.g. Beilock, 2010) to systematic reviews of relevant research (e.g. Hill et al., 2010).

Choking is ubiquitous among competitive athletes. As Tom Watson (the former world number one golfer) remarked, 'We all choke. You just try to choke last!' (cited in MacRury, 1997, p. 99). It is known as the 'yips' in golf, 'icing' or 'bricking' in basketball, 'dartitis' in darts and 'bottling' in soccer. Within such sports, choking is especially prevalent among performers of self-paced skills (i.e. actions that are executed largely at one's own speed and without interference from other performers). To illustrate, leading golfers like Greg Norman, Stewart Cink, Scott Hoch, and perhaps most famously, Jean van de Velde (who led by 3 strokes at the final hole of 1999 Open Championship at Carnoustie but who triple-bogied it before losing to Paul Lawrie in a play-off) have all admitted publicly that they have choked in major competitions (Dixon and Kidd, 2006). Choking has also precipitated dramatic collapses in tennis. To illustrate, consider what happened in the 1993 Wimbledon Ladies' Singles final between Jana Novotna (the Czech Republic) and Steffi Graf (Germany). Serving at 4–1 in the third set, with a point for 5–1, Novotna became anxious. She produced a double-fault and some wild shots to lose that game. Later, she served three consecutive double-faults in her attempt to increase her 4–3 lead over Graf. Interestingly, Novotna choked in a similar fashion in the third round of the 1995 French Open championship in Paris when she lost a match to the American player Chanda Rubin despite having nine match points when leading 5–0, 40–0 in the third set.

But choking is not confined solely to athletes engaged in individual sports. It is also evident in team games (e.g. soccer) when precise execution of a technical skill is crucial to the outcome of the match. To illustrate, many of the world's best footballers have crumbled under the pressure of penalty-taking. For example, Roberto Baggio (Italy) blazed his kick over the bar in a penalty shootout in the 1994 soccer World Cup final – a mistake that allowed Brazil to win the trophy. In attempting to explain this phenomenon of penalty misses by highly skilled players, Jordet (2009) discovered from analysis of video footage taken at major international soccer tournaments that publicly esteemed 'superstar' players (i.e. those who had received prestigious awards for their skills) tended to perform *worse* than less renowned players in penalty shootouts – presumably because of the additional pressure that they experienced in such situations.

What causes choking? Although most researchers agree that it is best regarded as an anxiety-based attentional difficulty, there is little consensus on the precise theoretical mechanisms underlying it. At present, two main attentional theories of choking are especially prominent in the research literature: *distraction* theories (e.g. processing efficiency theory or PET; Eysenck and Calvo, 1992) and *self-focus* theories (e.g. Masters, 1992; Beilock and Carr, 2001). In general, distraction theories postulate that perceived pressure induces anxiety which consumes working memory resources and causes inefficient processing of task-relevant information – thereby shifting attention away from task execution. By contrast, self-focus models of choking typically propose that anxiety increases athletes' levels of self-consciousness and causes them to focus their attention inwards. This shift to self-focused attention encourages athletes to attempt to consciously monitor and/or control their skill execution which may subsequently induce choking through a form of 'paralysis by analysis'. This term refers to skill failure that can occur when people think too much about actions that are usually executed automatically. As Beilock (2010) explained, just as thinking about where to place our feet as we rush downstairs may cause us to trip, focusing deliberately on activities that normally operate outside our conscious awareness can lead to choking.

One of the most influential distraction theories of choking is processing efficiency theory (PET) (Eysenck and Calvo, 1992). Briefly, PET distinguishes between processing *effectiveness* (the quality of task performance) and processing *efficiency* (the relationship between the effectiveness of performance and the effort or resources that have been invested in task performance). It predicts that the adverse effects of anxiety on performance effectiveness are often *less* than those on processing efficiency. This prediction stems from the assumption that increased effort by the performer can compensate for the reduction in attentional resources that are typically caused by anxiety. According to PET, anxious athletes may try to maintain their level of performance by investing extra effort in it. Although this increased effort investment may appear to generate immediate benefits, it soon reaches a point of diminishing returns. At this stage, the athlete may conclude that too much effort is required, and so he or she gives up. Then, his or her performance deteriorates rapidly.

Turning to self-focus accounts of choking, two theoretical models are especially prominent: the 'conscious processing' or reinvestment hypothesis (CPH) (Masters, 1992; Masters and Maxwell, 2008) and the 'explicit monitoring' hypothesis (EMH) (Beilock and Carr, 2001). Although these two approaches share many ideas, they differ in at least one important issue (Hill et al., 2010): whereas the EMH suggests that athletic performance is disrupted by performers *monitoring* their step-by-step execution of the skill, the CPH postulates that the disruption is caused by athletes consciously *controlling* the skill involved. Either way, self-focus models explain choking by postulating that when people experience a great deal of pressure to perform well, they tend to think more about themselves and the importance of the event in which they are competing than they would normally. This excessive self-consciousness causes people to attempt to gain conscious control over previously automatic skills – just as a novice would do. As a result of this attempt to invest automatic processes with conscious control, skilled performance tends to unravel. Interestingly, according to some athletes, this unravelling of skill, which is caused by thinking too much about automatic movements, may happen more frequently as one gets older. For example, consider the golfer Ian Woosnam's experience of trying to correct his putting stroke. Specifically, he said that 'putting shouldn't be hard … but that's where the mind comes in. So much is running through your mind – hold it this way, keep the blade square – whereas when you're young, you just get hold of it and hit it. When you get old too much goes through your mind' (cited in White, 2002, p. 22). As yet, however, this hypothesis that ageing increases the proclivity to think too much about one's sport skills remains speculative. But one individual difference variable that *has* been shown to be a reliable moderator of choking in sport is 'dispositional reinvestment' or a person's tendency to attempt to consciously control a well-learned skill under pressure (Masters et al., 1993). In an effort to measure this personality dimension, Masters et al. developed the 20-item Reinvestment Scale and found that athletes who scored lower on this test tended to perform better under pressure than counterparts who scored relatively higher. Similar results were reported by Jackson et al. (2006).

Overall, according to Gucciardi and Dimmock (2008), empirical support for distraction models of choking is strongest for tasks (e.g. mathematical computation) that depend heavily on working memory resources. By contrast, self-focus models of choking appear to be supported best by studies involving tasks that make few demands on working memory (e.g. golf putting). A good explanation for this finding comes from Beilock (2010). If we are performing a complex thinking task that drains our working memory resources, then anxiety alone can induce choking. But if we are performing a highly automatic motor skill, then worrying in itself will not lead to choking, but attempting to exert conscious control over one's automatic skills (which is a consequence of anxiety) *will* do so.

In summary, although choking under pressure is a pervasive problem in sport, no consensus has been reached as yet about the precise theoretical mechanisms that cause it. Nevertheless, most theories of this phenomenon agree that anxiety impairs performance by inducing the athlete to think too much, causing him or her to regress to an earlier stage of learning – effectively making him or her a beginner again.

How can we counteract choking under pressure? Until recently, little or no research had been conducted on theoretically-based interventions designed to alleviate this problem. However, this gap in the literature is gradually being filled. For example, Oudejans and Pijpers (2010) investigated whether or not exposing athletes to mild levels of anxiety (a form of simulation training) can help them to perform better under conditions that could give rise to choking. In this study, a sample of novices was assigned to one of two groups. In the experimental group, participants practiced darts throwing under experimentally induced levels of mild anxiety – achieved by requiring participants to hang high rather than low on an indoor climbing wall. In the control group, participants practised without any additional anxiety. Manipulation checks using heart-rate (an index of arousal/anxiety) were conducted to ensure that the anxiety manipulation had been effective. After training, participants were tested under conditions of low, mild and high anxiety. Results showed that despite systematic increases in anxiety, heart rate and effort from low to mid to high anxiety, the experimental group (i.e. the one that had trained under mild anxiety) performed equally well on all three tests, whereas the performance of the control group deteriorated in the high anxiety condition.

In summary, Oudejans and Pijper (2010) interpreted their results to indicate that training with mild anxiety may help to prevent performers from 'choking' under conditions of high anxiety. In a similar manner, Mesagno and Mullane-Grant (2010) examined which aspects of a pre-performance routine (PPR) (see also **2.7** and **4.19**) were most beneficial in alleviating choking among a sample of Australian football players. In this study, the footballers attempted kicks at scoring zones under conditions of low- and high-pressure. They were assigned to one of four different intervention groups which varied in the component of PPR used (e.g. diaphragmatic breathing, use of a 'trigger word', temporal consistency, and an extensive PPR) for 15-minute sessions. Results showed that the most effective pre-performance routine in alleviating choking was one that included psychological and behavioural components and that occupied the footballers' attention prior to kick-execution.

REFERENCES

Beilock, S.L. (2010) *Choke.* New York: Free Press.

Beilock, S.L. and Carr, T.H. (2001) On the fragility of skilled performance: What governs choking under pressure? *Journal of Experimental Psychology: General,* 130, 701–725.

Dixon, P. and Kidd, P. (2006) The golf pro who missed from 3ft and lost £230,000. *The Times,* 21 March, p. 5.

Eysenck, M.W. and Calvo, M. (1992) Anxiety and performance: The processing efficiency theory. *Cognition and Emotion,* 6, 409–434.

Gucciardi, D.F. and Dimmock, J.A. (2008) Choking under pressure in sensorimotor skills: Conscious processing or depleted attentional resources? *Psychology of Sport and Exercise,* 9, 45–59.

Hill, D., Hanton, S.M., Matthews, N. and Fleming, S. (2010) Choking in sport: A review. *International Review of Sport and Exercise Psychology,* 3, 24–39.

Jackson, R.C., Ashford, K.J. and Norsworthy, G. (2006) Attentional focus, dispositional reinvestment, and skilled motor performance under pressure. *Journal of Sport and Exercise Psychology,* 28, 49–68.

Jordet, G. (2009) When superstars flop: Public status and choking under pressure in international soccer penalty shootouts. *Journal of Applied Sport Psychology,* 21, 125–130.

MacRury, D. (1997) *Golfers on Golf.* London: Virgin Books.

Masters, R.S.W. (1992) Knowledge, 'knerves' and know-how: The role of explicit versus implicit knowledge in the breakdown of a complex motor skill under pressure. *British Journal of Psychology,* 83, 343–358.

Masters, R.S.W. and Maxwell, J.P. (2008) The theory of reinvestment. *International Review of Sport and Exercise Psychology,* 2, 160–183.

Masters, R.S.W., Polman, R.C.J. and Hammond, C.V. (1993) 'Reinvestment': A dimension of personality implicated in skill breakdown under pressure. *Personality and Individual Differences*, 14, 655–666.

Mesagno, C. and Mullane-Grant, T. (2010) A comparison of different pre-performance routines as possible choking interventions. *Journal of Applied Sport Psychology*, 22, 343–360.

Oudejans, R.R.D. and Pijpers, J.R. (2010) Training with mild anxiety may prevent choking under higher levels of anxiety. *Psychology of Sport and Exercise*, 11, 44–50.

White, J. (2002) 'Interview: Ian Woosnam'. The *Guardian*, 15 July, pp. 22–23 (Sport).

2.9: Coping Strategies

anxiety and stress

48

> **Definition:** Coping strategies are plans of actions that people follow, either in anticipation of encountering a stressor or as a direct response to stress as it occurs.

Competitive sport is a stressful experience for many athletes, regardless of their ability or experience. For example, although Pádraig Harrington has won three golf Majors and represented Europe in six Ryder Cup teams since 1999, he admits that he always feels anxious on the tee-box at the start of this latter competition: 'It all goes into a blur because you're so nervous and eventually you just have to go hit it … it's the height of nervousness' (cited in Clerkin, 2010, p. 3). Given the ubiquity of such competitive anxiety in sport (see **2.5** and **2.6**), it is vital for psychology researchers and practitioners to understand the nature and efficacy of the coping strategies used by athletes to alleviate stressful experiences.

According to Lazarus and Folkman (1984), coping involves 'constantly changing cognitive and behavioural efforts to manage specific external and/or internal demands that are appraised as taxing or exceeding the resources of the person' (p. 141). It is a dynamic ongoing process that can change from situation to situation and involves any methods that a person uses in an effort to master, reduce or otherwise tolerate stress. This emphasis on the ever-changing nature of coping raises an interesting methodological issue for research in this field. Specifically, Nicholls (2008) pointed out that in order to study coping as a dynamic process, researchers should collect data from repeated measures of the same person over time. However, most research on coping in sport uses static 'snapshot' designs in which participants are required to provide a single retrospective report on their coping experiences. Clearly, in order to rectify this methodological problem, researchers should prioritise the use of longitudinal designs in future studies of coping strategies.

In psychology, a *coping strategy* is 'a plan of action that we follow, either in anticipation of encountering a stressor or as a direct response to stress as it occurs' (Martin et al., 2009, p. 765) in an effort to reduce the level of stress that we experience. In their seminal work, Lazarus and Folkman (1984) postulated two main types of coping responses: 'problem-focused' and 'emotion-focused' strategies. Whereas *problem-focused* coping strategies attempt to reduce stress by tackling the stressful event or situation directly, *emotion-focused* coping strategies attempt to regulate the emotional distress that is normally elicited by a given stressor. Typical problem-focused coping strategies include obtaining as much information as possible about the stressful situation to be faced, making a plan of action by setting specific and relevant goals, increasing one's effort in the situation, and trying to block out the source of stress (e.g. boxers on the way to the ring often listen to headphones in order to drown out crowd noise). By contrast, emotion-focused coping includes such strategies as seeking emotional support from others, engaging in physical relaxation exercises (Williams, 2010) and/or trying to change one's perception of the stressful event or situation (also called 'cognitive reappraisal'). To illustrate cognitive reap-praisal in action, consider how Jack Nicklaus, who has won more golf major championships than any other player in history, changed the way he labelled the anxiety that he felt before competitions: 'Sure, you're nervous, but that's the difference between being able to win and not being able to win. And that's the fun of it, to put yourself in the position of being ner-vous, being excited. I never look on it as pressure. *I look on it as fun and excitement*' (cited in Gilleece, 1996, p. 7). A third general coping strategy proposed by Endler and Parker (1990) is *avoidance* or removing oneself from the stressful situation. Despite the negative (and possibly psycho-pathological) connotations of its name, avoidance coping may be helpful sometimes in competitive sport. For example, a tennis player who is worried about an impending match may seek to avoid meeting officials and other players (including his or her opponent) before the game itself by warming up alone in an effort to avoid being distracted. Although problem-focused, emotion-focused and avoidance coping strategies are distinguishable from each other on theoretical grounds, they may overlap considerably when practised in everyday life. To illustrate, using an example from Richards (2004), imagine an athlete who has just received bad news about an injury going out for a drink with a friend. If this friend happens to be a physiotherapist, then the athlete may be regarded as using a combination of problem-focused coping (seeking advice on the injury from an expert), emotion-focused coping (seeking social support from a friend) and/or perhaps even avoidance (using alcohol as a temporary distraction from the stressful news).

Over the past two decades, a considerable amount of research has been conducted on coping processes in athletes. For example, 64 studies were included in a review by Nicholls and Polman (2007) of research in this field. It is difficult either to compare or integrate the results of these studies, however, as investigators varied considerably in their choice of coping measures. For example, Anshel et al. (2001) used the Coping Strategies Inventory; Pensgaard and Roberts (2003) used a version of the COPE inventory (Carver et al., 1989); and Johnson (1997) used the General Coping Questionnaire. Nevertheless, based on this review and on subsequent studies, the following insights have emerged into the nature and efficacy of coping strategies in sport.

To begin with, research suggests that athletes use a wide variety of problem-focused coping strategies in responding to stressful situations. These strategies include concentrating on goals, learning time management skills, learning about opponents, and practising. In a similar vein, commonly reported emotion-focused coping strategies include seeking social support, using mental imagery (see **4.17**), relying on humour, and attempting to remain confident in the face of stressful situations. Sometimes, age-related changes are evident in strategy use. For example, Reeves et al. (2009) investigated stress and coping in adolescent academy soccer players. They found that although problem-focused coping strategies were common among all ages of players, the middle adolescent footballers used more social support coping strategies than did their early adolescent counterparts.

Second, another issue addressed in the relevant research literature concerns the attempt to identify functional relationships between specific stressors and particular coping strategies. In this regard, Weston et al. (2009) used in-depth interviews to explore the stressors faced, and coping strategies employed, by five single-handed, round-the-world sailors. Among the stressors experienced by these sailors were environmental hazards (e.g. isolation and sleep deprivation), competitive stressors (e.g. yacht-related difficulties) and personal issues (e.g. family problems). In response to these stressors, the sailors reported using a combination of problem-focused coping strategies (e.g. making detailed plans for what to do in various hypothetical scenarios) and emotion-focused coping strategies (e.g. relying on social support from family and supporters to counteract the isolation of single-handed sailing). Interestingly, Weston et al. acknowledged that their research did not establish specific causal or temporal links between the stressors experienced by these sailors and the resulting coping strategies adopted. However, they suggested that future research in this field could benefit from equipping participants with electronic diaries to log the time-course of their stressor-coping strategy interactions.

Third, there has been an upsurge of research interest in the coping strategies of elite coaches. For example, Olusoga et al. (2010) used in-depth interviews to investigate the responses to stress of, and coping techniques used by, a sample of world-class UK coaches from a range of sports (e.g. swimming, field hockey). Thematic analysis showed that the most frequently reported coping strategy was 'structuring and planning' – a problem-focused approach that involved using past experience to anticipate and circumvent likely stressors. Attending coaching courses and seeking continuous professional development were also widely cited as preferred coping strategies.

As a final theme in research in this field, some investigators have addressed the crucial issue of the *efficacy* of coping strategies in sport. According to Nicholls and Polman (2007), coping effectiveness refers to 'the extent to which a coping strategy, or combination of strategies, is successful in alleviating the negative emotions caused by stress' (p. 15). Unfortunately, there has been a dearth of theoretically-driven attempts to evaluate the efficacy of coping strategies in athletes. Nevertheless, some sport psychology researchers have tested Folkman's (1991) 'goodness of fit' proposal that problem-focused coping techniques should be used when people face personally *controllable* stressors (e.g. those arising from their own behaviour), whereas emotion-focused strategies may be more appropriate when the stressful situations are *uncontrollable* (e.g. in sport, those arising from an opponent's performance). This hypothesis was corroborated by Anshel (1996), who reported that high perceived controllability was linked to problem-focused coping strategies, whereas low perceived controllability was associated with emotion-focused coping strategies in competitive athletes. Similarly, Kim and Duda (2003) discovered that when stressors were perceived to be controllable, athletes tended to use problem-based coping strategies. Despite such findings, little progress has been made in understanding the theoretical mechanisms underlying the apparent efficacy of problem-focused and emotion-focused coping strategies. Clearly, additional studies are required in which theoretically-derived hypotheses concerning coping strategies are tested using longitudinal research designs.

REFERENCES

Anshel, M.H. (1996) Coping styles among adolescent competitive athletes. *Journal of Social Psychology*, 136, 311–324.

Anshel, M.H., Jamieson, J. and Raviv, S. (2001) Cognitive appraisals and coping strategies following acute stress among skilled competitive male and female athletes. *Journal of Sport Behavior*, 24, 128–143.

Carver, C.S., Scheier, M.F. and Weintraub, J.K. (1989) Assessing coping strategies: A theoretically based approach. *Journal of Personality and Social Psychology*, 56, 267–283.

Clerkin, M. (2010) 'Pressure makes diamonds and golfers like Harrington'. *Sunday Tribune*, 19 September, p. 2 (Sport).

Endler, N. and Parker, J. (1990) Multi-dimensional assessment of coping: A critical review. *Journal of Personality and Social Psychology*, 58, 844–854.

Folkman, S. (1991) Coping across the life span: Theoretical issues. In Cummings, E.H. and Karraker, K.H. (eds) *Life-span Developmental Psychology: Perspectives on Stress and Coping*. Hillsdale, NJ: Erlbaum. 3–19.

Gilleece, D. (1996) 'Breathe deeply and be happy with second'. *The Irish Times*, 27 September, p. 7.

Johnson, U. (1997) Coping strategies among long-term injured competitive athletes: A study of 81 men and women in team and individual sports. *Scandinavian Journal of Medicine and Science in Sports*, 7, 367–372.

Kim, K.A. and Duda, J.L. (2003) The coping process: Cognitive appraisals of stress, coping strategies, and coping effectiveness. *The Sport Psychologist*, 17, 406–425.

Lazarus, R.S. and Folkman, S. (1984) *Stress, Appraisal, and Coping*. New York: Springer.

Martin, G.N., Carlson, N.R. and Buskist, W. (2009) *Psychology*. 4th edn. Harlow: Pearson Education.

Nicholls, A.R. (2008) Coping in sport. In Kirk, D., Cooke, C., Flintoff, A. and McKenna, J. (eds) *Key Concepts in Sport and Exercise Sciences*. London: Sage. pp. 109–111.

Nicholls, A.R. and Polman, R.C. (2007) Coping in sport: A systematic review. *Journal of Sports Sciences*, 25, 11–31.

anxiety and stress

Olusoga, P., Butt, J., Maynard, I. and Hays, K. (2010) Stress and coping: A study of world-class coaches. *Journal of Applied Sport Psychology*, 22, 274–293.

Pensgaard, A.M. and Roberts, G.C. (2003) Achievement goal orientation and the use of coping strategies among Winter Olympians. *Psychology of Sport and Exercise*, 4, 101–116.

Reeves, C.W., Nicholls, A.R. and Polman, J. (2009) Stressors and coping strategies among early and middle adolescent Premier League academy soccer players: Differences according to age. *Journal of Applied Sport Psychology*, 21, 31–48.

Richards, H. (2004) Coping in sport. In Lavallee, D., Thatcher, J. and Jones, M.V. (eds) *Coping and Emotion in Sport*. New York: Nova Science. pp. 29–51.

Weston, N.J.V., Thelwell, R.C., Bond, S. and Hutchings, N.V. (2009) Stress and coping in single-handed round-the-world ocean sailing. *Journal of Applied Sport Psychology*, 21, 468–474.

Williams, J.M. (2010) Relaxation and energizing techniques for regulation of arousal. In J.M. Williams (ed.), *Applied Sport Psychology: Personal Growth to Peak Performance* (6th ed.) New York: McGraw-Hill. pp. 247–266.

3

Motivation and Commitment

3.10: Sport Participation Motives

Definition: The psychological forces and structural factors that act, either individually or collectively, to determine our willingness to engage with, and disengage from, sport over time.

The reasons for taking part in sport, and giving it up, have long pre-occupied sport psychologists. According to earlier writers in the 18th and early 19th centuries, the primary motive for taking part in sport was to satisfy base instincts, with many descriptions steeped in evolutionary or psychodynamic ideas including catharsis (see **5.28**). It was only in the 1960s that more systematic attention came to bear directly on the issue through work on intrinsic motivation (see **3.14**, **3.15** and **3.16**), although these approaches were in turn linked to earlier drive theories of motivation, such as those advanced by Hull and Spence in the 1950s.

The most important early model was derived from McClelland and Atkinson's research on achievement motivation (see **3.13**). The McClelland-Atkinson model in turn is based on a concept already described in Chapter 5, approach-avoidance or the fight–flight response. In other words, when faced with the perception of threat, danger or challenge we are caught literally in two minds – do we meet it or do we beat it.

Atkinson's work was part of a wider trend in psychology during the 1970s when several social cognitive paradigms all rose to prominence. One of the most important was causal attribution theory, concerned with how we explain our social world (see **5.24**). Research interest in attribution theory across psychology waned during the early 1990s with criticisms that the theory was too general and unable to account for either the role played by emotion or large individual differences. This led to a call for ever-more sophisticated models which would accommodate attribution processes alongside a wider range of psychological and contextual constructs and including those factors identified as significant motives for engagement in sport.

Since that time sport psychologists have been interested both in developing theoretical frameworks for understanding sport motivation (see **3.13**, **3.14**, **3.15** and **3.16**) as well as listing the motives that influence why people take up sport and then influence their continued engagement. This research has revealed changing motives over the life cycle. For example, the reasons that children typically give for playing sport usually relate to one or more of fun, competence, affiliation, fitness and success. It is interesting that while intrinsic motives associated with competence have attracted considerable research interest, the motive of what is actually meant by fun or enjoyment has been largely ignored, despite children often citing this as their most important reason for taking up a sport in the first place.

Several large scale surveys have shown that children's reasons for taking part in sport change as they grow older, with an increasing emphasis on competition and fitness at the expense of affiliation and fun. Foster et al. (2007) found that factors such as dislike of team sports, gender and cultural stereotyping of certain sports, costs of participation in organised sports, and increasing emphasis on technical and performance issues at the expense of fun are all 'turn-offs' for young children (under 8 years old), while the 'turn-ons' were enjoyment, parental and peer support, and age-appropriate activities.

Reasons for withdrawal from sport also begin to be identifiable, including a lack of improvement, interest in/conflict with other activities, lack of fun, boredom, lack of playing time, excessive pressure from significant others (including parents, teachers and coaches), and competing pressures on time (e.g. school work and exams). Around this time, withdrawal from sport can be temporary or permanent and it can be either specific to a particular activity or total rejection of sport in all its forms. Estimates of attrition rates from sport vary depending on the sport in question and the populations under scrutiny, but an average rate of withdrawal of around one-third is not uncommon across adolescent populations, with particular sports (e.g. swimming) revealing drop-out rates that are far higher (Butcher et al., 2002).

Other chapters will look more closely at the 'why' of participation, but for now we will focus attention on the 'what', or the primary motives that have been associated with engagement in sport.

MOOD STATE

Not surprisingly, the literature confirms a positive relationship between sport participation and positive moods (e.g. contentment, satisfaction and enjoyment), and also links negative mood states with disengagement (e.g. depression, anxiety, tension). Early reliance on only one measure of mood, the Profile of Mood States Questionnaire (POMS), may have hindered exploration of the complexities of the relationships between engagement and both positive and negative affect, as two independent factors. Furthermore, research often disregarded the issue of causality – does being in a good mood encourage physical exercise, or does exercise improve our mood? The answer is probably both, but later research using measures that make a clearer distinction between positive and negative states (e.g. Positive Affect Negative Affect Schedule or PANAS) has helped to advance understanding. For example, frequency of engagement in physical activity has been found to be associated with positive affect, whereas a reduction of negative affect is not necessarily associated with participation, but may be linked to withdrawal from an activity. Research looking at the links between mood state, exercise and the role played by mediating variables, both psychological (including self-efficacy) and structural (including significant others), would suggest that a complex interplay is at work where, for example, friendships can improve mood state, which in turn can increase the likelihood of taking part in sport, which in turn can enhance mood state even further.

ENJOYMENT

A construct closely related to positive mood is enjoyment although, in contrast with affect or mood, it remains poorly defined and under-researched (McCarthy et al., 2008). Among adults, the best predictors of enjoyment have been found to be mastery, good performance, effort, sports importance and socio-psychological well-being. It has been suggested that significant sources of sport enjoyment in physical activity among adolescents are somewhat different, and include greater task-orientation, greater perceived competence and increased number of years involved in the activity.

SIGNIFICANT OTHERS

Other people will often play a critical role in determining patterns of sport participation throughout life, but are of critical importance in determining early initiation into a sport. Hellstedt (1987) first referred to the critical role played by the 'athletic triangle' of athlete, coach and parent, although more recent research has shown how parents, and particularly mothers, are increasingly concerned about placing their children in unsafe environments and thus may discourage engagement with certain sports or activities regarded as unsafe (Porter, 2002). Over time, research would suggest that the relative importance of significant others changes. While adults, including parents, teachers and coaches, may be critical in the early stages of engagement, peers become increasingly important into adolescence, while among adults it is work colleagues, health professionals, family and friends who exert the strongest influence.

HEALTH AND FITNESS

Research consistently points to the significance of health-related motives for participation, and most especially as we grow older. However, according to Allender et al. (2006), health benefits per se are not usually the primary motive but instead weight management, enjoyment, social interaction and support are more likely to exert a direct influence.

ACTIVITY CHOICE

The extensive survey literature on leisure activity among young people reveals that certain types of activity remain more attractive than others. For example, traditionally boys have tended to opt for team sports while girls have been more inclined to choose individual, non-competitive activities (see **7.35**). Furthermore, among young people in general there has been a shift away from organised activities and towards individual activity, for example extreme sports (De Knop et al., 1999).

STRUCTURAL BARRIERS

Along with the psychological factors listed below, there are many real and concrete barriers that have an immediate effect on participation opportunities, and despite good intentions, it is these that practically prevent regular participation, including the local transport and recreational infrastructure (Davison and Lawson, 2006), and even family television viewing habits (Sallis et al., 2000). Among adolescents, lack of time and conflict with other activities are cited as the most important reasons for poor adherence to physical activity programmes, while Gebhardt et al. (1999) list four primary reasons for non-participation: chores, entertaining/socialising with friends, watching TV and 'being cosy at home'.

With age, perceived risk of injury becomes increasingly important (Biddle and Nigg, 2000), while gender differences constantly appear (see **7.35**). In a systematic review aimed at understanding participation in sport, Sport England (2005) concluded that important factors standing in the way of regular participation included several practical factors such as embarrassment at showing others an unfit body (e.g. 'the walk of shame' from changing room to swimming pool), appearing incompetent, appearing masculine (among women), difficulty in accessing facilities, poor state of facilities, and the costs attached to joining sporting clubs and fitness gyms. Also, critical stages in life (e.g. leaving school, having children, children leaving home, retirement) all had a significant impact on participation, drop-out and future reasons for participation.

REFERENCES

Allender, S., Cowburn, G. and Foster, C. (2006) Understanding participation in sport and physical activity among children and adults: A review of qualitative studies. *Health Education Research*, 21, 826–835.

Biddle, S.J.H. and Nigg, C.R. (2000) Theories of exercise behavior. *International Journal of Sport Psychology*, 31, 290–304.

Butcher, J., Lindner, K.J. and Johns, D.P. (2002) Withdrawal from competitive youth sport: A retrospective ten-year study. *Journal of Sport Behavior*, 24, 145–161.

Davison, K. and Lawson, C. (2006) Do attributes in the physical environment influence children's physical activity? A review of the literature. *International Journal of Behavioral Nutrition and Physical Activity*, 3, 3–19.

De Knop, P., Wylleman, P., Theeboom, M., De Martelaer, K., van Hoecke, J. and van Heddegem, L. (1999) The role of contextual factors in youth participation in organized sport. *European Physical Education Review*, 5 (2), 153–168.

Foster, C., Cowburn, G., Allender, S. and Pearce-Smith, N. (2007) *Physical Activity and Children Review 3: The Views of Children on the Barriers and Facilitators to Participation in Physical Activity: A Review of Qualitative Studies.* London: NICE Public Health Collaborating Centre – Physical Activity.

Gebhardt, W.A., van der Doef, M.P. and Maes, S. (1999) Conflicting activities for exercise. *Perceptual and Motor Skills*, 89 (3), 1159–1160.

Hellstedt, J.C. (1987) The coach/parent/athlete relationship. *The Sport Psychologist*, 1 (2), 151–160.

McCarthy, P.J., Jones, M.V. and Clark-Carter, D. (2008) Understanding enjoyment in youth sport: A developmental perspective. *Psychology of Sport and Exercise*, 9, 142–156.

Porter, S. (2002) *Physical Activity: An Exploration of the Issues and Attitudes of Parents of pre-Fives.* London: Scott Porter Research and Marketing.

Sallis, J.F., Prochaska, J.J. and Taylor, W.C. (2000) A review of correlates of physical activity of children and adolescents. *Medicine and Science in Sports and Exercise*, 32, 963–975.

Sport England (2005) *Understanding Participation in Sport: A Systematic Review.* London: Sport England.

> **Definitions:** Burnout is a chronic physical and mental state characterised by a reduced sense of accomplishment, a devaluing of, or resentment towards, sport, coupled with physical and emotional exhaustion. Dropout is either total or partial disengagement from sport.

There can be few labels in sport more difficult to shoulder than 'The next...'. Whether it be 'The next Tiger Woods', 'The next Michael Jordan' or 'The next Pelé', all sports are littered with athletes who were tipped to be 'The next big thing' – but never quite seem to hit the mark. A word often invoked to describe this scenario is *burnout*. But what precisely does burnout mean? Where does it come from? Is it different from *dropout*? And finally, what can be done to prevent it?

In a thought provoking article, Raedeke (1997) suggests that much of the appeal of the term 'burnout' is due to its intuitive sense. When it is coupled with descriptions of athletes as sports *stars*, this appeal is magnified further. One can be asked to imagine a young star, burning bright in the firmament, before the talent fades and dies. In short, the term itself is almost poetic. However, poetic terms rarely make for quantifiable scientific phenomena, and so it has proven with burnout. Much of the debate surrounding the definition and measurement of burnout in sport has been fuelled by the fact that the term originated outside the sport psychology literature. In fact, the early and influential studies into burnout are to be found in professional contexts that include drug rehabilitation volunteers and poverty lawyers. In these studies burnout was defined as the chronic experience of emotional exhaustion, depersonalisation and impaired performance. It has taken some time for sport-specific definitions of burnout to emerge, but in the recent past the picture has become somewhat clearer. It now appears broadly accepted that the experience of athlete burnout consists of three elements: a reduced sense of accomplishment; a devaluing of, or resentment towards sport; and physical and emotional exhaustion (Raedeke et al., 2002). This definition has recently led to the development of the Athlete Burnout

Questionnaire (ABQ), a validated measure of burnout (Raedeke and Smith, 2001). One key feature of the definition of burnout is that it is multidimensional. There has been much debate within the literature as to the potential overlap between the concepts of overtraining and burnout. It certainly would appear to be the case that physical exhaustion is a central characteristic of burnout (Davis et al., 2002). However, this must be tempered by the influence of athlete perception; that is, athletes may feel exhausted because they are feeling burnt out, as equally as they may feel burnt out because they feel exhausted. The importance of a multidimensional definition is that it extends burnout beyond overtraining. Additionally, it makes recognition of varying extents and experiences of burnout.

To understand these issues, it is important to establish the theoretical underpinnings of burnout. Historically, explanations of burnout have focused on stress models but additional factors have been suggested more recently, including commitment and motivation. In terms of the role of stress in burnout, Smith's (1986) cognitive-affective model has proven highly influential. The key to understanding the role of stress is to understand the central role of perception. Stress is the physiological response to the perception that the athlete lacks the resources to meet the demands of a given situation. When the athlete consistently and repeatedly perceives an inability to cope with demands it may ultimately lead them to feel that they lack control over the situation, leading to feelings such as resentment and reduced accomplishment, as well as feelings of physical and emotional exhaustion associated with chronic stress (see **2.5** and **2.8**). While there is a widely accepted value in this account of burnout, it is not without its limitations. As Raedeke (1997) points out, in the stress-based account of burnout, where is the line of demarcation between stress and burnout? Or to take the logic one step further, why does every stressed athlete not experience burnout, or ultimately dropout? One of the key additional theoretical explanations of burnout to emerge is the importance of commitment. Schmidt and Stein (1991) proposed that athletes may choose to remain in a chronically stressful situation due to their commitment levels. In this model commitment is defined by the interplay of satisfaction, alternative courses of action, and investments. It is at this point that the difference between dropout and burnout may be delineated. In a stressful situation, an individual with better options and limited investment is likely to walk away. However, the individual who has invested a great deal in their sport may begin to feel trapped. This precludes dropout, and may lead to the feelings associated with burnout. In support of this suggestion, Raedeke (1997) reports that athletes presenting higher levels of extrinsic (rather than intrinsic) motivation display higher levels of burnout. In short, this refers to athletes who feel they must continue in their sport, rather than wanting to remain in their sport. In practice the examples of extrinsic motivators are obvious. Money is one factor, while in adolescence the pressure of parents is another. There is a link here with self-determination theory (SDT) (see **3.14**). SDT states that individuals seek to fulfil their basic intrinsic needs for autonomy, competence and relatedness. Within this model motivation may vary in quality. In particular, behaviours that are externally regulated (i.e. lacking in autonomy), that do not result in feelings of competence, and are engaged in to avoid negative outcomes, perversely are then likely to be associated with negative outcomes (Lemyre et al., 2006). This leads to a final theory of burnout: Coakley (1992) proposes that a narrowly defined identity may lead to a feeling of entrapment in the role of an athlete (see **7.37**).

While there has undoubtedly been progress towards the development of theoretical models of athlete burnout, these models will eventually be of most benefit when they have come to have an impact on actual outcomes for athletes. One potential avenue that has been explored, but not fully, is prevention. This work has used the above theoretical frameworks to identify potential warning signs that burnout may be on the horizon. In terms of the stress models of burnout, two broad categories of burnout precursors have emerged: stressors and resources. In terms of stressors, Cresswell (2009) points to what he describes as 'hassles'. In particular it is reported that in longitudinal studies sport-specific hassles (in his example, within rugby) and money hassles are associated with future feelings of burnout. In terms of resources, Cresswell also reports that the perception of a low level of social support can also be associated with future feelings of burnout. Additional to this is the finding that exhaustion, in particular emotional exhaustion, is a central factor in burnout (Goodger et al., 2007).

In terms of individual motivation and commitment, Lemyre et al. (2006) report that a shift towards extrinsic motivation is associated with feelings of burnout. In practice the picture is of an athlete who has forgotten the enjoyment they first experienced when they started playing sport and have become distracted by other external factors, whether that be pressure from others, money, celebrity status, or the other numerous potential distractions that young elite athletes face daily. Other factors that have been associated with burnout include frustration due to injury or non-selection and feelings of limited performance improvement (Cresswell and Eklund, 2007). Finally, in terms of feelings of entrapment, it has been reported that financial constraints, as well as feelings of loyalty, can lead athletes to remain in stressful situations, potentially leading to burnout (Boiché and Sarrazin, 2008).

Reflecting back on the numerous athletes who never quite managed to be 'the next big thing', these are familiar stories. Some appear distracted by external factors, some seem to consistently pick up injuries, while others seem exhausted by the pressure placed on them at a young age. There can be little dispute that these stories of burnout are tragic not only on a sporting level but also on a human level. However, a review of the burnout literature gives much cause for hope. Research has progressed to the point that there is now a broadly accepted definition of burnout and a well validated measure to identify it. Additionally, future preventative work will be well informed by a growing research base that can help identify the precursors of burnout. What will serve the field, and athletes, well will be the appetite of practitioners and researchers to move towards the development of well validated intervention methods to help ensure that 'The next big thing' lives up to his or her potential, and if they do not, that their return to earth is gentle and dignified.

REFERENCES

Boiché, J.C.S. and Sarrazin, P.G. (2008) Proximal and distal factors associated with dropout versus maintained participation in organized sport. *Journal of Sports Science and Medicine*, 8 (1), 9–16.

Coakley, J. (1992) Burnout among adolescent athletes: A personal failure or social problem? *Sociology of Sport Journal*, 9, 271–285.

Cresswell, S.L. (2009) Possible early signs of athlete burnout: A prospective study. *Journal of Science and Medicine in Sport*, 12, 393–398.

Cresswell, S.L. and Eklund, R.C. (2007) Athlete burnout: A longitudinal qualitative study. *The Sport Psychologist*, 21, 1–20.

Davis, H., Botterill, C. and MacNeill, K. (2002) Mood and self-regulation changes in under-recovery: An intervention model. In Kellmann, M. (ed.) *Enhancing Recovery: Preventing Underperformance in Athletes*. Champaign, IL: Human Kinetics. 161–179.

Goodger, K., Gorely, T., Lavallee, D. and Harwood, C. (2007) Burnout in sport: A systematic review. *The Sport Psychologist*, 21, 127–151.

Lemyre, P., Treasure, D.C. and Roberts, G.C. (2006) Influence of variability in motivation and affect on elite athlete burnout susceptibility. *Journal of Sport and Exercise Psychology*, 28, 32–48.

Raedeke, T.D. (1997) Is athlete burnout more than stress? A sport commitment perspective. *Journal of Sport and Exercise Psychology*, 19, 396–417.

Raedeke, T.D. and Smith, A.L. (2001) Development and preliminary validation of an athlete burnout measure. *Journal of Sport and Exercise Psychology*, 23, 281–306.

Raedeke, T.D., Lunney, K. and Venables, K. (2002) Understanding athlete burnout: Coach perspectives. *Journal of Sport Behavior*, 25, 181–206.

Schmidt, G.W. and Stein, G.L. (1991) A commitment model of burnout. *Journal of Applied Sport Psychology*, 8, 323–345.

Smith, R.E. (1986) Toward a cognitive-affective model of athlete burnout. *Journal of Sport Psychology*, 8, 36–50.

3.12: Goal Setting

> **Definition:** Goal setting is a self-motivational technique based on the principle of establishing specific and challenging short-term goals in order to move towards the realisation of long-term targets or objectives.

Setting goals is something that most athletes do, and something that most believe to be effective in enhancing their performance (e.g. Burton et al., 1998). It is difficult to underestimate the range, diversity and scope of goals that modern athletes typically incorporate into their career development plans. In a recent magazine interview, basketball's latest megastar, Lebron James, revealed that he is learning Mandarin to aid his attempts to break into the lucrative Chinese basketball market. James is quoted as saying, 'It's tough, but it's important.' Reading such sentiments, the mind may wander to that most overt characterisation of the role of business in sport, Jerry Maguire imploring his client to 'Show me the money!'. To the purists these may be viewed as undesirable developments, but developments they remain. As such, goal setting strikes at a core question for athletes and those working with them: what is the ultimate goal of an athlete's career?

It is no coincidence that goals have been a longstanding concern of both the psychology of business and the psychology of sport. But what precisely constitutes a goal? Do the lessons of goal setting in the world of business apply to the world of sport? What are the various types of goals? Is it beneficial for an athlete to set goals, and if so, which type of goals? It is with these questions in mind that the goal setting literature will be examined.

To begin, in order to set goals systematically it is important to establish baselines and to identify personal strengths and weaknesses, and this is where performance profiling becomes critical. Linking with work on self-appraisal, Richard Butler popularised performance profiling with his visually appealing profiling dartboard (Butler, 1996). This involves listing the range of attributes around the rim of the dartboard and then shading each segment up to a maximum of ten with two colours, one showing 'where you are now', the other 'where you

motivation and commitment

want to be'. This profile then acts as a masterplan for subsequent goal setting, and allows change or improvement over time to be easily recorded.

Defining what constitutes a goal is not a difficult task. A goal may be defined as an outcome that an individual is seeking to achieve through a particular course of action. Goals may not always be conscious; indeed, it has been suggested that they are likely to drift in and out of conscious thoughts (Locke and Latham, 1990). Historically, Locke's theory of goal setting was a watershed for the field as it provided the basis for goal setting to be widely applied in business settings. Locke theorised that goals affect performance through four mechanisms: by focusing attention; by activating appropriate levels of effort; by enhancing persistence; and by encouraging the development of strategies to achieve the stated goal. Further to this, Locke proposed four key principles of effective goal setting: that more difficult goals lead to higher performance; that specific goals are more effective than vague goals; that the performer must accept the goals; and that goals will not be effective without feedback (Locke and Latham, 1994). In practice, these principles have been reflected in industry, sport and education by interventions such as SMART Goal Setting: that is, the setting of goals that are Specific, Measurable, Action-Orientated, Realistic and Timely.

In reviewing the vast literature that has developed around goal setting, Burton and Weiss (2008) conclude that goal setting does enhance performance, and particularly when specific yet difficult goals are established. The evidence base for such a conclusion is broad, incorporating evidence from various settings, including the experimental. While a broad base of support is undoubtedly to be welcomed, one must also be mindful that each context within which goal setting is applied is different. This is clearly the case in sport where practitioners should be aware of the particular concerns of the athlete (Hall and Kerr, 2001). For example, sport is likely to entail a more explicit focus on competition and individual athletes' desire to win. Business, by contrast, is more often characterised by corporate thinking, as well as a more hierarchical structure that can see certain goals dictated from above. This leads to the question, how effective is goal setting in sport-specific settings? Further to this, the question must also be asked, what particular considerations should be given to athletes seeking to set goals?

In terms of assessing the general effectiveness of goal setting in sport, meta-analytic research remains somewhat limited but it would appear that goal setting can be an effective intervention in sport, even if the effect is not as great as that observed in other contexts (Kyllo and Landers, 1995). This leads to the question, what particular considerations should be given to athlete goal setting? In their comprehensive review of 88 sport-specific studies into goal setting, Burton and Weiss (2008) report that 80 per cent of these studies found a moderate to strong effect on performance. Further to this, they outline findings from within the sporting field which may be used to guide athlete goal setting. First and foremost it is suggested that the type of goals an athlete sets may be characterised along a continuum that incorporates three key goal categories. These are process goals, performance goals and outcome goals. Each goal category effectively builds on the other, with process goals typically characterised as forming the foundation of the athlete's career. Process goals include concerns such as technique and strategy. They are the *how* of sport. Performance goals reflect the athletes' own personal application of their athletic skill. They are the *what* of sport, for example, a basketball player's free throw percentage. Outcome goals are, to a degree, the result of how well an athlete performs. They are victories, championships and financial rewards. Effectively, they are the *why* of sport. Based on their examination of the literature, Burton and Weiss suggest what they call the Fundamental Goal Concept, namely that process and performance goals are the path which leads to successful outcome goals. As such they suggest that process and performance goals are the most effective goals for an athlete to set. This is said to be the case for a number of reasons, but chiefly because outcome goals are rarely within the complete control of an athlete. Other factors such as conditions, officials and opponent's skill are likely to play a role. The benefit of the athlete focusing on process and performance is that it ensures that their criteria for success remain under their control, hopefully limiting the damage of any failures to achieve outcome goals. Additionally, it encourages an emphasis on intrinsic, rather than extrinsic, motivation. Crucially, the point is made that the setting of outcome goals is not discouraged; indeed, they are seen as vital components of athlete commitment. In this respect, Lebron James has got it right in that if his outcome goal is to break into the Chinese market, the learning of Mandarin is an appropriate process goal to help get him there. The question is one of focus and how one judges the success of goal-setting exercises. The research to date would suggest that a focus on skills and their application are more appropriate goals to set and to judge success against.

Further characteristics of effective goals have been examined in sport-specific contexts. In terms of Locke's suggestion that the more difficult a goal, the greater the effect on performance, this has not been consistently demonstrated in sporting contexts. Indeed, it has been reported that difficult goals may prove counterproductive by increasing stress and thereby impairing performance (Weinberg et al., 2001). In general, it would appear that moderately difficult goals are most desirable in sporting settings (Kyllo and Landers, 1995). Increasingly, the concept of difficulty has been associated with a second key concept: specificity. It would appear that the effect of goal specificity is dependent on goal difficulty. For example, a specific easy goal is unlikely to be as effective in increasing performance in comparison with a specific moderately difficult goal. However, it would appear that when difficulty is controlled, increased specificity is likely to increase performance. Finally, a key consideration is the proximity of a goal, that is, how quickly can success be evaluated? While this is not an area that has received a great deal of attention, it would appear that the success of long-term goals is contingent on short-term markers of success (Kyllo and Landers, 1995). This would sit well with Locke's emphasis on the importance of feedback in achieving goals. Additionally, it sits well with the fundamental goal concept as it suggests that longer-term outcome goals are contingent on shorter-term process and performance goals.

In summarising the literature of goal setting in sport, one would have to conclude that it remains an important performance enhancing tool. However, it comes with caveats. Consideration should be given to the finding that goal setting in sport is slightly less effective than goal setting in business. Additionally, consideration must be given to the particular idiosyncrasies of the sporting context and the nature of working with individual athletes. While the concept of setting goals would appear to be a relatively simple one, the process of guiding an athlete through the goal setting process rarely is. Recent conceptualisations of goal setting as a process, such as the Competitive Goal Setting Model (CGS-3) (Burton and Weiss, 2008), provide an insight into the complexities of the goal setting process. The success, or otherwise, of any goal setting intervention operates in a context that incorporates numerous important factors. These include cognitive factors, such as the athlete's beliefs regarding the nature of ability, social factors, such as the support an athlete receives, and situational factors, such as outcomes and the athlete's reactions to them. The importance of each of these factors should be recognised and none should be addressed in isolation. However, despite these caveats, the goal-setting literature stands as testimony to the importance of the development of a sport-specific literature. There would now appear to be some degree of consensus that, while athletes should be encouraged to be mindful of longer-term outcome goals, they are well served to focus on the means to achieving them. The key characteristic of goal setting in sport is to focus athletes on the means to achieving their desired outcome goals, through the practice and successful application of the particular skills of their sport. Upon reflection, rather than imploring his client to 'Show me the money', Jerry Maguire may have been better imploring him to 'Show me the process'!

REFERENCES

Burton, D. and Weiss, C. (2008) The fundamental goal concept: The path to process and performance success. In Horn, T. (ed.) *Advances in Sport Psychology*. 3rd edn. Leeds: Human Kinetics. pp. 339–375.

Burton, D., Weinberg, R.S., Yukelson, D. and Weigland, D. (1998) The goal effectiveness paradox in sport: Examining the goal practices of collegiate athletes. *The Sport Psychologist*, 12, 404–418.

Butler, R.J. (1996) *Sport Psychology in Action*. Oxford: Butterworth-Heinemann.

Hall, K. and Kerr, A.W. (2001) Goal setting in sport and physical activity: Tracing empirical development and establishing conceptual direction. In Roberts, G.C. (ed.) *Advances in Motivation in Sport and Exercise*. Champaign, IL: Human Kinetics. pp. 183–235.

Kyllo, L.B. and Landers, D.M. (1995) Goal setting in sport and exercise: A research synthesis to resolve the controversy. *Journal of Sport and Exercise Psychology*, 17, 117–137.

Locke, E.A. and Latham, G.P. (1990) *A Theory of Goal Setting and Task Performance*. Englewood Cliffs, NJ: Prentice Hall.

Locke, E.A. and Latham, G.P. (1994) Goal setting in theory. In O'Neill, H.F. and Drillings, M. (eds) *Motivation: Theory and Research*. Hillside, NJ: Lawrence Erlbaum. pp. 13–29.

Weinberg, R.S., Butt, J. and Knight, B. (2001) High school coaches' perceptions of the process of goal setting. *The Sport Psychologist*, 15, 20–47.

> **Definitions:** Fear of failure describes the motive to avoid those occasions where the prospect of failure is a possibility while the need to achieve characterises the desire to succeed in competitive situations.

Fear is a phenomenon that has long received substantial academic attention. As far back as 1915, Walter Cannon coined the key phrase that has characterised discussions of the psychology of fear: fight or flight. Cannon, a physiologist by training, examined animal responses to threat. His suggestion was that the bodily reactions associated with the perception of threat, essentially the activation of the sympathetic nervous system, prepared the organism to make one of two responses, to meet it or beat it (fight or flight). This central consideration, that the arousal associated with the perception of threat may have an adaptive purpose, would later inform drive theories of motivation that sought to examine the effects of increased arousal on performance. Once the contention is accepted that arousal may affect performance, the relevance to sport becomes obvious. Arguably the key theory to emerge in this respect is the McClelland–Atkinson Need Achievement Theory (NAT). Building on Cannon's idea that the stress reaction can elicit two differing responses (flight or fight), the NAT posited two key psychological constructs that continue to influence the field today: fear of failure and need to achieve.

The NAT is a theory of motivation cast in the tradition of other approaches that focus on intrinsic drives or forces (see **3.14**, **3.15** and **3.16**). Within its framework, motivation is conceptualised as a drive to meet challenges or, as termed in the theory, a need to achieve (NAch). The strength of this need is dependent on a number of factors. The first factor is the relative strengths of two motives: the motive to achieve success (MS) and the motive to avoid failure (MAF), also known as fear of failure (FF). The second factor is the combination of two perceptions:

the perception that success is likely (Ps) and the perception of the incentives available (Is). The final factor is the role of extrinsic rewards (MExt). The combination of these factors may be expressed as a formula:

$$NAch = (MS - MAF)(Ps \times Is) + MExt$$

The concept of fear of failure has received substantial attention across various domains within the psychological literature, including education, business and sport. It is now understood as a relatively stable disposition that may be established in childhood (Conroy and Coatsworth, 2004). The disposition is towards viewing situations in which the person is being evaluated as threatening (Conroy et al., 2002). This perception of threat, or fear, is likely to have a restrictive effect on performance in such situations, leading to the adoption of avoidance-based goals (Birney et al., 1969). The adoption of these negative goals is in turn associated with a number of negative consequences, including worry, stress and anxiety (Conroy et al., 2002), hostile self-concepts and lower self-esteem (Conroy at al., 2005), and, in young athletes, can affect interpersonal behaviour, school work, sporting performance and general well-being (Sagar et al., 2009).

In the light of these negative outcomes, recent years have seen a growing emphasis on understanding the developmental origins of fear of failure in young athletes (Sagar and Lavallee, 2010). The starting point for any discussion of the origin of fear of failure must be the recognition that fear itself is a natural reaction to perceived threat; the question then is why do some young athletes perceive competitive situations as threatening? What has been suggested is that while failure itself is unlikely to cause fear, what is likely is that the young athlete fears the *consequences* of failure. The central consequence highlighted by the literature has been that of the feeling of shame associated with failure (McGregor and Elliot, 2005). However, this contention raises a further question; why do some young athletes perceive failure as something to be ashamed of? This question may be answered by examining recent hierarchical models of fear of failure. Conroy (2001) has identified five aversive consequences associated with failure: experiencing shame/embarrassment; devaluing one's self-estimate; being uncertain of the future; significant others may lose interest; and significant others may be upset. In terms of evidence supporting the relevance of the factors highlighted above, the role of significant others has emerged as central. For example, it has been reported that young athletes experiencing a high level of fear of failure are likely to perceive parents and coaches as hostile (Conroy, 2003). In a related vein, athletes with a high fear of failure also report that they engage in critical self-talk that mirrors the criticism they receive from their coaches, suggesting that fear of failure may be socialised, or transferred from important others. Additionally, when one considers the potential aversive consequence of devaluing one's self-estimation, the suggestion may be made that normative referencing (i.e. comparing young athletes against their peers) may also contribute to fear of failure. While intuitively the suggestion that an increased emphasis on competition will increase fear of failure is appealing, it must be noted that existing research remains inconclusive (Conroy and Elliot, 2004). Indeed, it has been suggested that in general there remains a lack of research into the developmental origins of fear of failure, particularly in elite athletes (Sagar et al., 2009). While it would appear that there remains work to be done in identifying the aetiological factors that contribute to the fear of failure, once one accepts that the behaviour of significant others, as well as the measures of success given to the young athlete, may be important, practitioners have a focus for intervention. This has proven to be the case, with positive results being reported for programmes that target both coach and parent behaviours (Sagar et al., 2009).

A tempting contention to be made is that fear of failure may be reduced by increasing the need to achieve. However, the view that need to achieve and fear of failure are two sides of the same coin is inaccurate. The NAT posits that these two constructs are independent. In practice this means that it is possible for an athlete to possess both a high need to achieve and a high fear of failure. In fact, four theoretical combinations are possible, each of which make their own distinct predictions regarding motivation:

1. *Low need to achieve and high fear of failure* – this athlete is highly likely to withdraw from competition, viewing the stress associated with possible failure as more pertinent than any potential achievements.
2. *Low need to achieve and low fear of failure* – this athlete is likely to be quite indifferent to competition, being driven by neither fear nor a need to achieve.
3. *High need to achieve and low fear of failure* – this athlete is likely to enjoy competitive situations and not perceive them as a threat to their self-concept.
4. *High need to achieve and high fear of failure* – this athlete is likely to enjoy competition but perceive it as a potential threat to their self-concept.

The question these categories present to practitioners is which of the above types of motivation is most suitable for an elite athlete? It could certainly be suggested that Type 3 represents, in a sense, the *purest* form of motivation, and is likely to be associated with athletes in the early stages of their careers, before they are socialised into experiencing fear of failure. Indeed, studies of elite athletes would suggest that they possess the types of motivation that may be associated with a need to achieve, such as intrinsic motivation and a focus on task goals (Mallett and Hanrahan, 2004). However, when one considers the world of elite sport it would appear highly likely that extrinsic factors, such as the opinions of others, potential loss of income and comparing oneself against other athletes, will also be pertinent (Duda et al., 1995). Evidence would suggest this is the case, with it being reported that elite athletes may possess goals of both an intrinsic and extrinsic nature (Roberts, 2001). In such an instance, it may be expected that the motivation of an elite athlete will more closely reflect Type 4. As such, while it is useful that practitioners seek to lessen fear in young athletes, there must also be a recognition that, in top-level sport, the ability to handle fear is likely to be as useful an asset as possessing a need to achieve. As Mark Twain famously put it, 'Courage is resistance to fear, mastery of fear – not the absence of fear.'

REFERENCES

Birney, R.C., Budick, H. and Teevan, R.C. (1969) *Fear of Failure*. New York: Van Nostrand.

Cannon, W. (1915) *Bodily Changes in Pain, Hunger, Fear and Rage: An Account of Recent Researches into the Function of Emotional Excitement*. New York: Appleton.

Conroy, D.E. (2001) Fear of failure: An exemplar for social development research in sport. *Quest*, 53, 165–183.

Conroy, D.E. (2003) Representational models associated with fear of failure in adolescents and young. *Journal of Personality*, 71, 757–783.

Conroy, D.E. and Coatsworth, J.D. (2004) The effects of coach training on fear of failure in youth swimmers: A latent growth curve analysis from a randomized, controlled trial. *Journal of Applied Developmental Psychology*, 25, 193–214.

Conroy, D.E., Coatsworth, J.D. and Fifer, A.M. (2005) Testing dynamic relations between perceived competence and fear of failure in young athletes. *Revue Européenne de Psychologie Appliqué*, 55, 99–110.

Conroy, D.E. and Elliot, A.J. (2004) Fear of failure and achievement goals in sport: Addressing the issue of the chicken and the egg. *Anxiety, Stress and Coping*, 17, 271–285.

Conroy, D.E., Willow, J.P., and Metzler, J.N. (2002) Multidimensional fear of failure measurement: the performance failure appraisal inventory. *Journal of Applied Sport Psychology*, 14, 76–90.

Duda, J.L., Chi, L., Newton, M.L., Walling, M.D. and Catley, D. (1995) Task and ego orientation and intrinsic motivation in sport. *International Journal of Sport Psychology*, 26, 40–63.

Mallett, C.J. and Hanrahan, S.J. (2004) Elite athletes: why does the 'fire' burn so brightly? *Psychology of Sport and Exercise*, 5, 183–200.

McGregor, H.A. and Elliot, A.J. (2005) The shame of failure: examining the link between fear of failure and shame. *Personality and Social Psychology Bulletin*, 31, 218–231.

Roberts, G.C. (2001) Understanding the dynamics of motivation in physical activity: The influence of achievement goals on motivational processes. In Roberts, G.C. (ed.) *Advances in Motivation in Sport and Exercise*. Champaign, IL: Human Kinetics. 1–50.

Sagar, S.S. and Lavallee, D. (2010) The developmental origins of fear of failure in adolescent athletes: Examining parental practices. *Psychology of Sport and Exercise*, 11, 177–187.

Sagar, S.S., Lavallee, D. and Spray, C.M. (2009) Coping with the effects of fear of failure: A preliminary investigation of young elite athletes. *Journal of Clinical Sport Psychology*, 1, 1–27.

3.14: Self-Determination Theory

> **Definition:** A theory of human motivation that links our innate growth tendencies and psychological needs to motivational types, with a particular emphasis on intrinsic motivation and self-determination.

Following from the early work of McClelland and Atkinson on achievement motivation (see **3.13**), and set within the broader context of the social cognitive movement, Self-Determination Theory (SDT) emerged in the 1970s to offer an elaborate framework for considering how our innate growth tendencies are reflected in motivational types and subsequent behaviours (Ryan and Deci, 2002; Deci and Ryan, 2008). As an approach to understanding why we take part in both sport and physical exercise generally, and what we derive from that engagement, it has continued to enjoy support both in academia and in a variety of practical settings (Vallerand, 2008).

In the early days, SDT appeared relatively straightforward, suggesting that three basic psychological needs (competence, autonomy/self-determination and relatedness) reveal themselves in patterns of intrinsic and/or extrinsic motivations which then regulate our actions, and our willingness to continue to engage in the future. As time has passed so layers of complexity have continued to be added to SDT, and while the underlying postulates are now well established, the degree of sophistication attaching to the most recent versions of the theory can be confusing and complex to the uninitiated.

What can add to this confusion is the relationship between SDT and its sub-theories, including cognitive evaluation theory, causality orientation theory and organismic integration theory. Each of these sub-theories focuses attention only on certain elements within SDT, with cognitive evaluation theory generally regarded as the most significant and with the greatest practical utility.

Cognitive Evaluation Theory considers how various factors, and in particular environmental or contextual influences, impact on intrinsic motivation, with a particular focus on competence and autonomy. For example, some studies have considered how different types of reward systems (e.g. task completion v. engagement contingent v. performance contingent) may influence future motivation in different ways (see Hagger and Chatzisarantis, 2007). The theory highlights the importance of good feedback on performance, linked to the ability of the athlete to control that performance.

The core theory, SDT, proposes that our intrinsic motivation derives from three innate growth needs: competence, autonomy (or self-determination) and relatedness. These are seen as universal psychological needs, although it is argued that their salience will vary across time, place and life domain, including the physical. SDT next proposes that we need to distinguish between two types of motivation derived from these needs: the intrinsic and the extrinsic. Intrinsic motivation, the inherent pleasure or joy of doing something for its own sake, is qualitative distinct from those rewards that we often automatically associate with success, known as extrinsic incentives or motives. In turn these are distinguished from the state of amotivation, or the absence of motivation.

The theory suggests that the strength of intrinsic motivation is influenced principally by the person's degree of autonomy or self-determination, which normally has been operationalised as their locus of causality (either internal or external). An external locus of causality ('Things happen to me') reflects low control and is likely to decrease intrinsic motivation, while an internal locus of causality ('I make things happen') reflects a high degree of perceived control and is more likely to enhance intrinsic motivation.

Perceived competence (see **3.16**) and engagement with challenging activities also mediate our intrinsic motivation. This is because the level of challenge attached to an activity is critical in showing us how competent we actually are. Easy and difficult activities provide little feedback, but a challenge that is both difficult and demanding yet also attainable seems to strike the right balance (see **3.12**).

The relationship between extrinsic outcomes and intrinsic motivation in the theory is now far from straightforward. Originally it had been proposed as a negative relationship, then it was argued that outcomes can have both positive and negative relationships with motivation, before finally it was suggested that both feedback and reinforcement outcomes interact with intrinsic motivation in a relationship mediated by the functional significance or psychological meaning attached to each. Furthermore, the meaning of feedback and reinforcement can be perceived to be either informational or controlling, the former enhancing intrinsic motivation while the latter has little effect.

Nowadays, SDT is typically represented as a hierarchical model, with motivation influenced by a hierarchy of social factors that can be either global (e.g. personality), contextual (e.g. coach behaviour) or situational. In this hierarchical model the three types of motivation (intrinsic, extrinsic and amotivation) are placed along a continuum of self-determination, with amotivation being the least self-determining, intrinsic motivation the most, and extrinsic positioned midstream. *Amotivation* is the absence of motivation, purpose or expectation. *Extrinsic motivation* is subdivided into four types that vary in terms of the degree of self-determination from external regulation (to achieve a reward or avoid punishment, thus the lowest level of self-determination), to introjected regulation (participation out of pressure or coercion), identified regulation (participation from choice but not interest) and integrated regulation (the values of the behaviour are integrated into personal values and belief systems).

The last, integrated regulation, is the closest to intrinsic motivation but is still regarded as qualitatively different as it involves achieving a goal that is socially valued – without necessarily embracing those values within the self-concept. This is not quite the equivalent of *intrinsic motivation*, which is about engaging in an activity for its own inherent satisfaction rather than for any extrinsic reward or value. However, even intrinsic motivation has been further subdivided into three types: motivation towards knowledge, accomplishment and experiencing stimulation. Further, according to Vallerand (2007a), motivation is seen to exist at three levels of generality: the *global* (i.e. the environment as a whole), the *contextual* (i.e. usual response to a specific context, e.g. education, sport) and the *situational* (i.e. specific activity at a given time).

This multidimensional view of motivation has been measured in a variety of ways; one of the most popular is the Sport Motivation and Exercise Motivation Scales, based on the earlier Sport Motivation Scale, which in turn is based on the Intrinsic/Extrinsic Motivation Scale (see Li, 1999).

The early research on self-determination began from simple principles but rapidly moved to a position where it began to embrace more and more elements. Most recently, Vallerand has shifted ground yet again by arguing that the three basic psychological needs of autonomy, competence and relatedeness will influence both our choice of activity and our subsequent willingness to continue to engage, but then our attention will concentrate on a small number of activities that are seen as especially enjoyable and important, and which resonate strongly with our sense of identity. Vallerand's Dualistic Model of Passion (Vallerand, 2008), maintains that these activities become 'passionate activities' where passion is defined as a strong inclination toward a self-defining activity that one likes (or even loves), finds important, and in which one invests time and energy.

Past research has shown that values and regulations concerning non-interesting (dispassionate) activities can be internalised in either a controlled or an autonomous fashion (Sheldon, 2002). Similarly, activities that people are passionate about will also be internalised in these same two ways, leading to two distinct types of passion: obsessive and harmonious. Obsessive passion results from a controlled internalisation of the activity into one's identity where the values and regulations associated with the activity are taken on board but not embraced completely within the sense of self. This type of internalisation may develop because contingencies are attached to the activity, such as feelings of social acceptance or self-esteem, or because the sense of excitement derived from activity engagement is uncontrollable.

According to Vallerand (2007b), an obsessive passion can fuel an uncontrollable urge to participate. In contrast, harmonious passion develops naturally from the internalisation of the activity into the person's identity. It occurs when the activity is freely accepted as important, unfettered by any contingencies. Not surprisingly, harmonious passion is associated with positive engagement in sport, while obsessive passion can lead us down a much more difficult and dangerous path.

REFERENCES

Deci, E.L. and Ryan, R.M. (2008) Facilitating optimal motivation and psychological well-being across life's domains. *Canadian Psychology*, 49, 14–23.

Hagger, M.S. and Chatzisarantis, N.L.D. (eds) (2007) *Intrinsic Motivation and Self-Determination in Exercise and Sport*. Champaign, IL: Human Kinetics.

Li, F. (1999) The Exercise Motivation Scale: Its multifaceted structure and construct validity. *Journal of Applied Sport Psychology*, 11, 97–115.

Ryan, R.M. and Deci, E.L. (2002) An overview of self-determination theory. In Deci, E.L. and Ryan, R.M. (eds) *Handbook of Self-Determination Research*. Rochester, NY: University of Rochester Press. pp. 3–33.

Sheldon, K.M. (2002) The self-concordance model of healthy goal-striving: When personal goals correctly represent the person. In Deci, E.L. and Ryan, R.M. (eds.) *Handbook of Self-Determination Research*. Rochester, NY: University of Rochester Press. pp. 65–86.

Vallerand, R.J. (2007a) Intrinsic and extrinsic motivation in sport and physical activity: A review and a look at the future. In Tenenbaum, G. and Eklund, E. (eds) *Handbook of Sport Psychology*. 3rd ed. New York: Wiley. pp. 49–83.

Vallerand, R.J. (2007b) Passion for sport in athletics. In Jowett, S. and Lavallee, D. (eds) *Social Psychology in Sport*. Champaign, IL: Human Kinetics. pp. 249–264.

Vallerand, R.J. (2008) On the psychology of passion: In search of what makes people's lives most worth living. *Canadian Psychology*, 49, 1–13.

3.15: Achievement Goal Theory

> **Definition:** A psychological theory of intrinsic motivation that considers how beliefs and cognitions orient us towards achievement or success, especially in relation to two styles, task (mastery) and ego (performance).

As psychologists have become increasingly interested in cognitive approaches to understanding motivation, so Achievement Goal Theory (AGT) has emerged to play a prominent role in the contemporary sport psychology literature and is now one of the most popular theories applied in this context (Roberts et al., 2007). In contrast with many other models and theories that only highlight the positive side of intrinsic motivation, AGT instead makes a distinction between types of motives or goal orientations that could be either harmful or helpful.

As with many motivational models the origins of this approach originally lie outside sport, in the world of educational psychology, but it did not take long to see the potential application to sporting endeavours. AGT focuses attention on those beliefs or cognitions that energise us towards achievement or success (Wang and Biddle, 2007). It therefore considers our attitudes towards achievement, our motivation in achievement settings, and our achievement performances themselves. Sport psychologists have found the approach intuitively appealing for many reasons, not least because of its focus on achievement but also, in the early years, because it appeared to provide a clear way of distinguishing between those whose goal orientations are positive and concerned with mastery of skills, as opposed to those whose motives are less wholesome, being more concerned with self-advancement at the expense of others.

The two styles are characterised in the literature as representing two achievement goal orientations, either task (mastery) or ego (performance). These orientations are not seen as fixed (or traits) but are more like cognitive schema (or mental representations) that tend to be quite stable over time, unless feedback on performance suggests that a radical re-orientation is required. The two orientations are seen to be a function of three interacting factors: our underlying disposition; the climate created by significant others (or motivational climate, see later); and developmental influences during childhood (White, 2007).

'Task orientation' refers to those occasions where the person focuses primarily on improvement and mastery of a skill. The AGT suggests that those with a task (mastery) orientation are more likely to show persistence and to choose challenging activities that allow them to assess not only where they are but where they need to be. By contrast, those with an ego (performance) orientation use their sport to prove their worth against others, and often have an unhealthy preoccupation with competition and winning. This approach can reveal itself in an arrogance that masks underlying insecurities and where fear of failure can become the overriding concern (see **3.13**).

It is also argued that the two goal orientations differ significantly in relation to how competence is construed. Those with a task orientation tend to use self-referenced criteria to assess their competence, while those with an ego orientation are more inclined to use others as their primary reference point, thereby making them more vulnerable to dips in confidence (Roberts et al., 2007). In turn, this may reflect in lowered perceptions of success and effort, especially where self-confidence is already fragile.

Early research on either side of the Atlantic, as initially pioneered by Nicholls (1984), appeared to confirm the early enthusiasm for the theory (Duda, 2005). For example, it was found that young people with a high task orientation believed that their engagement with sport improved co-operation and mastery skills, while those with a high ego orientation looked on sport as a way of gaining social acceptance, and of bolstering their ego through competition. Further, a task orientation linked effort to success, teamwork and experience, while an ego orientation saw success as being dependent on natural skill or ability above all else. In other words, those with a task orientation generally feel they can improve and are in control of their own destiny (an internal attribution style, see **5.24**), while those with an ego orientation feel themselves more as the victims of fate or circumstance (an external attribution style, see **5.24**). It should therefore come as no surprise to learn that those with an ego orientation are more likely to resort to cheating, aggression and foul play in order to succeed.

To this point, the picture is straightforward. Someone with a task orientation is a better sporting prospect and is likely to be more highly motivated, and successful, over time. However, recent years have tended to cast doubt on this simple explanation and relationship, with research indicating that both task and ego orientations can each be helpful in the right circumstances (Harwood, 2002). More recently it has been suggested that it is the individual goal orientation profile in a particular context that should become the focus of future research, rather than a search for general patterns across wider populations. For example, evidence suggests that many elite athletes see an ego orientation as complementing, not competing with, a task orientation, as in concert the two help to give competition the edge that is necessary to ensure continued success, and which helps sustain motivation in the longer term. This finding confirms that both orientations must be seen as independent constructs; in other words, a person can be high on both, low on both, or any high/low combination of the two.

By 2000, an extensive research literature had grown to consider the many variables that interact with goal orientation and also the relationship between participation motives and goal orientation. For example, those who are task-oriented tend to choose to participate in sport in order to develop or master skills, or for social reasons or fun, while those with a strong ego orientation tend to take part principally for recognition and social status.

Such findings suggest that those with an ego-oriented outlook will tend to find competition more meaningful as it provides an opportunity for social comparison, a view supported by Harwood et al. (2000). However, those with either a task or an ego orientation have been shown to place a similar emphasis on competition, and it appears that it is their subjective evaluation of the competitive context that is important rather than the context itself (Treasure et al., 2001).

The theory suggests that early influences will make an impression not only on the goal orientation of the young person but also the motivational climate within which sport takes place (Parish and Treasure, 2003). Significant others, including parents, teachers and coaches, help create this climate which is typically characterised as being either mastery (task) or performance (ego) oriented (Ntoumanis and Biddle, 1999). By way of example, it has been found that parents and teachers high in task orientation tend to emphasise a mastery climate that values a team orientation, whereas those with an ego orientation nurture a climate or culture that focuses more on competition and winning. In time, the dominant orientation of the significant other can be internalised by the young person, and so the climate is perpetuated to the next generation.

The interplay between the motivational climate and the person's own goal orientation profile then becomes of primary concern, along with how the individual orientation changes depending on context, for example in and out of competition (Harwood, 2002).

Interestingly, neither parents nor children are always accurate in assessing what the achievement goal orientation of their respective parent/child actually is, but it is their perception that matters most and which comes to have the most profound influence. Those who perceive that their parents or coaches have an ego orientation are more likely to worry about making mistakes and winning at all costs, whereas significant others who are seen to have a task orientation generally place a greater emphasis on learning and fun.

Over time there is some evidence that our goal orientation may shift from a task orientation in early childhood to an ego orientation in adolescence, but large individual differences exist depending on the predominant motivational climate during childhood. Differences have also been noted between boys and girls, with boys (and men) being viewed as more ego-oriented than girls (or women).

Despite the rich history of research, recent years have witnessed a steady decline in interest, coupled with a more critical appraisal of findings to date. Research has still to explain if goal orientations change through the course of a sporting season or career and if they do, what factors act as antecedents and which are influenced by goal orientation. Sport and physical activity provide constant sources of feedback and information on performance, which undoubtedly change perceptions of competence, enjoyment and satisfaction over time.

Traditionally, goal orientations have been measured using scales such as the Perception of Sport Questionnaire (POSQ) or the Task and Ego Orientation Sports Questionnaire (TEOSQ), the latter measuring both sport-specific and domain-general goal orientation. These treat the two orientations as either entirely independent or orthogonally related, with scores on one not necessarily related to scores on the other.

Not unusually, as more and more research has been carried out, so the basic tenets of the theory have come under closer scrutiny and the limitations of the approach have been exposed. For example, it is now argued by authors including Andrew Elliot (Elliot and Conroy, 2005) that a simple distinction between ego and task orientation only tells half the story, and there may be a need to consider multiple achievement goals at the same time. Alongside the dichotomy between task and ego orientations it is argued that there is a need to consider whether the person is driven by approach (challenge) or avoidance (fear) motives.

Elliot argues that performance goals which focus on challenge or striving to be competent differ from those that fear showing incompetence. The former is an approach goal and is likely to encourage persistence, while the latter represents an avoidance goal, driven not by the desire to meet a challenge, but to avoid failing. This is not likely to sustain motivation in the long term. In combination these then allow for four distinct achievement goals; Mastery-approach (MAp); Performance-approach (PAp); Performance-avoidance (PAv); and Mastery-avoidance (MAv). Although the research evidence is not yet extensive it does suggest that this new dimension adds significantly to AGT and represents a promising way forward for future research dealing with achievement goals.

REFERENCES

Duda, J.L. (2005) Motivation in sport: The relevance of competence and achievement goals. In Elliot, A.J. and Dweck, C.S. (eds) *Handbook of Competence and Motivation*. New York: Guilford Publications. pp. 318–335.

Elliot, A.J. and Conroy, D.E. (2005) Beyond the dichotomous model of achievement goals in sport and exercise psychology. *Sport and Exercise Psychology Review*, 1, 17–25.

Harwood, C.G. (2002) Assessing achievement goals in sport: Caveats for consultants and a case for contextualisation. *Journal of Applied Sport Psychology*, 14, 106–119.

Harwood, C., Hardy, L. and Swain, A. (2000) Achievement goals in sport: A critique of conceptual and measurement issues. *Journal of Sport and Exercise Psychology*, 22, 235–255.

Nicholls, J.G. (1984) Achievement motivation: Conceptions of ability, subjective experience, task choice, and performance. *Psychological Review*, 91 (3), 328–346.

Ntoumanis, N. and Biddle, S.J.H. (1999) A review of motivational climate in physical activity. *Journal of Sport Sciences*, 17, 643–665.

Parish, L.E. and Treasure, D.C. (2003) Physical activity and situational motivation in physical education: Influence of the motivational climate and perceived ability. *Research Quarterly of Exercise and Sport*, 74, 173–182.

Roberts, G.C., Treasure, D.C. and Conroy, D. (2007) Understanding the dynamics of motivation in sport and physical activity: An achievement goal interpretation. In Tenenbaum, G. and Eklund, R.C. (eds) *Handbook of Sport Psychology*. Hoboken, NJ: Wiley. pp. 3–30.

Treasure, D.C., Duda, J.L., Hall, H.K., Roberts, G.C., Ames, C. and Maehr, M.L. (2001) Clarifying misconceptions and misrepresentations in achievement goals research in sport: A response to Harwood, Hardy and Swain. *Journal of Sport and Exercise Psychology*, 23, 317–329.

Wang, C.K.J. and Biddle, S.J.H. (2007) Understanding young people's motivation toward exercise: An integration of sport ability beliefs, achievement goals theory, and self-determination theory. In Hagger, M. and Chatzisarantis, N.L.D. (eds) *Self-Determination Theory in Exercise and Sport*. Champaign, IL: Human Kinetics. pp. 193–208.

White, S.A. (2007) Parent-created motivational climate. In Jowett, S. and Lavallee, D. (eds) *Social Psychology in Sport*. Champaign, IL: Human Kinetics. pp. 131–144.

3.16: Self-Efficacy and Perceived Competence

> **Definitions:** Self-efficacy is a person's judgements of his or her capabilities to organise and execute courses of actions required to attain designated types of performance. Perceived competence is the extent to which a person feels he or she has the necessary attributes in order to succeed.

Alongside the growth of interest in intrinsic influences on sport participation during the 1970s, it was inevitable that a focus would fall on the self and in particular on aspects of the self that have a direct bearing on our confidence and ability to perform well. At that time there were major developments regarding the self within psychology as a whole, typically driven from within the field of education, and these new ideas resonated strongly in the world of sport. Chief among these were the constructs of self-efficacy and perceived competence, the former most closely associated with social learning theory and Albert Bandura, the latter with Susan Harter. Although quite separate and distinct theories and research literatures later developed around each term, the underlying themes are not dissimilar. Both deal with our confidence or perceived ability to deal with new experiences and challenges, and both form an integral part of our self-concept.

Before looking at key research findings it may be useful to define each term and to see how they interrelate. To begin self-concept is defined as a person's self-perceptions that are formed through experience with, and interpretations of, his or her environment, including both the academic and non-academic (social, emotional, physical). This encompasses all self-perceptions, both positive and negative; in contrast, perceived competence and self-efficacy focus attention on the positive, or what is commonly known as confidence or self-confidence. Perceived competence is characterised as the extent to which we feel we possess the necessary attributes (including social, emotional, physical and intellectual/ cognitive skills) in order to succeed, while self-efficacy concerns our personal evaluation of our ability to perform, defined by Bandura as 'people's judgements of their capabilities to organise and execute courses of actions required to attain designated types of performance' (Bandura, 1997).

How do these constructs interrelate? Not an easy question and one which the majority of authors have sidestepped, perhaps because of the degree of overlap. To some the terms are used interchangeably, while others have at least attempted to map out their connections more systematically (Sundström, 2006), or to highlight distinctions, however subtle. According to Feltz et al. (2008), self-efficacy relates to state-specific perceptions that either vary across tasks or within tasks (depending on difficulty and context), while perceived competence relates to perceptions of abilities that have developed over time. Further, self-efficacy addresses what you *are* able to do with your abilities (e.g. 'How likely do you feel that *you are* better than others your age at soccer?'), while perceived competence focuses on the perception of what you *can* accomplish with your abilities (e.g. 'How confident are you that *you can* score from a penalty – from 1 out of 10 to 10 out of 10?').

SELF-EFFICACY

In Bandura's original formulation (Self-Efficacy Theory), self-efficacy was regarded as stable and determined by four primary sources of information – performance accomplishment, vicarious experience, verbal persuasion and physiological state – with the first, performance accomplishment, seen as the most significant. Later writers have modified the theory (see Maddux and Volkmann, 2010), for example adding a further two potential sources of information – imaginal experiences (i.e. seeing ourselves succeeding) and emotional states – while Vealey (2001) postulated that in the context of sport, as many as nine separate sources of information could be identified: mastery; demonstration of ability; physical and mental preparation; physical self-presentation; social support; coach's leadership; vicarious experience; environmental comfort; and situational favourableness.

In a later reformulation (Social-Cognitive Theory – Bandura, 1997), self-efficacy was broken down further into two components. The first relates to our ability to actually perform the skill or task in the first place (*efficacy expectations*), while the second concerns our judgements about the outcomes attaching to that performance, otherwise known as *outcome expectations*. He also argued that rather than being a stable predisposition, our self-efficacy may be more context dependent, suggesting that cognitions (including self-efficacy), actions and the environment interact in a reciprocal manner over time. He also maintained that any measure of self-efficacy must consider three dimensions: level (expected level of attainment); strength (certainty that the level will be attained); and generality (the domains across which the person feels capable).

Since that time, given the importance that athletes attach to confidence, it is no surprise that sport psychologists have not been slow to consider how self-efficacy reflects in performance (Feltz et al., 2008). For example, research has shown that self-efficacy does predict engagement with specific physical activities and that those who are more physically efficacious tend to exercise more regularly, expend greater effort, persist longer, enjoy greater success and achieve better health-related benefits from exercise than adults with a low sense of physical self-efficacy. That is, with high expectations of a successful outcome to participation and repeated success, a person will be more likely to repeat and sustain their involvement. In contrast, low self-efficacy and unfavourable experiences are more likely to lead to withdrawal.

Several variables including prior experience, social support and personality have been shown to impact on self-efficacy prior to engagement with the activity, while during participation itself the person's confidence is influenced by prior self-efficacy, personal goals, feedback and rewards; in turn these then influence self-efficacy and motivation toward sustained involvement. Overall, the influence of self-efficacy on exercise participation appears to be stronger in the early stages of exercise adoption. With repeated experience the activity often becomes more routine and the psychological demands are less taxing; in these circumstances the person relies less on self-efficacy and more on feedback (McAuley et al., 2001).

In terms of demographic variables, men and those with higher socio-economic status are often characterised by greater self-efficacy, while among adults self-efficacy tends to peak up to middle age. In childhood and adolescence, it would appear that different age groups rely on different sources of self-efficacy. For example, encouragement from coaches and peers is the most important source of self-efficacy for adolescents, while performance accomplishment remains significant for all ages.

The literature on self-efficacy continues to show the practical utility of the construct (Feltz et al., 2008), and strongly suggests the positive role that significant others, including parents and coaches, can make on improving self-efficacy. Also, self-efficacy increasingly makes an appearance in many contemporary theoretical perspectives, including those rooted in theories or reasoned action and planned behaviour (McAuley et al., 2001) and the Transtheoretical Model, an approach that attempts to understand not only an individual's willingness to pursue exercise but also strategies for ensuring the continuance of a healthy lifestyle (Prochaska and Velicer, 1997). In addition, a quite separate literature has developed considering not self-efficacy but collective efficacy. This deals with not the individual's but the team's belief in its collective capabilities to perform collective tasks (Beauchamp, 2007), and has been shown to have a considerable bearing on team performance and success (see **5.22**).

An approach that borrows heavily from both the work of Bandura and Achievement Goal Theory (see **3.15**) is Vealey's Theory of Sport Confidence (Vealey, 2001). The theory tracks the effect that underlying trait confidence (self-efficacy) will have on state confidence and ultimately performance, mediated by the competitive orientation (either task or ego) that the athlete brings to his or her sport.

PERCEIVED COMPETENCE

As with Albert Bandura's work on self-efficacy, the origins of research on perceived competence lie far outside the world of sport, but it did not take long for the ideas to be borrowed to help understand sport performance and motivation. According to Susan Harter (Harter, 1999), human motivation is mediated by the influence of our perceptions of competence and control in various domains, including the cognitive, the social and the physical (Weiss and Amorose, 2006). During the 1970s, work on perceived competence in a sporting context flourished, where it was found to exert an influence both on the initiation of activity and then on continued engagement, a pattern now commonly referred to as 'the success circle'.

Despite the strong assertion that perceived competence will positively link to participation, research in sport and exercise settings has not revealed a particularly strong relationship, hence the gradual decline in the volume of work that has been produced. In general terms, the available research does still suggest that perceived competence may be significant but not exclusive; instead, it acts as one of many reasons that individuals routinely cite for taking part in sport (Weiss et al., 2009).

Once the individual has engaged in a mastery attempt, that person will receive feedback on competence from a variety of sources, including significant others. This information will influence the individual's perceptions of competence, control and their emotional reactions, which then go on to influence the likelihood of the person choosing to either repeat or avoid the experience. Success is accompanied by pleasure, which raises perceived competence, which in turn increases achievement-striving behaviour – and so the success circle grows. In contrast, failure leads to dissatisfaction and a perception of incompetence, decreasing the likelihood of future attempts at mastery.

In common with Social-Cognitive Theory, Harter's theory suggests that perceptions of competence are strongly influenced by the feedback provided by significant others such as coaches, teachers, parents or peers. The available evidence strongly suggests that the nature of such feedback following from success or failure is critical in nurturing perceptions of competence.

A closely related approach adopted by Jacquelynne Eccles and her colleagues is the Expectancy-Value Theory (Eccles and Wigfield, 2002). Expectancy-value theorists consider perceived competence in terms of two belief systems, those relating to expectancy (of a certain performance) and those linked to ability or perceived competence in certain domains. Ability beliefs represent an individual's broad beliefs about their competence in a given domain (e.g. the physical), while expectancy beliefs for task performance are more domain-specific. Ability beliefs thus are distinguished conceptually from expectancy beliefs in at least two ways. First, ability beliefs are broad beliefs about one's competence and expectancy beliefs are domain-specific beliefs. Second, ability beliefs focus on present ability and expectancy beliefs focus on the future (Eccles and Wigfield, 2002).

REFERENCES

Bandura, A. (1997) *Self-Efficacy: The Exercise of Control.* Basingstoke: Freeman.

Beauchamp, M.R. (2007) Efficacy beliefs within relational and group contexts in sport. In Jowett, S. and Lavallee, D. (eds) *Social Psychology in Sport.* Champaign, IL: Human Kinetics. pp. 181–193.

Eccles, J.S. and Wigfield, A. (2002) Motivational beliefs, values, and goals. *Annual Review of Psychology,* 53, 109–132.

Feltz, D.L., Short, S.E. and Sullivan, P.J. (2008) *Self-Efficacy in Sport: Research and Strategies for Working with Athletes, Teams and Coaches.* Champaign, IL: Human Kinetics.

Harter, S. (1999) *The Construction of the Self: A Developmental Perspective.* New York: The Guilford Press.

Maddux, J.E. and Volkmann, J.R. (2010) Self-efficacy and self-regulation. In Hoyle, R. (ed.) *Handbook of Personality and Self-Regulation.* New York: Wiley-Blackwell. 210–245.

McAuley, E., Pena, M.M. and Jerome, G. (2001) Self-efficacy as a determinant and an outcome of exercise. In Roberts, G.C. (ed.) *Advances in Motivation in Sport and Exercise.* Champaign, IL: Human Kinetics. pp. 235–261.

Prochaska, J.O. and Velicer, W.F. (1997) The transtheoretical model of health behavior change. *American Journal of Health Promotion,* 12, 38–48.

Sundström, A. (2006) *Beliefs about Perceived Competence: A Literature Review.* Educational Measurement Report (EMR) No. 55, University of Umeå, Sweden.

Vealey, R.S. (2001) Understanding and enhancing self-confidence in athletes. In Singer, R.A., Hausenblas, H.A. and Jannelle, C. (eds) *Handbook of Sport Psychology.* 2nd ed. New York: Wiley. pp. 550–565.

Weiss, M.R. and Amorose, A.J. (2006) Motivational orientations and sport behavior. In Horn, T.S. (ed.) *Advances in Sport Psychology.* 3rd edn. Champaign, IL: Human Kinetics. pp. 115–155.

Weiss, M.R., Amorose, A.J. and Wilko, A.M. (2009) Coaching behaviors, motivational climate, and psychosocial outcomes among female adolescent athletes. *Journal of Pediatric Exercise Science,* 21, 475–492.

motivation and commitment

4

Cognitive Processes in Sport

4.17: Mental Imagery

> **Definition:** Mental imagery is the ability to simulate in the mind information that is not currently being perceived by the senses.

One of the most remarkable capacities of the mind is its ability to simulate sensations, actions and other types of experience. For example, if you close your eyes, you should be able to imagine the appearance of a tennis racket (a visual image), the sound of a tennis ball bouncing on the strings of the racket (an auditory image) and perhaps even the 'feeling' or weight of this racket in your hand (a kinaesthetic image). Mental imagery (or visualisation) is the ability to simulate in the mind information that is not currently being perceived by the senses. Put simply, it is a cognitive process that enables us to 'see', 'hear' and 'feel' things in our imagination. At a theoretical level, imagery involves perception without sensation. To explain, whereas perception occurs when we interpret sensory input obtained from the outside world, imagery arises from our interpretation of stored, memory-based information. So, the process of generating a mental image is rather like running perception backwards. Not surprisingly, different types of mental imagery exist – depending on the sensory modality involved. Apart from visual and auditory imagery, the most recent type of imagery investigated in sport psychology and cognitive neuroscience is motor imagery (also known as kinaesthetic imagery), which is used whenever people imagine actions without engaging in the actual physical movements involved (see also **4.18**).

At least three strands of evidence confirm the importance of mental imagery for the learning and performance of sport skills (Moran, 2011). First, anecdotal testimonials to the value of imagery come from world class athletes such as Tiger Woods (golf), Ronaldinho (soccer) and Michael Phelps (swimming). Second, descriptive evidence (e.g. survey data) suggests that elite athletes, coaches and psychologists use imagery extensively for a variety of purposes, including skill-learning, anxiety management and mental preparation for competitive performance. Third, experimental research on mental practice shows that the systematic use of mental imagery can improve skill-learning and skilled performance.

Although mental imagery processes are unobservable, they are measurable indirectly. In general, three different approaches have been used for this task: the psychometric, qualitative, and chronometric paradigms. To begin with, researchers using the psychometric approach have developed standardised self-report scales designed to measure athletes' imagery abilities and their imagery use (see review by Morris et al., 2005). Typically, imagery ability tests ask participants to evaluate certain aspects of their imagery experience (e.g. the *vividness* of an image or its clarity or sensory richness). Among the most popular and psychometrically impressive tests of imagery skills in athletes are the Vividness of Movement Imagery Questionnaire (VMIQ) (Isaac et al., 1986) and the revised version of the Movement Imagery Questionnaire (MIQ-R) (Hall and Martin, 1997). The VMIQ is a 24-item measure of 'visual imagery of movement itself and imagery of kinaesthetic sensations' (Isaac et al., 1986, p. 24). Each of the items presents a different movement or action to be imagined (e.g. riding a bicycle). Respondents are required to rate these items in two ways: 'watching somebody else' and 'doing it yourself'. The ratings are given on a five-point scale where 1 = 'perfectly clear and as vivid as normal vision' and 5 = 'no image at all'. The MIQ-R was designed to assess individual differences in *kinaesthetic* as well as visual imagery of movement. Briefly, this test contains eight items which assess people's ease of imaging specific movements either visually or kinaesthetically. In order to complete an item, respondents must execute a movement and rate it on a scale ranging from 1 (very hard to see/feel) to 7 (very easy to see/feel). Imagery scores are calculated as separate sums of the two sub-scales of visual and kinaesthetic imagery skills. Available evidence indicates that the MIQ-R displays adequate reliability and validity. The most recent psychometric test of imagery ability is the Vividness of Movement Imagery Questionnaire-2 (VMIQ-2) (Roberts et al., 2008). This test consists of 12 items and assesses the ability to form mental images of a variety of movements visually and kinaesthetically. The visual component is further subdivided into 'external' and 'internal' visual imagery. Respondents are required to imaging each of the 12 movements and to rate the vividness of each item on a Likert-type scale from 1 (perfectly clear and vivid) to 5 (no image at all). The VMIQ-2 displays impressive factorial validity and acceptable concurrent and discriminate validity. Turning to imagery use, the *Sport Imagery Questionnaire* (SIQ) (Hall et al., 1998) is a popular, theory-based and reliable tool for measuring the frequency with which athletes employ imagery for motivational and cognitive purposes. Based on Paivio's (1985) theory that imagery affects behaviour through motivational and cognitive mechanisms operating at general and specific levels, the SIQ is a 30-item instrument (with five sub-scales) that asks respondents to rate on a seven-point scale (where 1 = 'rarely' and 7 = 'often') how often they use five specific categories of imagery:

- Motivation general – mastery (e.g. imagining appearing confident in front of others)
- Motivation general – arousal (e.g. imagining the stress and/or excitement associated with competition)
- Motivation specific (e.g. imagining winning a medal)
- Cognitive general (e.g. imagining various strategies for a competitive event)
- Cognitive specific (e.g. mentally practising a skill)

Sample items from these sub-scales include:

- 'I imagine myself appearing self confident in front of my opponents' (motivational general-mastery)
- 'I imagine the stress and anxiety associated with competing' (motivation general-arousal)
- 'I imagine myself winning a medal' (motivation specific)
- 'I imagine alternative strategies in case my event/game plan fails' (cognitive general)
- 'I can mentally make corrections to physical skills' (cognitive specific)

The six items that comprise each sub-scale are averaged to yield a score that indicates to what extent respondents use each of the five functions of imagery.

Unfortunately, subjective self-report scales of imagery have certain limitations. For example, the movements that participants are required to form in these tests are quite complex and time-consuming, thereby making such tests administratively inconvenient.

Also, these tests are subject to contamination from response sets such as social desirability. Put simply, most people are eager to portray themselves as having a good or vivid imagination regardless of their true skills in that area. For this reason, objective tests of imagery have been developed. Thus, the controllability dimension of a visual mental image (which refers to the ease and accuracy with which it can be transformed symbolically) can be measured objectively by requesting people to complete tasks which are known to require visualisation abilities. For example, in the Group Mental Rotations Test (GMRT) (Vandenberg and Kuse, 1978), people have to make judgements about whether or not the spatial orientation of certain three-dimensional target figures matches (i.e. is congruent with) or does not match (i.e. is incompatible with) various alternative shapes. The higher people's score is on this test, the stronger are their image control skills.

The second approach to measuring mental imagery skills in sport is the qualitative paradigm. Using this method, in-depth interviews are employed to investigate the meaning and richness of people's imagery experiences. Although such methods have obvious weaknesses (e.g. they depend on introspective access to conscious awareness), they can provide valuable insights into athletes' *meta-imagery* processes – or their knowledge of, and control over, their *own* mental imagery skills and experiences (Moran, 2002). For example, MacIntyre and Moran (2007a, 2007b) investigated whether or not expert athletes have greater insight into and control over their use of imagery than their successful counterparts. In particular, these authors asked athletes about their knowledge of some common motor imagery effects. Results indicated that athletes were aware both of *mental practice* effects (see **4.18**) and *mental travel* effects – the fact that when one imagines a movement it should last the same duration as the actual executed action. Unfortunately, a weakness of the qualitative approach is that it is inherently subjective and hence difficult to validate empirically.

The final approach to measuring mental imagery is the chronometric pradigm (see reviews by Guillot and Collet, 2005, 2010). This approach allows researchers to investigate motor imagery objectively by comparing the duration required to execute real and imagined actions. The logic here is as follows. According to the functional equivalence hypothesis (e.g. Jeannerod, 1994) imagined and executed actions rely on similar motor representations and activate some common brain areas (e.g. the parietal and prefrontal cortices, the pre-motor and primary cortices). As the temporal organisation of imagined and actual actions is similar, there should be a close correspondence between the time required to mentally perform simulated actions and that required for actual performance. In a typical study, Calmels et al. (2006) examined the temporal congruence between actual and imagined movements in gymnastics. They found that the overall times required to perform and imagine a complex gymnastic vault were broadly similar – regardless of whether participants used 'first person' or 'third person' imagery perspectives. However, the temporal congruence between actual and imagined actions is mediated by a number of factors. For example, Guillot and Collet (2005) concluded that when the skills in question are largely automatic (e.g. reaching, grasping) or occur in cyclical movements (e.g. walking, rowing), there is usually a high degree of temporal congruence between actual and imagined performance. But when the skill being performed involves complex, attention-demanding movements (e.g. golf putting, tennis serving), people tend to *over-estimate* imagined duration. Guillot and Collet (2010) have shown that methods based on recording motor imagery times and measuring the temporal congruence between imagery and actual times are powerful and versatile tools for the assessment of mental imagery ability. However, a limitation of this approach is that it does not consider imagery vividness.

Although considerable progress has been made in understanding the mechanisms underlying, and measuring, mental imagery processes in athletes, a potentially important gap in this field may be identified. Specifically, although a wealth of evidence has been gathered on imagery use in athletes (e.g. see Weinberg, 2008), imagery researchers in sport have largely neglected *meta-imagery* processes or athletes' knowledge of, and control over, their *own* mental imagery skills and experiences. However, MacIntyre and Moran (2007a, 2007b) explored such meta-imagery processes in elite athletes. An interesting discovery from these studies was that these athletes sometimes deliberately generated *negative* imagery content based on the belief that it would help them to cope with possible future adversity.

REFERENCES

Calmels, C., Holmes, P., Lopez, E. and Naman, V. (2006) Chronometric comparison of actual and imaged complex movement patterns. *Journal of Motor Behavior*, 38, 339–348.

Guillot, A. and Collet, C. (2010) (eds) *The Neurophysiological Foundations of Mental and Motor Imagery*. Oxford: Oxford University Press.

Hall, C.R. and Martin, K.A. (1997) Measuring movement imagery abilities: A revision of the Movement Imagery Questionnaire. *Journal of Mental Imagery*, 21, 143–154.

Hall, C., Mack, D., Paivio, A. and Hausenblas, H.A. (1998) Imagery use by athletes: Development of the Sport Imagery Questionnaire. *International Journal of Sport Psychology*, 29, 73–89.

Isaac, A., Marks, D. and Russell, E. (1986) An instrument for assessing imagery of movement: The Vividness of Movement Imagery Questionnaire (VMIQ). *Journal of Mental Imagery*, 10, 23–30.

Jeannerod, M. (1994) The representing brain: Neural correlates of motor intention and imagery. *Behavioral and Brain Sciences*, 17, 187–245.

MacIntyre, T. and Moran, A. (2007a) A qualitative investigation of imagery use and meta-imagery processes among elite canoe-slalom competitors. *Journal of Imagery Research in Sport and Physical Activity*, 2, 1–23.

MacIntyre, T. and Moran, A. (2007b) A qualitative investigation of meta-imagery processes and imagery direction among elite athletes. *Journal of Imagery Research in Sport and Physical Activity*, 2, 1–20.

Moran, A.P. (2002) In the mind's eye. *The Psychologist*, 15, 414–415.

Moran, A. (2011) *Sport and Exercise Psychology: A Critical Introduction.* 2nd edn. London: Routledge.

Morris, T., Spittle, M. and Watt, A.P. (2005) *Imagery in Sport.* Champaign, IL: Human Kinetics.

Paivio, A. (1985) Cognitive and motivational functions of imagery in human performance. *Canadian Journal of Applied Sport Science*, 10, 22–28.

Roberts, R., Callow, N., Hardy, L., Markland, D. and Bringer, J. (2008) Movement imagery ability: Development and assessment of a revised version of the Vividness of Movement Imagery Questionnaire. *Journal of Sport and Exercise Psychology*, 30, 200–221.

Vandenberg, S. and Kuse, A.R. (1978) Mental rotations: A group test of three-dimensional spatial visualization. *Perceptual and Motor Skills*, 47, 599–604.

Weinberg, R.S. (2008) Does imagery work? Effects on performance and mental skills. *Journal of Imagery Research in Sport and Physical Activity*, 3 (1), 1–21.

4.18: Mental Practice

Definition: Mental practice is the systematic use of mental imagery to rehearse an action in one's imagination without engaging in the actual physical movements involved.

The term 'mental practice' (MP) refers to the systematic use of mental imagery to 'see' and 'feel' an action in one's imagination without engaging in the actual physical movements involved. Because it relies on *simulated* movements, MP is sometimes known as 'symbolic rehearsal', 'covert rehearsal' or 'imaginary practice'. Psychological interest in mental practice is as old as the discipline of psychology itself. For example, William James

(1890) suggested rather counter-intuitively that by anticipating experiences imaginatively, people actually learn to skate in the summer and to swim in the winter! For well over a century, the effects of MP on skilled performance have been investigated by psychology researchers (e.g. see review by Driskell et al., 1994). Typically, these investigators use an experimental paradigm that involves a comparison of the pre- and post-intervention performance of four groups of participants: those who have been engaged only in physical practice of the skill in question (the physical practice group, PP); those who have mentally practised it (the mental practice group, MP); those who have alternated between physical and mental practice (PP/MP); and participants in a non-practice control condition. After a pre-treatment baseline test has been conducted on a designated skill, participants are randomly assigned to one of these conditions (PP, MP, PP/MP or control). Normally, the cognitive rehearsal that occurs in the MP treatment condition is guided by a mental imagery 'script' that describes the motor actions to be executed in clear and vivid detail (see Morris et al., 2005). After this MP intervention has been applied, the participants' performance on the target skill is tested again. If the performance of the MP group is significantly superior to that of the control group, then a positive effect of mental practice is deemed to have occurred.

Using this experimental paradigm, imagery researchers have established a number of conclusions about the efficacy of mental practice. First, MP has been shown to improve the learning and performance of a variety of motor skills in sport (e.g. self-paced skills such as golf-putting and 'reactive' skills such as tackling in rugby), music and medical surgery. MP has also been found to increase physical strength performance and to facilitate rehabilitation from physical injury or neurological damage. Second, research suggests that MP, when combined and alternated with physical practice, tends to produce superior skill-learning to that resulting from either mental or physical practice conducted alone. Third, there is evidence that mental practice improves the performance of cognitive skills (i.e. those that involve sequential processing activities, e.g. mirror drawing tasks) more than it does for motor skills (e.g. as balancing on a stabilometer). Fourth, expert athletes tend to benefit more from MP than do novices, regardless of the type of skill being practised (either cognitive or physical). Fifth, the positive effects of MP on task performance tend to decline sharply over time. Indeed, according to Driskell et al. (1994), the beneficial effects of motor imagery training are reduced to *half* of their original value after approximately two weeks of time has elapsed. A practical implication of this finding is that in order to gain optimal benefits from mental practice, 'refresher' training should be implemented after this critical two-week period. Finally, there is evidence that imagery ability mediates the relationship between MP and motor skill performance. Thus, athletes who are proficient in generating and controlling vivid images tend to benefit more from visualisation than do counterparts who lack such abilities.

Despite the proliferation of research on MP, a key validation problem afflicts many studies in this field. Specifically, how do we know that people who *claim* to be using imagery when engaged in mental practice are actually doing so? Put differently, how can we validate people's subjective reports about their imagery experiences? One way of addressing this issue is to use custom-designed 'manipulation checks' or verification procedures that attempt to assess the ease and accuracy with which participants adhered to the imagery instructions/script that they had received. Another potential solution to this validation problem comes from research on the *mental travel* chronometric paradigm (see review by Guillot and Collet, 2005). To explain, according to the functional equivalence hypothesis (see **4.17**), imagined and executed actions rely on similar motor representations and activate some common brain areas (e.g. the pre-motor and primary cortices). Because the temporal organisation of imagined and actual actions is similar, there should be a close correspondence between the time required to *mentally* perform simulated actions and that required for *actual* performance. This hypothesis has been corroborated empirically (Guillot and Collet, 2005, 2010). Using this mental chronometry approach, Moran and MacIntyre (1998) validated the veracity of canoe-slalomists' imagery reports by comparing the congruence between the imagined time and 'real' time required by these athletes to navigate their courses in competition.

In general, four main theories have been postulated to explain MP effects: the neuromuscular model (e.g. Jacobson, 1932); the cognitive or symbolic approach (e.g. Denis, 1985); the bio-informational theory (e.g. Lang, 1979); and most recently the PETTLEP approach (Holmes and Collins, 2001). These theories may be summarised briefly as follows (Moran, 2011).

To begin with, the neuromuscular model proposes that mental practice effects are mediated by faint activity in the peripheral musculature. This theory postulates that there is a strong positive relationship between the muscular activity elicited by imagining a given skill and that detected during actual execution of this skill. Unfortunately, there is little empirical support for this hypothesis or, more generally, for neuromuscular theories of mental practice.

Next, the cognitive approach suggests that mental practice facilitates the coding and rehearsal of key elements of the skilled task. By contrast with neuromuscular accounts of MP, cognitive models attach little importance to what happens in the *peripheral* musculature of the performer. Instead, they focus on the possibility that mental rehearsal strengthens the brain's *central* representation or cognitive 'blueprint' of the skill being imagined. Although this approach has a plausible theoretical rationale, it is challenged by evidence that MP can improve people's performance of strength tasks which, by definition, contain few cognitive components. Another problem for symbolic theories is that they find it difficult to explain how MP can enhance the performance of expert athletes who, presumably, already possess well-established blueprints or motor schemata for the movements being imagined.

Third, the bio-informational theory postulates that MP effects reflect an interaction of three different factors: the environment in which a given movement is performed ('stimulus' information such as 'feeling' the soft ground as one imagines teeing up a ball in golf); what is felt by the performer while the movement occurs ('response' information such as feeling a slow, smooth practice swing on the imaginary tee-box); and the perceived importance of this skill to the performer ('meaning' information such as feeling slightly anxious because other people are watching as one prepares to drive the ball). Of these factors, the *response* propositions are held to be especially significant because they are believed to reflect how a person would *actually* react in the real-life situation being imagined. Therefore, bio-informational theorists postulate that imagery scripts that are heavily laden with response propositions should elicit greater MP effects than those without such information. Despite a dearth of empirical evidence to support this hypothesis, the bio-informational approach has been influential among imagery researchers in highlighting the value of 'individualising' imagery scripts so that they take account of the personal meaning which people attribute to the skills or movements that they wish to rehearse.

Fourth, the most recent theoretical approach to mental practice is called PETTLEP (Holmes and Collins, 2001) – an acronym referring to Physical, Environment, Task, Timing, Learning, Emotion and Perspective aspects of mental imagery. In this model, 'P' refers to the athlete's physical response to the sporting situation imagined, 'E' is the environment in which the imagery is performed, 'T' is the imagined task, 'T' refs to timing (i.e. the pace at which the imagery is performed), 'L' is a learning or memory component of imagery, 'E' refers to the emotions elicited by the imagery and 'P' designates the type of visual imagery perspective used by the practitioner (i.e. whether he or she imagines the movement from a 'first-person' perspective or from a 'third-person' perspective). Overall, the PETTLEP model proposes that in order to produce optimal functional equivalence (see **4.17**) between imagery and motor production, and thereby to enhance subsequent sport performance, imagery interventions should replicate not only athletes' sporting situation but also the emotions that they experience when performing their skills. Although the predictions of the PETTLEP model have not been tested extensively to date, available empirical results are generally supportive. For example, Smith et al. (2007) compared the use of PETTLEP imagery training with traditional mental practice techniques and also with physical practice in developing gymnastics jump skills. Results showed that the PETTLEP group improved its proficiency in these skills whereas the traditional imagery group did not.

Unfortunately, few studies have been conducted to arbitrate empirically between the preceding theories of mental practice. However, progress has been made in identifying some of the neural substrates of MP effects. For example, neuroimaging studies indicate that there is a great deal of overlap between the neural substrates of physical and imagined movement execution. Specifically, motor imagery and movement execution activate such neural regions as the premotor cortex, primary motor cortex, basal ganglia and cerebellum (Jeannerod, 2001). This overlap of neural substrates is not complete, however. Overall, based on available neuroscientific evidence, it seems plausible to postulate that mental practice (MP) is best understood as a centrally mediated cognitive activity that mimics perceptual, motor and certain emotional experiences in the brain.

REFERENCES

Denis, M. (1985) Visual imagery and the use of mental practice in the development of motor skills. *Canadian Journal of Applied Sport Sciences*, 10, 4s–16s.

Driskell, J., Copper, C. and Moran, A. (1994) Does mental practice enhance performance? A meta-analysis. *Journal of Applied Psychology*, 79, 481–492.

Guillot, A. and Collet, C. (2005) Duration of mentally simulated movement: A review. *Journal of Motor Behavior*, 37, 10–20.

Guillot, A., and Collet, C. (2010) (eds) *The Neurophysiological Foundations of Mental and Motor Imagery*. Oxford: Oxford University Press.

Holmes, P. and Collins, D. (2001) The PETTLEP approach to motor imagery: A functional equivalence model for sport psychologists. *Journal of Applied Sport Psychology*, 13, 60–83.

Jacobson, E. (1932) Electrophysiology of mental activities. *American Journal of Psychology*, 44, 677–694.

James, W. (1890) *Principles of Psychology*. New York: Holt, Rinehart and Winston.

Jeannerod, M. (2001) Neural simulation of action: A unifying mechanism for motor cognition. *NeuroImage*, 14, S103–S109.

Lang, P.J. (1979) A bio-informational theory of emotional imagery. *Psychophysiology*, 17, 495–512.

Moran, A.P. (2011) *Sport and Exercise Psychology*. 2nd edn. London: Routledge.

Moran, A.P. and MacIntyre, T. (1998) 'There's more to an image than meets the eye': A qualitative analysis of kinaesthetic imagery among elite canoe-slalomists. *The Irish Journal of Psychology*, 19, 406–423.

Morris, T., Spittle, M. and Watt, A.P. (2005) *Imagery in Sport*. Champaign, IL: Human Kinetics.

Smith, D., Wright, C.J., Allsopp, A. and Westhead, H. (2007) It's all in the mind: PETTLEP-based imagery and sports performance. *Journal of Applied Sport Psychology*, 19, 80–92.

4.19: Attention and Concentration

Definitions: Attention is the process of exerting mental effort on specific features of the environment or on certain thoughts or activities. Concentration is an attentional process that involves the ability to focus on the task at hand while ignoring distractions.

The ability to concentrate, or focus on the task at hand while ignoring distractions (Moran, 1996), is a crucial prerequisite of successful performance in sport. Evidence to support this claim comes from anecdotal, descriptive and experimental evidence. First, anecdotally, athletes often highlight the role that concentration played in their success. For example,

Trevor Immelman (South Africa) attributed his victory in the US Open golf championship in 2008 to the fact that he had been 'totally in the present' in his final round (McRae, 2008, p. 6). Second, correlational studies indicate that the capacity to become absorbed in the present moment is a key component of peak performance experiences in athletes (Jackson and Kimiecik, 2008). Third, laboratory experiments show that there is a relationship between people's focus of attention and skilled performance. Specifically, Wulf (2007) showed that an external focus of attention (where performers direct their attention to the effects that their movements have on the environment) is usually more effective than an internal one (where performers focus on their own body movements) in the learning and performance of motor skills.

For psychologists, concentration (i.e. the decision to invest mental effort in what is most important in any situation) is one component of the multidimensional construct of 'attention', or the process of exerting mental effort 'on specific features of the environment, or on certain thoughts or activities' (Goldstein, 2008, p. 100). Two other dimensions of this construct are *selective attention* and *divided attention*. Selective attention is the perceptual ability to 'zoom in' on task-relevant information while ignoring distractions. For example, a soccer goalkeeper who is preparing to defend against a corner-kick has to learn to focus only on the flight of the incoming ball, rather than on the movements of players in the penalty area. Divided attention is a form of mental time-sharing or multi-tasking through which performers learn, as a result of extensive practice, to perform two or more concurrent actions equally well. To illustrate, a skilled basketball player can dribble with the ball while simultaneously looking around for a team-mate who is in a good position to receive a pass. In summary, attention refers to three different cognitive processes: concentration or effortful awareness; selectivity of perception; and/or the ability to co-ordinate two or more actions at the same time.

As scientists, psychology researchers use metaphors to explain the unknown in terms of the known. Of the various metaphors of attention postulated since the 1950s, the 'spotlight' approach (Posner, 1980) has probably been the most influential in sport psychology. According to this metaphor, concentration resembles a mental spotlight that we shine at things that are important to us at a given moment. These targets of our concentration beam can be *external* (i.e. in the world around us) or *internal* (i.e. in the private domain of our own thoughts and feelings). For example, aiming one's golf drive at a specific target on the fairway involves an external focus of attention, whereas concentrating on rhythm or feeling of one's golf swing involves an internal focus of attention. Although the spotlight metaphor has several weaknesses (e.g. it neglects emotional influences on attentional processes; see **2.8**), it has two important practical implications. First, it shows us that our concentration is never truly 'lost' because our mental spotlight is always shining somewhere – externally or internally. Second, it suggests that whenever we focus on the 'wrong' target (i.e. something irrelevant to the task at hand or that lies outside our control), our performance is likely to deteriorate. This latter point raises the issue of distractions in sport.

Competitive sport offers an abundance of distractions that can divert athletes' mental spotlight from its intended target. Whereas external distractions are objective stimuli from the world around us, internal distractions include a vast array of thoughts, feelings and/or bodily sensations (e.g. fatigue) that can disrupt our focus. Typical external distractions include such factors as spectator movements, sudden changes in ambient noise levels (e.g. the click of a camera), gamesmanship (e.g. trying to block a goalkeeper in soccer from seeing the ball at a corner-kick) and unpredictable weather conditions (e.g. tennis players can get distracted when windy conditions affect their ball-toss before serving). Usually, these distractions impair athletic performance. For example, Roger Federer's victory over Robin Söderling in the final of the 2009 French Open tennis championship was jeopardised by the sudden appearance of a spectator who jumped on to the court and approached him. Clearly rattled by this distraction, Federer lost the next three points and admitted afterwards, 'it definitely threw me out of my rhythm' (cited in Sarkar, 2009). Fortunately, he regained his concentration and won the match. In soccer, noisy supporters can distract players. For example, fans of the Turkish soccer club, Galatasaray, are infamous for using flares, drums, smoke and incessant shouting to intimidate visiting teams at their home ground, which is known to visitors as 'Hell'! Not surprisingly, some of the world's leading soccer teams (e.g. AC Milan, Barcelona, Manchester United, Real Madrid) have been defeated in this hostile environment (see **5.27**). Internal distractions stem mainly from thoughts such as wondering what might happen in the future, regretting what has happened in the past or worrying about what other people might think, say or do. A classic example of a costly internal distraction occurred in the case of the golfer Doug Sanders who missed a putt of less than three feet that prevented him winning the 1970 British Open championship in St. Andrews, Scotland, his first major tournament, and also deprived him of millions of pounds in prize money, tournament invitations and advertising endorsements. Remarkably, Sanders' attentional lapse was precipitated by thinking too far ahead: 'I had the victory speech prepared before the battle was over' (cited in G. Moran, 2005, p. 21). Unfortunately, despite such dramatic lapses, little research has been conducted to date on the mechanisms by which internal distractions disrupt performance. Nevertheless, Wegner (1994) developed a model which attempted to explain why attentional lapses occur 'ironically' – or precisely at the most inopportune moment for the person involved. Briefly, this model postulated that when our working memory system is overloaded because we are anxious or tired, trying *not* to think about something may paradoxically increase the prominence of this idea in our consciousness. This ironic rebound effect applies to actions as well as thoughts. For example, trying *not* to miss a penalty or overshoot the hole in golf can cause the exact opposite of what was intended. Thus Woodman and Davis (2008) discovered that when golfers were in pressure situations (arising from the opportunity to win a financial prize), they made more ironic errors in a putting task than when no pressure was evident.

In an effort to achieve a focused state of mind where there is no difference between what they are thinking about and what they are doing, athletes tend to use some of the following concentration strategies (Kremer and Moran, 2008; Moran, 2011). First, they set specific performance or action goals for themselves every time they compete. These goals (e.g. 'keep up with play' in soccer or 'first serve in' in tennis) encourage athletes to focus on task-relevant information and on controllable actions. Second, athletes make extensive use of pre-performance routines (PPRs) (Cotterill, 2010) or characteristic sequences of preparatory thoughts and actions before executing self-paced skills (i.e. actions that are carried out largely at one's own speed and without interference from other people) such as place-kicking in rugby or serving in tennis. PPRs are helpful because they encourage performers to focus, step-by-step, on task-relevant information. For example, many soccer goalkeepers follow pre-kick routines in an effort to block out any jeering that is directed at them by supporters of opposing teams. Recently, Cotterill et al. (2010) investigated PPR use among amateur international golfers. Results showed that these players used routines for attentional purposes such as attempting to 'switch on and off' (p. 55) and 'staying in the present and not dwelling on the past or engaging in fortune telling' (p. 55). A third concentration strategy used by athletes involves 'trigger words' or short, vivid and positively phrased verbal reminders to focus on a specific target or action. For example, the British Olympic athlete Paula Radcliffe, who won the 2007 New York City Marathon, reported counting her steps silently to herself in an effort to maintain her concentration in a race. As she explained afterwards, 'when

I count to 100 three times, it's a mile. It helps me to focus on the moment and not to think about how many miles I have to go. I concentrate on breathing and striding, and I go within myself' (cited in Kolata, 2007, p. 1). The fourth popular concentration technique is mental practice (see **4.17**) or the systematic use of mental imagery to 'see' and 'feel' a skill in one's imagination before actually executing it. For example, Mike Atherton, the former England cricket captain, used to prepare to concentrate in test matches by going to the match venue and visualising 'who's going to bowl, how they are going to bowl … so that nothing can come as a surprise' (cited in Selvey, 1998, p. 2). From this quote, it seems that imagery can help athletes to anticipate hypothetical scenarios, thereby ensuring that they will not be distracted by unexpected events on the day itself. The final concentration strategy that is used increasingly by athletes and coaches is simulation training (i.e. practising under conditions that replicate key aspects of an impending competitive situation). For example, the renowned US swimming coach Bob Bowman admitted deliberately breaking the goggles of Michael Phelps (who has won more Olympic gold medals than any other athlete in history) during practice so that he could learn to swim calmly without them if necessary in a competition. Remarkably, this later situation actually arose in the 2008 Olympics when Phelps won the 200 m butterfly event even though his goggles had been broken for the last 100 m of the race (Whitworth, 2008).

In summary, attentional processes such as concentration are vital determinants of athletic success. Although considerable progress has been made in understanding the principles underlying an optimal focus for sport performance, research is urgently required to evaluate which concentration strategies work best in enhancing different types of sport skills.

REFERENCES

Cotterill, S.T. (2010) Pre-performance routines in sport: Current understanding and future directions. *International Review of Sport and Exercise Psychology*, 3, 132–153.

Cotterill, S.T., Sanders, R. and Collins, D. (2010) Developing effective pre-performance routines in golf: Why don't we ask the golfer? *Journal of Applied Sport Psychology*, 22, 51–64.

Goldstein, E.B. (2008) *Cognitive Psychology: Connecting Mind, Research, and Everyday Experience*. 2nd edn. Belmont, CA: Thompson/Wadsworth.

Jackson, S.A. and Kimiecik, J.C. (2008) The flow perspective of optimal experience in sport and physical activity. In Horn, T.S. (ed.) *Advances in Sport Psychology*. 3rd edn. Champaign, IL: Human Kinetics, pp. 377–399; 474–477.

Kolata, P. (2007) 'I'm not really running, I'm not really running ...'. *The New York Times*, 6 December, available at www.nytimes.com/2007/12/06/health/nutrition/06Best.html

Kremer, J. and Moran, A. (2008) *Pure Sport: Practical Sport Psychology*. Hove: Routledge.

McRae, D. (2008) 'Even great players have tortured minds'. The *Guardian* (Sport), 15 July, p. 6.

Moran, A.P. (1996) *The Psychology of Concentration in Sport Performers: A Cognitive Analysis*. Hove: Psychology Press.

Moran, A. P. (2011) *Sport and Exercise Psychology*. 2nd edn. London: Routledge.

Moran, G. (2005) 'Oh dear, so near but yet so far away'. *The Irish Times*, 12 July, p. 2.

Posner, M.I. (1980) Orienting of attention: The VIIth Sir Frederic Bartlett lecture. *Quarterly Journal of Experimental Psychology*, 32A, 3–25.

Sarkar, P. (2009) 'Open – Federer unnerved by spectator intrusion'. The *Guardian*, 7 June, available at www.guardian.co.uk/sport/feedarticle/8546123.

Selvey, M. (1998) 'Getting up for the Ashes'. The *Guardian* (Sport), 20 November, p. 2.

Wegner, D.M. (1994) Ironic processes of mental control. *Psychological Review*, 101, 34–52.

Whitworth, D. (2008) 'On the waterfront'. *The Times* (magazine), 13 September, pp. 20–25.

Woodman, T. and Davis, P.A. (2008) The role of repression in the incidence of ironic errors. *The Sport Psychologist*, 22, 183–196.

Wulf, G. (2007) Attentional focus and motor learning: A review of 10 years of research. *Bewegung and Training*, 1, 4–14.

4.20: Positive Self-Talk and Thought Control

Definition: Self-talk is a cognitive self-regulation strategy which involves the use of vividly phrased cue-words to help athletes to control their thoughts and to instruct and motivate themselves.

It has long been known that athletes talk to themselves either silently or out loud when they train and compete – usually in an effort to improve their thinking, concentration and performance. For example, during the 2002 Wimbledon ladies' singles tennis final between the Williams sisters,

Serena Williams (who defeated Venus 7–6, 6–3) was observed by millions of viewers to be reading hand-written notes as she sat down during the change-overs between games. Afterwards, she explained that she had been reading notes as reminders to think about cues such as 'hit in front' or 'stay low' during the match (Williams, 2002, p. 6). Supporting such anecdotal examples, empirical research has confirmed the relationship between self-talk usage and athletic success. For example, Taylor et al. (2008) discovered that instructional self-talk (e.g. 'I have specific cue words or phrases that I say to myself to help my performance during competition') was one of the strongest predictors of successful Olympic performance among US athletes. Not surprisingly, in view of such evidence, a great deal of research has been conducted since the early 1990s on the nature, functions and efficacy of self-talk in athletes. Before we summarise this research, however, a brief clarification of terminology is required.

The term 'self-talk' refers to 'those automatic statements reflective of, and deliberate techniques (e.g. thought stopping) athletes use to direct, sports-related thinking' (Hardy et al., 2009a, p. 38). Put simply, self-talk is a cognitive self-regulation strategy. More precisely, it involves the use of vividly phrased cue-words to help athletes to control their thoughts and to instruct and motivate themselves (Zinsser et al., 2010). In sport psychology, self-talk is regarded as a multidimensional construct with at least three dimensions: overtness (i.e. whether self-talk is expressed explicitly or covertly); valence (i.e. whether self-talk is positive or negative); and functions (e.g. either cognitive/instructional or motivational) (Hardy, 2006). Two main types of self-talk have been identified. *Instructional* self-talk (e.g. as exemplified by Serena Williams) refers to covert self-directed statements that are intended to enhance athletic performance through adoption of a task-relevant attentional focus (see also **4.19**). *Motivational* self-talk involves similar statements intended to facilitate performance by increasing effort and energy expenditure and by boosting one's confidence and mood. With regard to instructional self-talk, considerable research has accumulated on the use of 'associative' thinking in sport or the use of attentional strategies whereby athletes focus deliberately on bodily signals such as breathing, heart-beat and kinaesthetic sensations when competing in arduous endurance events. This research was spawned by Morgan and Pollock's (1977) discovery that elite marathon runners tended to use associative cognitive strategies whereas non-elite runners tended to prefer dissociative strategies which involved attempting to block out sensations of pain and discomfort. For Morgan (1978), an athlete who dissociates 'purposefully cuts himself off from the sensory feedback he normally receives from his body' (p. 39). Early research on this topic showed that associative attentional strategies, when compared with dissociative equivalents, were linked with faster performance in sports such as running and swimming. From such evidence, Masters and Ogles (1998) concluded that whereas associative techniques facilitated comparatively faster performances by athletes, dissociative techniques were linked to a reduction in perceived exertion in endurance events. However, this conclusion was challenged by Salmon et al. (2010) in a recent review of the relevant research literature. Briefly, these latter investigators pointed out that studies in this field have been hampered by conceptual confusion (e.g. inconsistency in the definitions of association and dissociation) and methodological problems (e.g. the use of unvalidated measures of key constructs). Despite such difficulties, the use of associative and dissociative cognitive strategies has attracted increasing research interest in exercise endurance settings (e.g. see review by Lind et al., 2009).

The efficacy of self-talk in enhancing athletic performance has been demonstrated using observational studies (e.g. Van Raalte et al., 1994), laboratory-based experiments (e.g. Van Raalte et al., 1995), intervention studies (e.g. Johnson et al., 2004) and research using single-case designs (e.g. Hamilton et al., 2007). To illustrate, in a study of the dimensions of overtness and valence, Van Raalte et al. (1994) found that a large proportion of the overt self-talk of young tennis players was negative in content. Furthermore, such negative self-talk was associated with losing. These researchers also noted that players who reported believing in the utility of self-talk won more points than players who did not share this belief. More recently, Hamilton et al. (2007) showed that athletes who used *positive* self-talk consistently improved their cycling time-trial performance significantly more than did counterparts who used *negative* self-talk. Theoretically, the content of self-talk may involve praise (e.g. 'Well done! That's good'), criticism ('You idiot – that's a stupid mistake') and/or instruction ('Swing slowly').

Accordingly, self-talk may be positive, negative or neutral. Exploring this idea psychometrically, Zourbanos et al. (2009) developed an instrument entitled the Automatic Self-Talk Questionnaire for Sports (ASTQS) in an effort to measure the content of athletes' self-talk. Factor analysis revealed eight factors or distinct dimensions of thoughts in athletes – four measuring positive self-talk, three tapping negative self-talk and one indicating neutral self-talk. Among the positive self-talk items were statements used by athletes to 'psych up' (e.g. 'Let's go'), boost confidence ('I can make it'), instruct themselves (e.g. 'Concentrate on your game') and control their anxiety levels (e.g. 'Relax', 'Calm down'). For the factors measuring negative self-talk, typical items reflected worrying (e.g. 'I am going to lose'), disengagement (e.g. 'I can't keep going') and feeling somatic fatigue (e.g. 'I am tired'). Finally, a sample item from the neutral self-talk factor concerned irrelevant thoughts (e.g. 'What will I do later tonight?'). Although further construct validation of the ASTQS is required, preliminary analysis indicates that this test possesses adequate psychometric characteristics.

In summary, there is substantial evidence that positive self-talk is beneficial to performance and should be encouraged in athletes and that negative self-talk is detrimental to performance and hence, should be discouraged. But how can this latter objective be achieved? Logically, the first step in changing self-talk is to become more aware of it (Zinsser et al., 2010). So, in a recent study, Hardy et al. (2009b) evaluated the efficacy of two intervention strategies purported to increase athletes' awareness of their negative self-talk. The intervention strategies involved a thought awareness logbook and an exercise requiring athletes to transfer paper-clips from one pocket to another whenever they used a negative self-statement. Results showed that although both treatment groups showed increased awareness of the *content* of their negative self-talk, the logbook group showed greater awareness than the control group of the *use* of negative self-talk. Accordingly, Hardy et al. recommended that logbook maintenance may be a useful tool for increasing awareness of negative self-talk among athletes in applied settings.

Unfortunately, as Hardy et al. (2009b) acknowledged, if applied sport psychology consultants seek to build on increased awareness of negative self-talk with the use of a thought control technique such as 'thought stopping' (whereby a verbal cue such as 'stop' is stated aloud every time an undesired thought is encountered), problems may occur. Specifically, research based on Wegner's (1994) ironic processes model shows that when our working memory is overloaded due to anxiety or fatigue, the attempt to suppress a thought may paradoxically increase the prominence of that thought in our consciousness. In such circumstances, the attempt to engage in thought stopping may lead to a 'rebound' experience whereby the suppressed thought becomes even more prominent in our consciousness. This tendency for a suppressed thought to come to mind more readily than a thought that is the focus of intentional concentration is called 'hyperaccessibility' and is especially likely to occur under conditions of heavy mental load. In summary, a key implication of the theory of ironic processes is that thought stopping should be used with great caution in attempting to reduce negative self-talk in athletes.

To conclude, research on self-talk is a vibrant and fertile ground for the study of cognitive self-regulation. With regard to future research directions in this field, a potentially fruitful line of inquiry concerns research on the comparative evaluation of instructional and motivational self-talk on skilled performance. For example, Kolovelonis et al. (2011) found partial support for the hypothesis (Hardy et al., 2009b) that whereas instructional self-talk is especially beneficial for the performance of tasks that require precision or timing, motivational self-talk is beneficial for performance of tasks that require strength or endurance. Research is also required urgently to establish the precise theoretical mechanisms that underlie the effects of self-talk on athletic performance.

REFERENCES

Hamilton, R.A., Scott, D. and MacDougall, M.P. (2007) Assessing the effectiveness of self-talk interventions on endurance performance. *Journal of Applied Sport Psychology*, 19, 226–239.

Hardy, J. (2006) Speaking clearly: A critical review of the self-talk literature. *Psychology of Sport and Exercise*, 7, 81–97.

Hardy, J., Oliver, E. and Tod, D. (2009a) A framework for the study and application of self-talk within sport. In Mellalieu, S. and Hanton, S. (eds) *Advances in Applied Sport Psychology: A Review*. London: Routledge. pp. 37–74.

Hardy, J., Roberts, R. and Hardy, L. (2009b) Awareness and motivation to change negative self-talk. *The Sport Psychologist*, 23, 435–450.

Johnson, J.J.M., Hrycaiko, D.W., Johnson, G.V. and Halas, J.M. (2004) Self-talk and female youth soccer performance. *The Sport Psychologist*, 18, 44–59.

Kolovelonis, A., Goudas, M. and Dermitzaki, I. (2011) The effects of instructional and motivational self-talk on students' motor task performance in physical education. *Psychology of Sport and Exercise*, 12, 153–158.

Lind, E., Welch, A.S. and Ekkekakis, P. (2009) Do 'mind over muscle' strategies work? Examining the effects of attentional association and dissociation on exertional, affective and physiological responses to exercise. *Sports Medicine*, 39, 743–764.

Masters, K.S. and Ogles, B.M. (1998) Associative and dissociative cognitive strategies in exercise and running: 20 years later, what do we know? *The Sport Psychologist*, 12, 253–270.

Morgan, W.P. (1978) The mind of the marathoner. *Psychology Today*, 11, 38–49.

Morgan, W.P. and Pollock, M.L. (1977) Psychological characterization of the elite distance runner. *Annals of the New York Academy of Sciences*, 301, 382–403.

Salmon, P., Hanneman, S. and Harwood, B. (2010) Associative/dissociative cognitive strategies in sustained physical activity: Literature review and proposal for a mindfulness-based conceptual model. *The Sport Psychologist*, 24, 127–156.

cognitive processes in sport

Taylor, M.K., Gould, D. and Rolo, C. (2008) Performance strategies of US Olympians in practice and competition. *High Ability Studies*, 19, 19–36.

Van Raalte, J., Brewer, B.W., Rivera, P.M. and Petitpas, A.J. (1994) The relationship between observable self-talk and competitive junior tennis players' match performance. *Journal of Sport and Exercise Psychology*, 16, 400–415.

Van Raalte, J., Brewer, B.W., Lewis, B.P., Linder, D.E., Wildman, G. and Kozimor, J. (1995) The effects of positive and negative self-talk on dart throwing performance. *Journal of Sport Behavior*, 18, 50–57.

Wegner, D.M. (1994) Ironic processes of mental control. *Psychological Review*, 101, 34–52.

Williams, R. (2002) Sublime Serena celebrates the crucial difference. The *Guardian*, 8 July, p. 6 (Sport).

Zinsser, N., Bunker, L. and Williams, J. (2010) Cognitive techniques for building confidence and enhancing performance. In Williams, J.M. (ed.) *Applied Sport Psychology: From Personal Growth to Peak Performance*. 6th edn. New York: McGraw-Hill. pp. 305–335.

Zourbanos, N., Hatzigeorgiadis, A., Chroni, S., Theodorakis, Y. and Papaioannou, A. (2009) Automatic Self-Talk Questionnaire for Sports (ASTQS): Development and preliminary validation of a measure identifying the structure of athletes' self-talk. *The Sport Psychologist*, 23, 233–251.

4.21: Mental Toughness

> **Definition:** Mental toughness is a multidimensional personality construct that defines the ability to persevere towards goal accomplishment through the display of resilience and hardiness, and irrespective of circumstance, success or failure.

Mental toughness is central to the public understanding of sporting performance and the psychology of sport. As Sheard (2010) suggests, mental toughness is a term associated with the greatest champions, it appears in numerous guises in the sporting media (such as 'spine', 'guts', 'cojones' or 'character') and, at times, has been synonymous with perceptions of what sport psychology seeks to achieve with an athlete (Pain and

Harwood, 2004). Given the apparent centrality of mental toughness within sport, it would appear to have much to offer the discipline of sport psychology; however, over the years the relationship between the public understanding of the concept and the academic attention it has received has been complex. The difficulty is that by appearing in so many different guises, mental toughness becomes increasingly evasive. Like sand through the fingers of the discipline, a strong grasp of this vital concept has often slipped away. Perhaps in response to this, the past decade has seen a growth in the academic attention directed towards the concept.

The starting point for the discussion of any academic concept has to be definition. The difficulty is that for writers in this field, definition has taken on the role of a *bête noire*. As mentioned previously, mental toughness has appeared in numerous forms in the sporting media. Any sports' fan will have an understanding of what phrases such as 'resolve', 'desire' and 'steel' refer to, but each will have their own pet theories of what that may involve. Similarly, each sport psychologist will know what the term 'mental toughness' means – but ask them to agree on a common definition and you are likely to be disappointed. A comprehensive review of these definitions is beyond the remit of this chapter (see Sheard, 2010), however, typical phrases associated with mental toughness include belief (Bull et al., 2005), resilience (Clough et al., 2002) and persistence (Cashmore, 2002). The difficulty with such definitions is that they are each narrow and, by consequence, circular. In other words, if mental toughness is resilience, does this mean resilience is mental toughness? The danger of such circularity is that it can render the concept in question (in this case, mental toughness) meaningless. Further to this, when examining discussions of what characterises mental toughness it becomes apparent why a focused, one may say narrow, definition of the concept has proven so elusive.

One of the first domains within the psychology literature to make mention of mental toughness was personality theory. Within his seminal theory of personality, Cattell (1957) made reference to tough mindedness (as the polar opposite of tender mindedness) as a trait of the personality factor of sensitivity. That mental toughness makes an appearance in a seminal psychological theory of personality hints towards why it has proven such a difficult concept to define within the sport psychology literature; namely because it is a pervasive concept that may not be restricted to sport but is more likely reflective of wide-ranging aspects of the athlete's (or any individual's) personality. Indeed, investigations into the characteristics of mental toughness have confirmed this assumption. Qualitative investigations of 'super-elite' athletes, coaches and sport psychologists' understandings of mental toughness have highlighted four common dimensions: attitude/mindset (including belief and focus); training (including motivation); competition (including coping with pressure); and post-competition (including perceptions of success and failure) (Jones et al., 2007). Reflection on these four dimensions suggests that any narrow definition will be partial and instead a multidimensional, hierarchical model of mental toughness is called for. Recognition of this fact is not new. In particular, Loeher's (1986) highly influential description of mental toughness suggested seven characteristics: self-confidence, negative energy control, attention control, imagery control, motivation, positive energy and attitudinal control. Recent years have witnessed attempts to subsume these numerous dimensions into hierarchical models of mental toughness, allowing for the classification of the key characteristics of the mentally tough athlete. Much of this work has had its genesis outside the sport psychology, literature, being influenced by models from developmental psychology, including Michael Rutter's (1999) concept of resilience and Kobasa's (1979) theory of hardiness. Essentially, resilience and hardiness as psychological constructs help us understand the capacity to deal with difficult circumstances. Kobasa suggested three key aspects to an individual's world view that will allow them to meet difficult circumstances with courage and a belief that they can cope. Commonly referred to as 'the three Cs':

- *Commitment* – how prepared the individual is to become involved and attempt to tackle the circumstances they find themselves in.
- *Control* – the extent to which the individual wants to, and believes they can, influence their circumstances.
- *Challenge* – the tendency to see unexpected events as exciting and to feel unthreatened by evaluative situations.

The '3 Cs' model has proven particularly influential in sport psychology, later being adapted by Clough et al. (2002) to a '4 Cs' sport-specific model that incorporates *Confidence* and has been used to inform the development of a measurement tool for mental toughness, The Mental Toughness 48. Most recently, Middleton et al. (2005) have provided a hierarchical model that takes on board the numerous characteristics that have been associated with mental toughness. This model is at once a summation and a consolidation of the theory of mental toughness. Through its definition of mental toughness as perseverance towards a goal in the face of adversity, it incorporates much of the general understanding of what mental toughness actually *is*. However, this model moves further, by highlighting through the characteristics of mental toughness what it *does*. The 12 characteristics listed are: self-efficacy; a belief in one's own potential; a positive mental self-concept; task familiarity; task value; intrinsic motivation to achieve one's own personal best; goal commitment; perseverance; task-specific attention; positivity; stress minimisation; and positive self-comparison to opponents. Again a similar theme emerges, namely that mental toughness touches on almost every aspect of the athlete's life. This has been taken a step further by Sheard's (2010) suggestion that mental toughness is about more than dealing with adversity, that it is in fact present during the good times as well as the difficult times. This is an appealing suggestion, particularly when one considers the athletes who have dominated their fields. Mental toughness, in all probability, enables the athlete who reaches the top to stay there. Famous examples must include Michael Schumacher's seven world Formula One titles, Roger Federer's 23 consecutive tennis Grand Slam semi-final appearances and Lance Armstrong's seven consecutive Tour de France cycling victories. Even at the peak of their careers, with all seemingly well in their sporting world, few would argue that these athletes had not remained mentally tough.

A crucial theme within the literature is the role that mental toughness plays in enabling the athlete to cope with stress. Increasingly athletes, particularly at the elite level, are required to cope with stress, in both the good and the challenging times, on a daily basis. As such, any suggestion that mental toughness may serve as a moderator of an athlete's reaction to stress is worthy of investigation. It has been suggested that mental toughness may serve as a composite or global reflection of an athlete's stress coping skills (Fletcher, 2005). In other words, we may deem an athlete as mentally tough if they have a capacity to cope with stress. Indeed, it may be suggested that the mentally tough athlete does not only *cope* with stress, they actually *thrive* on stress (see **2.5**). This is suggestive of the athlete who deliberately seeks out challenges, who values skill improvement, has a low fear of failure, and who is committed to their sport (Mischel and Shoda, 1995). Again, consideration should be given to the suggestion that attributes of this nature, while undoubtedly useful in sport, may also be characterised as life skills (Connaughton et al., 2008). Particularly at the highest levels of sport, it can be difficult to delineate where an athlete's sporting life ends and their private life begins. In such a sporting world it may be contended that an athlete will require mental toughness in every domain of his or her life if he or she is to maximise potential. In many respects this brings us to the crux of any discussion of mental toughness. Much of the debate surrounding the concept has seen the field jumping through its own definitional, and at times tautological and circular, hoops. However, any athlete or coach will be seeking the bottom line of this debate, namely, can mental toughness, as it is generally understood, be increased?

Much of the progress in recent years towards an answer to this question has been in the development of valid and reliable measures of mental toughness. Two particular measures, the Psychological Performance Inventory (Golby et al., 2007) and the Sports Mental Toughness Questionnaire (Sheard et al., 2009), would appear to have gone some way towards addressing Moran's (2004) contention that mental toughness as a concept requires an independent index. The development of such indices allows for greater measurement of the effect of interventions on mental toughness. Returning to the contention that mental toughness reflects an athlete's coping skills, Sheard and Golby (2006) report promising findings regarding the impact of psychological skills training on the development of mental toughness. It is reported that athletes who receive training in goal setting (see **3.12**), visualisation (see **4.17**), relaxation (see **2.9**), concentration (see **4.19**) and thought stopping (see **4.20**) display higher levels of mental toughness post-intervention. While research in this field remains in its infancy and further work is required, there can be no doubting the potential importance of such findings; they suggest that mental toughness can be practised and improved. There can be few individuals working in sport who have not heard sentiments such as 'He lacks the bottle' or 'She doesn't have the winning mentality'. The great promise of mental toughness research is that it appears to offer a means to address, and overcome, such labels and stereotypes. Indeed, it has been suggested that the development of mental toughness should be placed in the context of the overall development of the athlete's career (Connaughton et al., 2008). Within this model the athlete's early years should be characterised by a supportive environment that allows him or her to learn from critical early experiences. Moving into their middle years the athlete will learn to apply the skills and lessons learnt, allowing them to reach their optimum mental toughness in their later years, when they should be reaching peak performance. Of course, there are numerous factors that will determine when athletes begin to display optimum levels of mental toughness, including their innate temperament, the significant others surrounding them, and the skills they are taught. A further factor that is yet to receive much attention, but which remains intriguing none the less, is the possibility that mental toughness may be socialised. As Sheard (2010) suggests, it would appear that certain sporting institutions exude mental toughness. The Australian cricket team of the late 1990s and early part of this century and the New Zealand rugby union team would be two such examples. The mechanisms by which these institutions manage to transmit their apparent mental toughness to new members are likely to prove fertile ground for investigation.

In answering the question 'Can mental toughness be increased?', the answer would appear to be a tentative 'yes'. That the mechanisms for doing so are so broad, incorporating general psychological skills training, the athlete's developmental profile and socialisation, returns us to a familiar theme – the pervasive nature of mental toughness in the life of the athlete. Mental toughness, at present, is not characterised as a distinct, singular skill; as Sheard (2010, p. 61) suggests, it is more likely 'a lived and experienced philosophy, applied to each situation encountered'. To succinctly define such a philosophy is a difficult challenge. This is not to suggest that sport psychologists should abandon any attempts to develop mental toughness, far from it. Rather, it is a call to recognise the importance of mental toughness not only for an athlete's profession but also for life. As the American football coach Tom Landry famously remarked: 'First become a winner in life – then it's easier to become a winner on the field.'

REFERENCES

Bull, S.J., Shambrook, C.J., James, W. and Brooks, J.E. (2005) Towards an understanding of mental toughness in elite English cricketers. *Journal of Applied Sport Psychology*, 17, 209–227.

Cashmore, E. (2002) *Sport Psychology: The Key Concepts*. London: Routledge.

Cattell, R.B. (1957) *Personality and Motivation Structure and Measurement*. New York: Harcourt, Brace and World.

Clough, P., Earle, K. and Sewell, D. (2002) Mental toughness: The concept and its measurement. In Cockerill, I. (ed.) *Solutions in Sport Psychology*. London: Thomson. pp. 32–46.

Connaughton, D., Wadney, R., Hanton, S. and Jones, G. (2008) The development and maintenance of mental toughness. *Journal of Sports Sciences*, 26, 83–95.

Fletcher, D. (2005) 'Mental toughness' and human performance: Definitional, conceptual and theoretical issues. *Journal of Sports Sciences*, 23, 1246–1247.

Golby, J., Sheard, M. and van Wersch, A. (2007) Evaluating the structure of the Psychological Performance Inventory. *Perceptual and Motor Skills*, 105, 309–325.

Jones, G., Hanton, S. and Connaughton, D. (2007) A framework of mental toughness in the world's best performers. *The Sport Psychologist*, 21, 243–264.

Kobasa, S.C. (1979) 'Stressful life events, personality, and health: An inquiry into hardiness', *Journal of Personality & Social Psychology*, 37 (1), 1–11.

Loeher, J.E. (1986) *Mental Toughness Training for Sports: Achieving Athletic Excellence.* Lexington, MA: Stephen Greene Press.

Middleton, S.C., Marsh, H.W., Martin, A.J., Richards, G.E. and Perry, C. (2005) Discovering mental toughness: A qualitative study of mental toughness in elite athletes. *Psychology Today*, 22, 60–72.

Mischel, W. and Shoda, Y. (1995) A cognitive-affective system theory of personality: Reconceptualizing situations, dispositions, dynamics, and invariance in personality structure. *Psychological Review*, 102, 246–268.

Moran, A. (2004) *Sport and Exercise Psychology: A Critical Introduction.* London: Routledge.

Pain, M.A. and Harwood, C.G. (2004) Knowledge and perceptions of sport psychology within English soccer. *Journal of Sports Sciences*, 22, 813–826.

Rutter, M. (1999) 'Resilience concepts and findings: Implications for family therapy', *Journal of Family Therapy*, 21, 119–144.

Sheard, M. (2010) *Mental Toughness: The Mindset Behind Sporting Achievement.* London: Routledge.

Sheard, M. and Golby, J. (2006) Effect of a psychological skills training program on swimming performance and positive psychological development. *International Journal of Sport and Exercise Psychology*, 4, 149–169.

Sheard, M., Golby, J. and van Wersch, A. (2009) Progress toward construct validation of the Sports Mental Toughness Questionnaire (SMTQ). *European Journal of Psychological Assessment*, 25, 184–191.

4.21: mental toughness

5

Social Psychology of Sport

> **Definition:** A dynamic process that reflects in the tendency for a group to remain united in the pursuit of its task objectives and/or the satisfaction of member's affective needs.

It is difficult to question the notion that good team dynamics play a vital role in successful sport. As the basketball star Michael Jordan said, 'Talent wins games but teamwork and intelligence wins championships'. In many respects this quotation captures the essence of why team dynamics are given such prominence in sport. History tells us that it is not always the most talented teams that succeed, but rather it is the teams who appear to operate as a strong unit. One example is the Greek national soccer team that won the European Championships in 2004, defeating a Portugal team that included the talents of Luis Figo and Christiano Ronaldo. While there may have been more talented teams at Euro 2004, Greece ultimately proved to be the strongest team (conceding no goals in the tournament's knockout stage). This illustrates the point – a good team is greater than the sum of its parts. Why this should be the case is one of the most fascinating, and complex, questions in sport psychology. Any team is a complex, dynamic and unique entity. However, as with many issues in sport, discussions regarding the nature of team dynamics are prone to over-simplification. Often the importance of these complex, dynamic, unique entities is subsumed into two words: team spirit. The purpose of this chapter is to deconstruct these two words through the lens of the psychological literature in the hope of illuminating the precise mechanisms and concepts that make team dynamics such a vital aspect of the psychology of sport.

The first task is to clarify precisely what is meant by the word 'team'. In many respects, doing so may appear unnecessary, but given the confusion that can accompany discussions of team dynamics, it is important that the boundaries of discussion are clear from the outset. A team is more than simply a collection of individuals; a team is a collection of individuals that share a purpose, whether this is characterised by a specific goal or the nature of the relationships within the team (e.g. providing support for each other). Implicit in this definition are a number of additional features that must be present in order to facilitate the pursuit of a common purpose. It is these features that typically define the nature of a team. They are the nature of interactions within the team, the structure of the team, how cohesive the team is, the goals that the team is pursuing, and the team identity (Forsyth, 2009). Each of these factors is a complex, multifaceted element that influences team dynamics. However, one of these factors has dominated the psychological literature associated with teams. It would appear to be a widely held belief within sport that cohesion and team spirit are intertwined. There is also a temptation to view cohesion as either positive or negative, that is, a team is either cohesive (i.e. has good team spirit) or it is not. However, team cohesion is a complex concept and, at times, one that would appear to go against the grain of conventional sporting wisdom.

Team cohesion has been defined as a process that sees a group of individuals stick together to pursue a common goal and/or satisfy group member needs (Carron and Hausenblas, 1998). The key distinction normally made is between task cohesion and social cohesion. The nature of these two types of cohesion is self-explanatory: *task cohesion* is a measure of how well integrated the team is when they are working towards their goals; *social cohesion* is how well integrated the team is on a personal level. Further work by Albert Carron and his colleagues has subdivided the categories of cohesion yet further to four measures of cohesion. Both task and social cohesion may be subdivided into members' perceptions of group integration and the extent to which members are attracted to the group (Widmeyer et al., 1992). So, for example, in terms of individual member's attraction to the group in terms of social cohesion, this is an indicator of how much team members wish to socialise together. On the other hand, members' perceptions of task integration is an indicator of how well the team feels they work together in achieving their goals. These distinctions are useful as they provide a framework for deconstructing the global concept of team cohesion into meaningful and discrete units, and thereby have helped the development of standardised measures of team cohesion. Whereas in the past researchers and practitioners relied on a wide range of indicators of cohesion (Hogg, 1992), the delineation of four specific subtypes of cohesion has facilitated the development of a clear and widely accepted measure of team cohesion. The Group Environment Questionnaire (GEQ) is a self-report measure of the four subtypes of cohesion.

However, arriving at the point where a concept may be defined and measured is only half the battle – the task remaining is to explain what influences team cohesion, and ultimately to arrive at an understanding of how important it really is. Turning first to the question of what exactly influences team cohesion, Carron (1982) originally proposed four categories of factors: situational, leadership, personal and team. While these may prove a useful framework for structuring research, it would appear that empirical support for the importance of these factors is limited (Lavallee et al., 2004). This is not to suggest that there is no empirical evidence but rather that conclusive evidence remains hard to find. For example, numerous correlates of team cohesion have been reported, including group size, the pursuit of shared goals, and role clarity. However, the difficulty in achieving a comprehensive evidence base is at least partly due to the difficulties associated with measuring the development of team cohesion. Studies into cohesion tend, by necessity, to be correlational in design. It is a well-worn phrase that correlation does not imply causality, and so it proves here. In short, is a team cohesive because it shares goals, or does it share goals because it is cohesive? This question of causality also impacts on a second key issue: just how important is team cohesion in determining team performance?

In answering this question, the primary concern typically has been the relationship between team cohesion and team success. It has been noted that this is a somewhat narrow focus and fails to take into account variables such as player mood and team stability (Lavallee et al., 2004). However, given the continued professionalisation of sport, it is perhaps not surprising that the bottom line remains – does cohesion produce results? What may be said is that there would appear to be a relationship of some sort between cohesion and success, even if the nature of this relationship is equivocal and, at times, contradictory. For example, Widmeyer et al. (1992) report that 83 per cent of studies show a positive relationship between cohesion and success. However, this impressive figure should be tempered by the conclusion of Mullen and Copper (1994) that, while significant, any effect could only be characterised as small. While Carron et al.'s (2002) meta-analysis reported a moderate to large effect, this finding too should be tempered by their finding that when examining professional sports, as compared to high school sports, the relationship between cohesion and performance was much weaker. There are also a number of mediating factors to be considered when interpreting these results. For example, Mullen and Copper report that the relationship between cohesion and performance exists only for task cohesion. However, Carron et al. report that the relationship also holds in terms of social cohesion. Even if these relationships are present, the question of causality remains a difficult one to answer. Mullen and Copper report that the direction of the effect appears to be from success to cohesion, that is, a successful team is more likely to create a cohesive team, as compared to a cohesive team creating a successful team. However, Carron et al. report no tendency in either direction. In answering the question of how beneficial cohesion is, the literature provides few clear findings. A relationship appears to exist, but it appears more likely that cohesion follows success.

Any discussion of the potential benefits of cohesion should also be balanced with a recognition of the potential pitfalls of cohesion. There is certainly enough evidence in the psychological literature to suggest that there is such a thing as too much cohesion. In terms of social cohesion, it has been reported that athletes see high levels as potentially damaging to team performance, citing factors such as a loss of focus on task goals and the added pressure of not wanting to disappoint peers (Hardy et al., 2005). In a related vein, it is vital to be mindful of the suggestion that a cohesive group will be unproductive if group members do not have high expectations of each other (Forsyth, 2009). In other words, in an overly cohesive group there is a danger that individuals will not wish to stand out. This brings into focus the role of conflict in teams. While historically, cohesion and conflict have been seen as mutually exclusive, it would now appear that the relationship between the two is much more subtle. In particular, it has been suggested that a constructive attitude towards conflict resolution within a team may increase cohesion, whereas avoiding disputes (perhaps due to an overly socially cohesive environment) may in fact damage task cohesion (Sullivan and Feltz, 2001). The suggestion may be made that, at times, it is likely that teams may benefit from leaving social concerns to one side and focusing on task cohesion.

Recent research dealing with collective efficacy within sport teams, or the shared belief among team members of their collective capabilities (Beauchamp, 2007), would suggest that along with factors including success, appropriate leadership behaviours, group size, vicarious experiences and motivational climate, team cohesion also impacts on perceptions of collective efficacy. This would appear to be a relationship that is worthy of further consideration (Chow and Feltz, 2007).

In seeking to reach a conclusion on the importance of team cohesion, it is important to bear in mind the suggestion made at the outset; each team is a complex, dynamic and unique entity. There is no such thing as a 'good' team, or the right type of team spirit. However, in practice, the key question for practitioners and coaches would appear to be one of priority, a team must be fit for purpose. In this regard task cohesion, rather than social cohesion, is likely to be of primary concern. Should an appropriate level of social cohesion follow, this may be a benefit but only to a point, and practitioners should be mindful of the potential damage to task cohesion of too much 'team spirit'. And finally, in terms of task cohesion, hard and fast rules cannot be applied – each situation is likely to vary as a factor of the individuals involved. This is the mystery of teams and what makes them such a fascinating part of the sporting landscape. The task for those working with teams is to find the right balance that will ultimately help their teams become something greater than the sum of its parts.

REFERENCES

Beauchamp, M.R. (2007) Efficacy beliefs within relational and group contexts in sport. In Jowett, S. and Lavallee, D. (eds) *Social Psychology in Sport*. Champaign, IL: Human Kinetics. pp. 181–195.

Carron, A.V. (1982) Cohesiveness in sports groups: Interpretations & considerations, *Journal of Sport Psychology*, 4, 123–128.

Carron, A.V. and Hausenblas, H. A. (1998) *Group Dynamics in Sport* (2nd edn.). Morgantown, WV: Fitness Information Technology.

Carron, A.V., Colman, M.M., Wheeler, J. and Stevens, D. (2002) Cohesion and performance in sport: A meta analysis. *Journal of Sport and Exercise Psychology*, 24, 168–188.

Chow, G.M. and Feltz, D.L. (2007) Exploring new directions in collective efficacy and sport. In Beauchamp, M.R. and Eys, M.A. (eds) *Group Dynamics in Exercise and Sport Psychology: Contemporary Themes*. New York: Routledge. pp. 221–248.

Forsyth, D. (2009). *Group Dynamics*. 5th edn. Belmont, CA: Wadsworth Cengage Learning. pp. 7–11.

Hardy, J., Eys, M.A. and Carron, A.V. (2005) Exploring the potential disadvantages of high cohesion in sports teams. *Small Group Research*, 36, 166–187.

Hogg, M.A. (1992) *The Social Psychology of Group Cohesiveness: From Attraction to Social Identity*. London: Harvester Wheatsheaf.

Lavallee, D., Kremer, J., Moran, A. and Williams, M. (2004) *Sport Psychology: Contemporary Themes*. London: Palgrave Macmillan.

Mullen, B. and Copper, C. (1994) The relation between group cohesiveness and performance: An integration. *Psychological Bulletin*, 115, 210–227.

Sullivan, P.J. and Feltz, D.L. (2001) The relationship between intra-team conflict and cohesion within hockey teams. *Small Group Research*, 32, 342–355.

Widmeyer, W.N., Brawley, L.R. and Carron, A.V. (1992) Group cohesion in sport and exercise. In Singer, R., Murphy, M. and Tennant, L. (eds) *Handbook on Research in Sport Psychology*. New York: MacMillan. pp. 672–692.

> **Definition:** The employment of a range of techniques designed to help foster a sense of collective efficacy within the team and to strengthen relationships between team members.

'To be the ultimate team, you must use your body and your mind. Draw up on the resources of your team-mates ... Remember, only teams succeed' (attributed to the soccer manager, José Mourinho, 2008).

Finding statements from top coaches that advocate the importance of teams in building success is not a difficult task. It is a firmly established maxim within sport that coaches and managers are responsible for building teams; indeed, this is an expectation that coaches seem to be highly aware of (Bloom et al., 2003). When teams do not appear to be functioning to their maximum capacity it is the manager who is held to account, often by the use of well-worn clichés such as 'He has lost the dressing room'. Over the years this sense of responsibility has led coaches to implement numerous strategies that fall under the umbrella term of 'team building'. As such, an understanding of which team building strategies are beneficial is likely to be valuable to sport in general and to coaches in particular.

It is useful at the outset to define the term 'team building'. As mentioned previously, it is an overarching term and, as such, there are broad definitions that span the gamut of activities that have been described as team building. In the broadest sense of the term, team building may be viewed as any intervention that improves the functioning of a team. The difficulty with such a global definition is that it borders on the tautological, that is, it is close to saying team building is building the team. Consequently, more precise definitions of team building are required. Schein (1999) defines team building as a means of analysing and changing intergroup relations and behaviours. However, there are numerous opinions as to how precisely teams should be analysed and how behaviour should be changed. Consequently, when one seeks to open out the umbrella term it seems that it has been covering shades of ambiguity.

For example, some definitions make explicit reference to cohesion while others refer to the importance of satisfying group member needs (Brawley and Paskevich, 1997). Such ambiguity may reflect on the differences that exist in the focus of team-building interventions, the means of delivery and the outcome measures that are employed. Therefore, when referring to any team-building activity it is important to be clear what exactly it is seeking to achieve, and how it is seeking to achieve it.

Three broad categories of team-building intervention have been suggested: interventions that are task focused; interventions that are socially focused; and interventions that are based on outdoor pursuits/shared experiences (Martin et al., 2009). Within these broad categories there is room for a variety of different approaches. For example, in terms of task-focused interventions, there may be a focus on either one or many factors that influence team functioning, such as cohesiveness, team identity, goal setting and team communication (Yukelson, 1998). Within the socially focused category there is room for a broad range of approaches, from the traditional team night out to a focus on social support within a team. However, there is a difficulty in allowing team building to be such a promiscuous term. Without careful definition it will be difficult to measure the effectiveness of team building and consequently it will then be difficult to make recommendations as to which approaches are more or less effective. This danger has been acknowledged in recent years, leading to clearer definitions as to what exactly constitutes team building. First, there has been a growing consensus in terms of defining the main approaches to team building. The four widely accepted approaches appear to be goal setting interventions, the development of interpersonal relationships, clarifying roles, and creating a capacity for problem-solving (Salas et al., 1999). Second, there are now clear lines of distinction regarding the methods of delivering team building. For example, it is recognised that interventions may be formally or informally delivered (Klein et al., 2009), and that they may be directly delivered (i.e. by the sport psychologist) or indirectly (i.e. through the coach under the guidance of the sport psychologist) (Carron and Hausenblas, 1998). A further distinction that should be made concerns the duration of the intervention (Martin et al., 2009). Finally, there is a need to clarify exactly what the intervention is trying to achieve. Four main measures have been suggested: cognitive outcomes (including knowledge of team processes), team processes (e.g. cohesion), performance outcomes and affective outcomes (Klein et al., 2009). It should be noted that while there has been undoubted progress in defining team-building interventions at a theoretical level, in practice, interventions are rarely 'pure' in their approach (Buller, 1986). Often this is by necessity as teams are such complex, interactive entities and hence interventions designed to improve their functioning, by necessity, end up being characterised by a more diagnostic, problem-solving approach. The benefit then is that team-building interventions are thereby tailored to suit individual situations – but even then, does team building really work?

In answering this question it is important to be aware of the history of team-building interventions throughout the psychological literature. Team building has long been seen as an important aspect of the psychology of business where any intervention that may increase the productivity of workers, or more specifically teams of workers, is highly valued. As such, team building is often considered de rigueur in corporate and industrial settings. While there are undoubtedly comparisons to be drawn between work teams and sport teams, there is a danger in the wholesale export of principles from one setting to another. What is required is a careful analysis of the evidence for effectiveness, in both settings, before any judgement regarding the transfer of team-building techniques from business to sport can be reached. However, the difficulty lies in the fact that both in business and in sport there has been a shortage of research dealing with the effectiveness of team building (Bloom et al., 2003; Klein et al., 2009). Thankfully, recent studies, particularly those employing meta-analytic techniques, are starting to address this issue. In terms of team building in the business setting, there is now evidence to suggest that team building does have a positive effect. More specifically it has been reported that the strongest effects appear to be associated with interventions using goal setting and/or role clarification approaches and that, in terms of outcome measures, the greatest effects appear to be on team processes and affective outcomes (Klein et al., 2009). The implication from this evidence would appear to be that task focused approaches to team building are most valuable.

In more ways than one, it would appear that the evidence from the sporting world mirrors the evidence from the business world. In their comprehensive meta-analysis Martin et al. (2009) report that goal setting is the most effective of the team-building approaches (see **3.12**). Again it is notable that this intervention is distinctly task oriented in nature. It should be borne in mind, though, that a smaller but statistically significant effect was found to exist for interventions with an outdoor pursuits/ adventure focus. In terms of outcome measures that are positively related to team-building interventions, Martin et al. (2009) report the greatest impact to be on cognitive and performance outcomes. Interestingly, it is also reported that team building has little effect on task cohesion (see 5.22). While the authors suggest this may be due to difficulties in measuring task cohesion, an alternative suggestion may be advanced. Task cohesion is about how well a team carries out its duties on the pitch. In a sporting context it may be that this is something that is learnt on the training pitch, not in a conference room. In terms of method of delivery, it was found that there was little difference in effectiveness between direct and indirect methods. What appeared more important was intervention length. Interventions of fewer than two weeks were found to be ineffective, with effectiveness rising after 20 weeks. This tallies with previous suggestions that team building should be carried out throughout the entire season (Brawley and Paskevich, 1997). Intriguingly, it is also reported that greater effects are present in individual sports compared to team sports. While apparently counter-intuitive, this suggestion contains a certain degree of logic. Team sports by definition require a measure of interaction between members, whereas in individual sports, individuals may be in a team but not interact (e.g. Ryder Cup golf). In this respect there is more to be gained, as the level of support within a team of individuals is starting from a lower level.

In examining the evidence above, one thing is clear: many of the activities that have been identified as team building in the past need not be a priority for the coach seeking to build their team. Traditional views of teams being built by socialising together, particularly where alcohol is involved, do not appear to be validated by careful scrutiny of the evidence. Ultimately, the purpose of a team is to achieve defined goals. The evidence would suggest that assisting teams in clarifying those goals, assessing the steps required to achieve those goals, and assisting teams in developing a healthy and helpful focus on those goals, is likely to improve the team's ability to achieve their goals. When José Mourinho speaks of drawing on the resources of team mates, one would imagine he is referring to what happens on the football pitch, not what happens in the bar. It is unsurprising then that, for coaches and sports psychologists alike, a focus on task concerns appears the most effective path towards building a successful team.

REFERENCES

Bloom, G., Stevens, D. and Wickwire, T. (2003) Expert coaches' perceptions of team building. *Journal of Applied Sport Psychology*, 15 (2), 129–143.

Brawley, L.R. and Paskevich, D.M. (1997) Conducting team building research in the context of sport and exercise. *Journal of Applied Sport Psychology*, 9, 11–40.

Buller, P.F. (1986) The team building–task performance relation: Some conceptual and methodological refinements. *Group and Organization Studies*, 11, 147–168.

Carron, A.V. and Hausenblas, H.A. (1998) *Group Dynamics in Sport*. 2nd edn. Morgantown, WV: Fitness Information Technology.

Klein, C., DiazGranados, D., Salas, E., Huy Le, C., Burke, S., Lyons, R. and Goodwin, G.F. (2009) Does team building work? *Small Group Research*, 40 (2), 181–222.

Martin, L.J., Carron, A.V. and Burke, S.M. (2009) Team building interventions in sport: A meta-analysis. *Sport and Exercise Psychology Review*, 5 (2), 3–18.

Salas, E., Rozell, D., Mullen, B. and Driskell, J.E. (1999) The effect of team building on performance: An integration. *Small Group Research*, 30, 309–329.

Schein, E.H. (1999) *Process Consultation Revisited: Building the Helping Relationship*. Reading, MA: Addison-Wesley.

Yukelson, D. (1998) Communicating effectively. In Williams, J.M. (ed.) *Applied Sport Psychology*. 3rd edn. Palo Alto, CA: Mayfield. pp. 142–157.

5.24: Causal Attribution

social psychology of sport

Definition: The psychological processes that are employed to help explain why events take place, normally with reference to either internal or external factors that vary in relation to stability and control.

In 1918 the Boston Red Sox were on top of the baseball world. Led by one of the sport's iconic players, Babe Ruth, they had just won their fourth World Series in seven years. Few would have believed that it would be 2004 before another World Series triumph. In the 1918 close season Babe Ruth was sold to bitter rivals, the New York Yankees. The Yankees went on to win 26 World Series titles while the Sox waited in the wings. Many Red Sox fans attributed this lack of silverware to a curse placed on the club as punishment for selling Babe Ruth to New York – the infamous 'Curse of the Bambino'. This example serves to illustrate the point that those who are involved with sport are constantly seeking explanation. Coaches and athletes are repeatedly asked to explain their successes and failures. As illustrated by the Curse of the Bambino, these explanations are not always logical. The purpose of this chapter is to place these explanations, or attributions, under the microscope, to understand why and how they are made and why they matter so much.

It is adaptive for human beings to seek out explanations. When an event can be attributed to a cause it provides us with the basis to understand and predict future events and so increases our sense of mastery. Essentially this is an attribution, the perceived cause of an event which may, of course, be different from the actual cause (Hanrahan and Biddle, 2008). The process of making attributions is such a fundamentally human characteristic that it has been studied across the various psychology subdisciplines for a number of years. As far back as 1944, Fritz Heider was highlighting the desire of human beings to understand causality. Heider (1944) portrayed humans as lay psychologists, seeking to understand the behaviour of others. Building on this work, Jones and Davis (1965) then examined the importance of attributions in how we make inferences about the personalities of others. This would lead to one of the key findings of attribution theory, the fundamental attribution error, which states that we tend to attribute others' behaviour to their personality dispositions, rather than the circumstances that they find themselves in, while the actors themselves are more inclined to blame circumstances.

As the field developed the emphasis began to move from examining the attributions that people make about others to understanding the attributions that they make about themselves (Kelley, 1972). Kelley's theory suggests that we examine how accompanying conditions or events vary as outcomes vary. This information is then analysed in terms of its consistency, distinctiveness and consensus. So a golfer who plays distinctively worse in the rain, on a consistent basis, who is told by his caddy that he struggles in the rain, is likely to form the attribution that rain affects his game. This example also hints at a further key distinction that is made in the attribution literature – the difference between internal and external attributions (Weiner, 1972). Weiner suggested that, when making attributions, we are faced with something of a dilemma: do we look to ourselves or to external factors? This distinction would inform a key finding from attribution theory – the attributional or self-serving bias (e.g. Miller and Ross, 1975). This is the tendency to attribute success to internal factors (such as ability) and failure to external factors (typically luck). Further to this, Weiner suggested a second dimension to attributions: stability. This is the tendency to examine the likelihood of the perceived cause remaining consistent. For example, ability is likely to be perceived as fairly constant, whereas individuals may perceive an abstract concept, such as luck, to be more variable. Weiner explicitly applied his theory to achievement settings, initially focusing on academic achievements. Weiner posited that outcomes (e.g. test results) lead to emotions (positive or negative), which in turn lead to a search for reasons for the outcome. Our understanding of the reasons will in turn affect our psychological state. For example, if poor test results are perceived to be due to a lack of ability, this may lead to the conclusion that there is no point trying. This will ultimately have a behavioural consequence; in this instance it may be a lack of effort in the future.

While early studies of attribution tended to focus on discrete factors, primarily ability, effort, task difficulty and luck, Weiner's theory focused on attribution dimensions. Initially this consisted of two dimensions, internality and stability, with the additional dimensions of globality, intentionality and controllability only later receiving attention (Hanrahan and Biddle, 2008). 'Globality' refers to the perceived breadth of effect of the perceived cause, that is, how likely is it to remain a factor across different settings. 'Intentionality' refers to whether or not the cause was present through the desire of the individual, in turn overlapping with controllability or the degree of control that the individual perceives they have. By conceptualising attribution dimensions in this way it becomes possible to reflect on the endless number of discrete factors that athletes may perceive as important. Not that this is always an easy task. As Hanrahan and Biddle suggest, grey areas still exist. For example, in certain closed-skill sports (e.g. diving, darts, pistol shooting) task difficulty remains stable. However, in a sport such as golf, task difficulty could be seen as unstable, being influenced by both the course and the conditions. This highlights the strength of the dimensional concept of attribution theory, it provides a mechanism to recognise the influence of the particular sport in question and the influence of the athlete's perception of attribution dimensions. It is through the lens of these dimensions that attribution research in the sporting domain has been conducted and it is through this lens that we now move on to examine how attributions are made and why they are so important.

In understanding how attributions are made, the primary focus has been on seeking to identify factors that predict the types of attributions that individuals are likely to make. For example, in children's sport, self-perception has been identified as an important factor. It is reported that children with higher levels of self-esteem are more likely to make attributions that are internal, stable and controllable. Additionally, children with higher levels of self-efficacy are more likely to attribute failures to a lack of effort, rather than a lack of ability (see **3.16**). A further factor that has been identified as a predictor of attributions is goal orientation (see **3.15**) (Hanrahan and Gross, 2005). In this instance it is reported that a higher task orientation is likely to lead to global and stable attributions. It is also reported that expertise is likely to affect attributions, with expert basketball players appearing more likely to make strategic attributions (i.e. blaming poor strategy for failures) than novice basketball players (Clearly and Zimmerman, 2001). A particularly interesting finding is the absence of an influence of intelligence on the types of attributions made (Kozub, 2002). This would support the assertion made at the outset that explanations in sport are often lacking in logic or rationale. Of course, these findings only matter if the attributions that athletes make have a direct effect on their performance, that is, if attributions have consequences. It is with this in mind that we move to examine why attributions are so important.

One of the primary reasons that attributions are so important is that they influence future expectancies. For example, an athlete who attributes their failures to internal, unstable and controllable causes is likely to have more positive expectancies of future performance. They are likely to form the belief that they are capable of altering the circumstances that led to their failure. For example, athletes who attribute failure to a lack of effort (an internal, unstable and controllable factor) are more likely to believe that they can perform better in the future. This may be contrasted with attributions that cite external, stable and uncontrollable factors for failure. The classic example is the player who believes 'his name was never on the trophy'. In such an example the athlete is likely to feel helpless and at the mercy of fate when it comes to future performances. Stability in particular seems important in this regard in that it has been found to influence athlete self-efficacy, with those who attribute success to stable factors displaying higher levels of self-efficacy (see **3.16**) (Bond et al., 2001). A similar effect has been noted on perceptions of performance, with both athletes and coaches displaying increased perceptions of performance and higher levels of persistence when they attribute success to internal, stable, controllable and intentional causes.

In practical terms, what these findings mean is that athletes' attributions are likely to prove fertile ground for intervention and in particular around cognitive restructuring (see **4.20**). If certain attributions lead to more desirable outcomes, then it would make sense that athletes should be instructed in how best to explain their successes and failures. Across the discipline of psychology this type of intervention has been labelled as 'attribution retraining'. The central premise of attribution retraining is that objective information may be used to challenge unhelpful attributions. In sport this has tended to focus on ensuring that athletes attribute failure to something which they believe they can change, as supposed to more stable causes such as ability (Rees et al., 2005). One potential attribution that athletes may be encouraged to make is that failure was due to a lack of effort, as this is something they can change. Coaches employ this technique on a regular basis. Instead of telling their players they are not good enough, they may encourage them to try harder, in the belief that this will lead to improved results. However, this suggestion comes with a warning that, at times, failure may actually be due to uncontrollable circumstances (including superior opposition) and the athlete may have tried as hard as they could. In this instance, an attribution associated with lack of effort is likely to prove demoralising to the athlete. As such, positive results have been reported for programmes which focus on other unstable, controllable factors, in particular, strategy. An example of this type of thinking is the coach who tells his players that they are good enough but that they need to stick to the game plan in order to win. Such attributions are designed to protect self-efficacy and self-esteem while at the same time ensuring that athletes still believe that success is under their control.

Such a viewpoint stands in stark contrast to the type of superstition typified by our example of the Curse of the Bambino. However, the attribution literature does provide us with some clues as to why sport is littered with such irrational attributions. Faulkner and Finlay (2002) point out that attributions occur in a social context and as such should be seen as much as an action as a belief. In other words, attributions often serve a social function, for example, justifying oneself to the media (or a psychologist!). With this in mind it may have suited Red Sox fans to blame their team's repeated failures on the Curse of the Bambino rather than admit that their team was not good enough for almost 70 years! As such, attributions are important not only to the people who make them, but also to the people who hear them. This is a central distinction in attribution theory. While we may make excuses to others, our appraisal of ourselves must be both accurate and helpful. This is the challenge for practitioners and athletes alike when they seek to put attribution theory into practice.

REFERENCES

Bond, K.A., Biddle, S.J.H. and Ntoumanis, N. (2001) Self-efficacy and causal attribution in female golfers. *International Journal of Sport Psychology*, 32, 243–256.

Clearly, T.J. and Zimmerman, B.J. (2001) Self-regulation differences during athletic practice by experts, non-experts, and novices. *Journal of Applied Sport Psychology*, 13, 185–206.

Faulkner, G. and Finlay, S.J. (2002) It's not what you say, it's the way you say it! Conversation analysis: A discursive methodology for sport, exercise, and physical education. *Quest*, 54, 49–66.

Hanrahan, S.J. and Biddle, S.J.H. (2008) Attributions and perceived control. In Horn, T.S. (ed.) *Advances in Sport Psychology* 3rd edn. Leeds, UK: Human Kinetics. 99–114.

Hanrahan, S.J. and Gross, J. (2005) Attributions and goal orientations in masters athletes: Performance versus outcome. *Revista de Psicologia del Deporte*, 14 (1), 43–56.

Heider, F. (1944) Social perception and phenomenal causality. *Psychological Review*, 51, 358–374.

Jones, E.E. and Davis, K.E. (1965) From acts to dispositions: The attribution process in person perception. In Berkowitz, L. (ed.) *Advances in Experimental Social Psychology*. Vol. 2. London: Academic Press. pp. 219–266.

Kelley, H.H. (1972) Causal schemata and the attribution process. In Jones, E.E., Kanouse, D.E., Kelley, H.H., Nisbett, R.E., Valins, S. and Weiner, B. (eds) *Attribution: Perceiving the Causes of Behaviour*. Morristown, NJ: General Learning Press. pp. 1–26.

Kozub, F.M. (2002) Expectations, task persistence, and attributions in children with mental retardation during integrated physical education. *Adapted Physical Activity Quarterly*, 19, 334–349.

Miller, D.T. and Ross, M. (1975) Self-serving biases in the attribution of causality: Fact or fiction? *Psychological Bulletin*, 82 (2), 213–225.

Rees, T., Ingledew, D.K. and Hardy, L. (2005) Attribution in sport psychology: Seeking congruence between theory, research and practice. *Psychology of Sport and Exercise*, 6, 189–204.

Weiner, B. (1972) *Theories of Motivation: From Mechanism to Cognition*. Chicago, IL: Rand McNally.

5.25: Social Facilitation and Social Loafing

Definitions: Social facilitation is a change in individual effort and subsequent performance in the real or imagined presence of either co-actors or an audience. Social loafing is a reduction in individual effort when acting as part of a group or collective.

'Fabio Capello's side headed to South Africa with high hopes, so where did it all go so wrong for the boys of 2010?' (*Guardian*, 2010). The story of England's demise from the 2010 football World Cup is not unfamiliar. Time and again faithful fans follow their team with passionate and unrealistic expectations, only to return with their dreams left in tatters. Why is this the case – or in fact, are the supporters the root cause of the problem?

Over the last 100 years (see 1.1), the world of sport and exercise has presented itself as an ideal venue for exploring how the presence of others, whether as spectators, fellow competitors or teammates, impacts on motivation and performance. Social influence can reveal itself in many ways, but the primary focus of much of this work has been on two related themes, social facilitation and social loafing. That is, how the presence of others either helps or hinders individual effort and, in turn, performance.

Is it mere coincidence that so many world records and outstanding feats occur not in training but under the gaze of millions of spectators? Equally, in team sports do we subconsciously ease back on the throttle when we know we can hide ourselves in the group or collective? In actual fact, in both cases the earliest studies date back to the roots of experimental psychology. In the case of social facilitation, this can be traced to Norman Triplett's fishing-line experiment with children in 1898 (see 1.1), while the first social loafing experiment was carried out by a French agricultural engineer called Max Ringelmann in 1913 (Kravitz and Martin, 1986). Using a rope attached to a tree, he measured the force exerted by either one, two, three or up to eight men. By the time that eight men were pulling on the rope the average force that each exerted (31 kg) was less than half that they had shown they were capable of when acting alone (63 kg). Later experiments have confirmed this effect by taking account of co-ordination losses; even so the losses that could be explained by social loafing alone accounted for between 10 per cent and 15 per cent reduction in effort.

Both experiments generated a great deal of interest and started long research traditions, while also triggering other lines of enquiry. For example, Triplett was aware that the presence of others did not have the same effect on everyone, as some coped better than others (Triplett 1898). Some children wound faster alongside another child while others went to pieces, suggesting the significant role that stress or arousal had played (see **2.5**). Equally, later work on social influence across social psychology, including that dealing with topics such as conformity, compliance and obedience, all point to the non-conscious ways in which the presence of others influences our motives and behaviour.

SOCIAL FACILITATION

Triplett's work was taken up by eminent social psychologists including Floyd Allport in the 1920s and from that time until the 1980s there followed a multitude of human and animal studies, both in the field and the laboratory (Aiello and Douthill, 2001; Strauss, 2002). Some were truly ingenious. For example, one involved looking at the speed with which cockroaches ran from a bright light, either alone or in pairs, and either in a straight line (a dominant response) or around a corner (a non-dominant response). Across this research the results have been generally consistent, if not spectacular. In a nutshell, the presence of others leads to enhanced performance on certain tasks, and specifically tasks which call for well learnt, dominant responses. If you can do something well, the presence of others will improve performance. On the other hand, if you are incompetent, learning a skill or attempting something for the first time, then you may perform worse in company than alone. While the phenomenon is very important in the context of competitive sport, the number of applied studies is surprisingly small. One exception involved secretly rating players in a US pool hall according to their shot accuracy. Four spectators (confederates of the experimenter) then stood and watched games. As you may expect, those who were above average improved in front of an audience (from 71 per cent accuracy to 80 per cent), while those who were below average potted even fewer shots (from 36 per cent to 25 per cent) (Michaels et al., 1982).

Despite these isolated examples, by the 1980s interest in researching the phenomenon had waned. At the same time interest grew in trying to explain not the *what* but the *why* of social facilitation (Strauss, 2002). Zajonc's original explanation (Zajonc, 1965) had held sway for two decades, arguing that the mere presence of an audience (or co-actors) was somehow sufficient to increase drive or motivation, and this would improve well learned performance but at the same time interfere with newly acquired skills, whatever the circumstance. Later work suggested that the type of audience was critical and raised the possibility that the prospect of evaluation could not be ignored. Cottrell et al. (1968) maintained that social facilitation increased in proportion to the extent that the person felt he or she was being evaluated by either spectators or competitors. While evaluation apprehension does appear to be important to some degree (and hence explains why some teams have always played better away from the critical gaze of home 'supporters'), the larger 'why' questions still remain more elusive. Evaluation apprehension has been connected at different times with a host of 'self' variables such as self-awareness, self-consciousness, self-presentational concern, self-monitoring and self-attention. Meanwhile it was also suggested that the effect could be explained by the conflict that is generated when we are performing in the presence of others – the conflict between attending to the task and attending to the other people. This raises anxiety which then leads to social facilitation (Baron, 1986).

As to which theory offers the most valid explanation, the answer probably lies in the fact that all contain a kernel of truth – but fundamentally the effect may not be as profound as some would have suggested. In a meta-analysis of over 241 studies, involving nearly 24,000 participants, Bond and Titus (1983) found that the presence of others had only marginal effects on performance overall, to the order of only 2–3 per cent. They concluded that the presence of others may increase arousal but only if the individual is performing a complex task, and this may lead to a knock-on effect on both speed (increased) and accuracy (decreased). However, the effect of evaluation on performance was not shown to be strong across these published experiments.

SOCIAL LOAFING

On the other side of the coin from social facilitation lies social loafing, where the presence of others does not increase drive or arousal but instead provides an opportunity to coast. A substantial literature shows a variety of factors that impact on the extent of social loafing (Hardy, 1990). Factors that have been shown to decrease loafing effects include: smaller size of group; the extent to which individual effort can be identified; the strength of group identity; the nature and attractiveness of the task; the degree of trust between group members; the interdependence of group members; the extent of involvement with the group; group cohesiveness; intergroup comparisons; collective efficacy; and personal responsibility. Most recently, Heuze and Brunel (2003) found that when playing darts against opponents of varying degrees of ability, loafing was greatest when the opponent was superior and least when the other player was thought to be of a similar standard and hence competition was most fierce.

The overlap between many of the constructs described above is considerable, and hence it should come as no surprise to learn that there have been repeated calls to integrate the literature (Karau and Williams, 1993; Carron and Brawley, 2008).

As to why loafing occurs, a number of explanations have been offered, all generally pointing to two dominant concerns. First, the potential to share responsibility when individual effort is not identifiable, and in particular, on tasks or in games that are not seen as important. Second, the extent to which the person identifies with the collective and feels bound to the values and goals of the group or team.

By now it should be apparent that there are obvious connections between the two phenomena, social loafing and social facilitation, as both deal with how we are influenced by others in social situations, including teams. With this in mind a number of approaches have emerged to try to offer an overarching framework. For example, both Harkins and Szymanski (1987) and Mullen and Baumeister (1987) describe social loafing and social loafing in relation to self-concept; the former emphasising evaluation by self and others, the latter our self-awareness in a variety of social contexts. In a very different way, Sanna (1992) used self-efficacy theory (see **3.16**) to model four possible outcomes attaching to the interaction between loafing and facilitation. They proposed that when the presence of others *increases* evaluation then dominant responses will be enhanced (social facilitation) but difficult tasks will be impaired (social inhibition), while when the presence of others *decreases* evaluation then we will be inclined to 'sit back' on less demanding or easy tasks (social loafing) but our performance may actually improve on more difficult tasks as we are less anxious (social security). In a similar vein, Karau and Williams (2001) developed their Collective Effort Model to help explain the social phenomena, arguing that effort will only be expended when the individual values the task and their personal contribution to the group, and when their performance is being evaluated. At the same time, Aiello and Douthill (2001) outlined an integrative unifying theory, principally to consider social facilitation effects but with the potential to include social loafing as well. The model considers how situational (e.g. sensory cues, proximity of others, feedback and climate), presence (e.g. type of presence, roles of others, salience of presence, relationships and length of presence) and task (e.g. difficulty, cognitive/motor characteristics and time) factors combine to influence the individual's perceptions, cognitions, reactions and performance. This model represents a useful way forward.

REFERENCES

Aiello, J.R. and Douthill, E.A. (2001) Social facilitation from Triplett to electronic performance monitoring. *Group Dynamics*, 5, 163–180.

Baron, R.A. (1986) Distraction-conflict theory: Progress and problems. In Berkowitz, L. (ed.) *Advances in Experimental Social Psychology*. Vol. 19. Orlando, FL: Academic Press. pp. 1–39.

Bond, C.F. and Titus, L.J. (1983) Social facilitation: A meta-analysis of 241 studies. *Psychological Bulletin*, 94 (2), 265–292.

Carron, A.V. and Brawley, F.R. (2008) Group dynamics in sport and physical activity. In Horn, T.S. (ed.) *Advances in Sport Psychology*. Champaign, IL: Human Kinetics. pp. 213–238.

Cottrell, N.B., Sekerak, G.J. Wack, D.L. and Rittle, R.H. (1968) Social facilitation of dominant responses by the presence of an audience and the mere presence of others. *Journal of Personality and Social Psychology*, 9 (3), 245–250.

Guardian, The (2010) World Cup 2010: Five Reasons for England's Failure, 28 June, p. 7 (Sport).

Hardy, C.J. (1990) Social loafing: Motivational losses in collective performance. *International Journal of Sport Psychology*, 21, 305–327.

Harkins, S.G. and Szymanski, K. (1987) Social loafing and social facilitation: New wine in old bottles. In Hendrick, C. (ed.) *Review of Personality and Social Psychology: Group Processes and Intergroup Relations*. Newbury Park, CA: Sage. pp. 167–188.

Heuze, J-P. and Brunel, P.C. (2003) Social loafing in a competitive context. *International Journal of Sport and Exercise Psychology*, 1 (3), 246–263.

Karau, S.J. and Williams, K.D. (1993) Social loafing: A meta-analytic review and theoretical integration. *Journal of Personality and Social Psychology*, 65, 681–706.

Karau, S.J. and Williams, K.D. (2001) Understanding individual motivation in groups: The Collective Effort Model. In Turner, M.E. (ed.) *Groups at Work: Theory and Research*. Mahwah, NJ: Erlbaum. pp. 113–141.

Kravitz, D.A. and Martin, B. (1986) Ringelmann rediscovered: The original article. *Journal of Personality and Social Psychology*, 50, 936–941.

Michaels, J.W., Blommel, J.M., Brocato, R.M., Linkous, R.A. and Rowe, J.S. (1982) Social facilitation and inhibition in a natural setting. *Replications in Social Psychology*, 2, 21–24.

Mullen, B. and Baumeister, R.F. (1987) Group effects on self-attention and performance: Social loafing, social facilitation, and social impairment. In Hendrick, C. (ed.) Review of Personality and Social Psychology: Group Processes and Intergroup Relations. Newbury Park, CA: Sage. pp. 189–205.

Sanna, L.J. (1992) Self-efficacy theory: Implications for social facilitation and social loafing. *Journal of Personality and Social Psychology*, 62, 774–786.

Strauss, B. (2002) Social facilitation in motor tasks. *Psychology of Sport and Exercise*, 3, 237–256.

Triplett, N. (1898) The dynamogenic factors in pacemaking and competition. *American Journal of Psychology*, 9, 507–533.

Zajonc, R.B. (1965) Social facilitation. *Science*, 149, 269–274.

5.26: Leadership and Effective Coaching

Definition: The delivery of effective sport leadership and coaching styles that accommodate the contingencies of the situation and the sport along with the characteristics of those being coached or managed.

Whether prowling the touchline in an expensive suit or barking out instructions on a windy training ground, one of the most enigmatic figures in sport is the coach. Leading an elite sporting squad has become a high-profile, high-pressure vocation. Never was President Truman's phrase 'The buck stops here' more appropriate than when applied to the sport's coach. Coaches' careers stand or fall on the performances of their players, with the modern sporting media placing a huge onus on the importance of the leadership role. But why should this be the case? What exactly is the role of the coach? What makes an effective coach?

In truth there are as many questions as answers within the field. In many respects, the attire of these enigmatic figures reflects the contradictions and idiosyncrasies of the psychological literature that examines their role. On the one hand we have the literature that examines the role of leadership in sport – the expensive, made-to-measure suit of the literature as it were. On the other hand we have the literature examining coaching behaviour – or the tracksuit of the literature. While links undoubtedly exist between these two literatures, to a large extent there has been a historical fissure between them. This will be reflected in the structure of this review. Initially the psychological literature on leadership in sport will be examined before moving on to consider the literature concerned with effective coaching. While doing so it is hoped that some of the enigma surrounding the coach will be subject to close scrutiny, and greater clarity regarding the remit of the role will hopefully emerge.

It is unsurprising that sport psychology turned to organisational and occupational psychology when searching for theoretical models to apply to the sport leader. Within industry settings, there has been a longstanding interest in how best to manage teams. This interest has led to an extensive literature examining the importance of leadership. Current definitions characterise leadership as a process, during which a group is influenced towards achieving their goals by an individual (Northouse, 2001). Much of this work may be traced back to Kurt Lewin's (1951) highly influential research into leadership styles. Lewin's was the first of many theories to be taken from the occupational psychology literature and applied in the sporting context. Other influential models included Fiedler's Contingency Model of Situational Control, Normative Theory, Path-Goal Theory, and Situational Leadership Theory. Expositions of these theories are well rehearsed and numerous, and while there remains undoubted applied value in elements of these non-sport specific theories, it was not until the early 1990s that a comprehensive model of leadership in the sporting setting was proposed, the highly influential Multidimensional Model of Leadership (MML) (Chelladurai, 1993). MML is at once an attempt at synthesising, extending and testing the applicability of the models listed previous to the sporting context (Riemer, 2008). By drawing on these models, Chelladurai posited three central elements to leadership in sport: first, circumstantial expectations placed on the leader; second, the behaviour displayed by the leader and third, the preferences of the athletes being led. The interplay between these factors will ultimately affect the two primary outcomes of leadership behaviour, athlete performance and athlete satisfaction. Of central importance is how closely the leader's preferred behaviour corresponds with both the demands of the situation and the preference of the athlete. So, for example, an expert youth coach may find that his or her approaches and preferences may not quite match the requirements of leading a highly experienced, elite-level squad. This is not to say that a change in approach is not possible in different situations, rather it is to say that it is *required*.

While an appealing model in both its intuition and its scope, the research literature surrounding MML could not be described as definitive. While some promising findings have been reported, the picture is not clear (Riemer and Toon, 2001). A relatively recent adaptation to MML has come in the form of transformational leadership (Chelladurai, 2001; Hoption et al., 2007). Transformational leadership highlights the importance of the coach's ability to ensure that athletes buy into their vision for the team, to engage athletes in an emotional capacity, for want of a better expression, to bring something special to a team. 'Charisma', 'inspiration' and 'vision' are terms typically associated with this approach to leadership. Any follower of sport will be highly familiar with such a notion. This is the concept of the coach as a *leader* in the almost mystical sense of the term. However, even despite the widespread attention that this notion receives in both the media and supporters' perceptions of team performance, the concept of transformational leadership remains under-researched in sport. In truth this is unsurprising. The mystical figures of sport leadership are afforded this status because they are perceived to be unique, because they are what they appear to be – one in a million. This is not to say that transformational leadership is an undesirable characteristic in a coach, far from it. The danger is in concentrating on such a nebulous concept as charisma when there are so many elements to the role of the coach that are more concrete and ultimately open to improvement. This hints at a flaw within the leadership approaches in the sporting context; that is, they don't tell the whole truth. While a coach may benefit from having the expensive suit of leadership, they should be wary of neglecting the tracksuit of coaching.

Before turning to our examination of coaching behaviour, it is worth pausing to make one final comment on the leadership literature. Recently it has been acknowledged that the task of leadership extends beyond the role of the coach to include other athletes. The Leadership Scale for Sports (LSS) is a tool developed to measure five dimensions of leadership behaviour in sport (Chelladurai and Saleh, 1980). The five suggested dimensions are: training and instruction, democratic behaviour, autocratic behaviour, social support and positive feedback. As we move on to examine the coaching literature in more detail, the broad range of expectations placed on a coach should be noted. However, recent research has suggested that some of the leadership functions expected of the coach may be fulfilled by other leadership figures within a team. Specifically, it has been reported that teams may recognise up to a quarter of their members as informal leaders (Loughead and Hardy, 2005). It has been found that these informal leaders are more likely to fulfil the roles of social support, positive feedback and democratic decision-making. This is then reported to leave coaches with more time to concentrate on training and instruction, as well as autocratic behaviour. In other words, allowing them to focus on the big picture. This highlights an important point. Leadership is not something to be guarded by the coach but rather something to be encouraged by them. By doing this they are likely to increase the effectiveness of their coaching.

As mentioned previously, there has been an historical fissure between the leadership and coaching literatures. This is due, at least in part, to the fact that coaching spans numerous disciplines, including teaching, management and psychology. While there is undoubted strength in drawing information from such a broad base, it would appear that this broad base has often contributed to a lack of focus (Gilbert and Trudel, 2004). Examinations of coaching have tended to be descriptive in their approach, focusing on discrete coaching behaviours, for example how often the coach gives positive feedback. The difficulty in this approach is two-fold. First, coaching behaviour is the result of a complex inter-action of situational demands, personality traits and the demands of the particular sport. In short, rigidly following a list of prescribed behav-iours will not lead to effective coaching. Second, an over-focus on describing coach behaviour appears to have led to a neglect of the theoretical frameworks that may be used to understand it (Gilbert and Trudel, 2004). However, it would appear that this is a concern that is being addressed. Recent years have seen the emergence of a number of theories that seek to clarify the nature of the relationship between coaches and athletes. Jowett and Poczwardowski (2008) recently pro-posed an integrated research model of four of these theories. This framework recognises the complexity of the coaching relationship, delineating three key categories of concern. First, recognition is given to the role of antecedents to the coach–athlete relationship. Factors such as age, ability, experience and cultural norms will all play a role in determining which coaching approaches are appropriate. Second, consideration is given to the nature of the coach-athlete relationship. Jowett's (2005) description of the key components of the coach–athlete relationship (closeness, commitment, co-ordination and complementarity) is incorporated at this stage of the model. This factor also incorporates actual coaching behaviour. Third, the relative importance of the desired outcomes is considered. In other words, appropriate coaching behaviour will be determined by what the coach and athlete are seeking to achieve. For example, is the relationship mainly a social one, or is it predicated on achieving a specific sporting goal? Underpinning these three factors is the nature of communication between the coach and the athlete, communication being characterised as the driving force within the relationship, influencing every aspect of it. The scale of this framework highlights the challenge facing the coaching literature. Any research into effective coaching must be placed in context, making recognition of the particular demands and outcomes relevant in any given situation.

In terms of the elite sporting context, some interesting work has been carried out recently examining the cognitive demands that this complex relationship places on the coach. Particularly in sports that require the coach to take major decisions in the game situation, problem-solving skills are likely to be an important consideration in effective coaching. Indeed, research has borne this out. It has been reported that higher-level coaches possess a higher level of problem-solving competence than lower-level coaches (Hagemann et al., 2008). Perhaps most interestingly, it is reported that this reflects on a general capacity for problem-solving and is not dependent on sporting experience or knowledge. The idea of problem-solving being crucial in effective coaching has also been reflected in the behavioural literature, where it has been reported that elite-level coaches spend the majority of game time deliberately engaging in silent monitoring before intervening as and when required (Smith and Cushion, 2006).

It is not a surprising finding that coaches are often reflective, and this review would suggest that there is a lot for them to reflect on! Recent years have seen much progress in the development of sport-specific models of both leadership and effective coaching, both of which are broad in their scope. While the development of models is crucial, the next step for the field should be the placement of empirical findings within these frameworks. By doing so, further clarity will emerge regarding the role of the coach. However, the recognition of the development of the literature examining the role of the coach must be tempered with some caution. While the coach undoubtedly remains an important, and often enigmatic, figure, the best coach can achieve nothing on his or her own. Coaching is a two-way relationship. As one of the most decorated and enigmatic soccer coaches, Brian Clough, once put it, 'Players lose you games, not tactics'. Whether monitoring them from the sidelines in an expensive suit or instructing them on the training pitch, any coach is dependent on the athletes they are leading. Given the broad range of expectations placed on the coach, their ultimate frustration is likely to remain that they are dependent on the performance of others for their success. Considered in this light, it is perhaps a little unfair that the buck always stops with them.

REFERENCES

Chelladurai, P. (1993) Leadership. In Singer, R.N., Murphey, M. and Tennant, L.K. (eds) *Handbook of Research on Sport Psychology*. New York: Macmillan. pp. 647–671.

Chelladurai, P. (2001) *Managing Organisation for Sport and Physical Activity: A Systems Perspective*. Scottsdale, AZ: Holcomb-Hathaway.

Chelladurai, P. and Saleh, S.D. (1980) Dimensions of leader behaviour in sports: Development of a leadership scale. *Canadian Journal of Applied Sports Sciences*, 3, 85–90.

Gilbert, W.D. and Trudel, P. (2004) Analysis of coaching science research published from 1970–2001. *Research Quarterly for Exercise and Sport*, 75 (4), 388–399.

Hagemann, N., Strauss, B. and Busch, D. (2008) The complex problem-solving competence of team coaches. *Psychology of Sport and Exercise*, 9, 301–317.

Hoption, C., Phelan, J. and Barling, J. (2007) Transformational leadership in sport. In Beauchamp, M.R. and Eys, M.A. (eds) *Group Dynamics in Exercise and Sport Psychology: Contemporary Themes*. New York: Routledge. pp. 45–60.

Jowett, S. (2005) On repairing and enhancing the coach–athlete relationship. In Jowett, S. and Jones, M. (eds) *The Psychology of Coaching*. Leicester: British Psychological Society. pp. 14–26.

Jowett, S. and Poczwardowski, A. (2008) Understanding the coach–athlete relationship. In Horn, T.S. (ed.) *Advances in Sport Psychology*. 3rd edn. Champaign, IL: Human Kinetics. pp. 4–14.

Lewin, K. (1951) *Field Theory in Social Science*. New York: Harper.

Loughead, T.M. and Hardy, J. (2005) A comparison of coach and peer leader behaviours in sport. *Psychology of Sport and Exercise*, 6, 303–312.

Northouse, P.G. (2001) *Leadership: Theory and Practice*. 2nd edn. Thousand Oaks, CA: Sage.

Riemer, H.A. (2008) Multidimensional model of coach leadership. In Horn, T.S. (ed.) *Advances in Sport Psychology*. 3rd edn. Champaign, IL: Human Kinetics. pp. 58–73.

social psychology of sport

Riemer, H.A. and Toon, K. (2001) Leadership and satisfaction in tennis: Examination of congruence, gender and ability. *Research Quarterly for Exercise and Sport*, 72, 243–256.

Smith, M. and Cushion, J. (2006) An investigation of the in-game behaviours of professional, top-level youth soccer coaches. *Journal of Sports Sciences*, 24, 355–366.

5.27: Home Advantage

Definition: The advantages, actual and perceived, that teams and individuals feel are associated with playing at home venues.

A visit to any of the great stadiums reveals the importance that sports invest in the places that they call home. Stadiums such as Camp Nou (soccer: Barcelona FC), Fenway Park (baseball: Boston Red Sox) and Lords (cricket: Middlesex and England) are not so much pitches but rather shrines where the faithful gather to will their teams on to glory. To say that sports teams benefit from playing at home will surprise no sports fan. What may prove more surprising is how difficult it is to say why.

What is meant by the term 'home advantage'? In the simplest of terms, home advantage means that home teams win more than half of their games (Courneya and Carron, 1992b). Nevill and Holder (1999) provide an overview of home win percentages (hwp) across various sports. The five sports they report are: baseball (54.3 hwp); American football (57.3 hwp); ice hockey (61.2 hwp); basketball (64.4 hwp); and soccer (68.3 hwp). Further specific examples reported since are that all teams in the Six Nations score more points at home compared to when they play away (Thomas et al., 2008), and that teams who play the second leg of UEFA Champions League ties at home are more likely to progress (Page and Page, 2007). It is important to stress that teams of all ability experience home advantage, although it seems that the top teams enjoy a greater home advantage (Madrigal and James, 1999). While the research into the effect of teams playing at home is clear, the effect on individual sports is more difficult to untangle. Some research has identified a home advantage, especially when subjective judgements are made, for example in boxing (Balmer et al., 2005). However, other studies have suggested that the pressure of playing at home may negatively affect performance (Bray and Martin, 2003). Anecdotally, this may be part of the reason that English tennis players have found it so difficult to win at Wimbledon, and why French tennis players have found it difficult to win at Roland Garros.

The next question is what are the factors underlying home advantage? In their seminal literature review Courneya and Carron (1992a) concluded that the existence of a home advantage was so well established that researchers should no longer be looking for it, rather they should be looking to explain it. To this end they suggested potential avenues of investigation which may be divided into two broad categories: location effects and psychological effects.

The first potential location factor is the influence of travel. Anyone who has travelled in a cramped mini-bus to a sporting fixture can attest to the particular challenges that come from playing away from home, particularly in terms of fatigue. However, given the continuing professionalisation of sports, do we expect mundane factors such as travel to exert an influence at the highest level of sport? Travel factors have been found to play only a minor role in explaining home advantage, even when taking into account the distance travelled and the number of time zones crossed by away teams. A second location factor posited is the familiarity effect, that is, familiarity with a pitch and its facilities is advantageous. However, there is evidence to question the influence of this factor. For example, when English soccer was examined from 1981–84, only minimal effects of pitch size and even the use of an artificial surface were found (Pollard, 1986). The location effect has received the most attention, and has garnered that the most supporting evidence is the effect of the crowd (Nevill and Holder, 1999). While some studies have failed to identify an influence of crowd size (Dowie, 1982), it now appears that the key factor mediating the influence of a crowd is its density. Crowd density is essentially a measure of how full a stadium is. Intuitively, this is unsurprising – after all, 15,000 spectators at Wembley Stadium is an entirely different proposition to 15,000 spectators at Wimbledon Centre Court. Schwartz and Barsky (1977) reported that hwp rose from 48 per cent for matches played in front of a less than 20 per cent full stadium, to 57 per cent in front of a stadium that is more than 40 per cent full. Such findings have obvious implications for stadium design, as perhaps does the finding that playing in a stadium with a roof may lead to a greater hwp.

The conclusion that impassioned supporters will jump to is that they drive their team on to greater performance, that they are the classic 'twelfth man'. However, the evidence is inconclusive. Some evidence has suggested that a higher motivation is present when athletes perform at home while others have found higher testosterone levels. This has led to the territoriality argument (Neave and Wolfson, 2003), the suggestion that home advantage is related to a primitive desire to defend one's own territory. However, findings into individual responses to home advantage have not been consistently demonstrated (Carron et al., 2005). It may be that the psychological effects of playing at home are more subtle and idiosyncratic. For example, coaches commonly believe that familiarity with the home pitch is an advantage (Gayton et al., 2001). While the accuracy of this assessment may be questioned, the perception cannot be. In other words, believing you have an advantage may be enough to give you an advantage.

The final psychological factor that has been examined is the effect of home advantage on match officials. Soccer provides two main indicators of referee bias that are easily examinable: the extra time added to matches and disciplinary actions (e.g. yellow cards and penalties). In terms of the extra time added on to the end of matches, research has clearly indicated that there is a home advantage in this respect. On average, it has been shown that Spanish referees add around two more minutes of extra time when the home team is trailing by a goal, compared to when they are leading by a goal. However, the chances of scoring in stoppage time are slim compared to the chances of scoring from a penalty. Nevill et al. (1996) report that home teams receive more penalties than away teams. The obvious response to this finding is that home teams receive more penalties as they attack more. However, Sutter and Kocher (2004) report that home teams receive a penalty from 81 per cent of their penalty appeals, whereas away teams receive a penalty from 51 per cent of their appeals. Commonsense suggests what may be at play here. At a packed Old Trafford, 70,000 people will be calling for a home penalty, compared to around 5,000 calling for an away one. The research supports this view, but not as equivocally as may be expected. Using television replays of tackles from an English Premier League match, Nevill et al. (2002) asked qualified referees to decide whether they constituted a foul or not. Half the referees heard the accompanying crowd noise, half heard silence. This study found that crowd noise reduced the number of fouls given against the home team but did not significantly increase the number of fouls given against the away team. The authors take this as evidence that referees may avoid making decisions that may be unpopular. It is also suggested that this may relate to the star player effect, the finding that fewer fouls are given against star players (compared to non-star players) at home (Lehman and Reifman, 1987). Interestingly, Nevill et al. (2002) report that the effect of crowd noise appears to decrease as refereeing experience increases. It may be the case that increased experience provides referees with the confidence to make unpopular decisions.

Taking all of the research reported above, the finding that crowd noise influencing officials is a key part of home advantage is logical for a number of reasons. First, it explains the central role of crowd density (and the influence of a roof keeping sound in a stadium). Second, it may explain the varying degrees of influence of home advantage across sports. Examining Nevill and Holder's hwps, it could reasonably be argued that the sport with the greatest hwp (soccer) is the sport that includes the greatest number of subjective referring decisions. Additionally, it may explain why home advantage emerges in individual sports where subjective decisions determine the outcome (e.g. boxing), compared to sports where outcome is more objective (e.g. tennis). However, as suggested at the outset, the home advantage may not be so easily distilled. A particularly interesting finding is that home advantage appears to disappear for a team's first season in a new stadium (Wilkinson and Pollard, 2006). It may be the case that home advantage does entail something more than referees making mistakes and that numerous factors (familiarity, perceived advantage, territoriality, the crowd) are interacting in creating the home advantage. Given the mystery, and the difficulty of untangling home advantage, it perhaps isn't so surprising that sports fans treat home as reverentially as they do.

REFERENCES

Balmer, N.J., Nevill, A.M. and Lane, A. (2005) Do judges enhance home advantage in European championship boxing? *Journal of Sport Sciences*, 23, 409–416.

Bray, S.R. and Martin, K.A. (2003) The effect of competition location on individual athlete performance and psychological states. *Psychology of Sport and Exercise*, 4 (2), 117–123.

Carron, A.V., Loughhead, T.M. and Bray, S.R. (2005) The home advantage in sport competitions: Courneya and Carron's (1992) conceptual framework a decade later. *Journal of Sports Sciences*, 23, 395–407.

Courneya, K.S. and Carron, A.V. (1992a) Effects of travel and length of home stand/road trip on the home advantage. *Journal of Sport and Exercise Psychology*, 13, 42–49.

Courneya, K.S. and Carron, A.V. (1992b) The home advantage in sport competitions: A literature review. *Journal of Sport and Exercise Psychology*, 14, 13–27.

Dowie, J. (1982) Why Spain should win the world cup. *New Scientist*, 94, 693–695.

Gayton, W.F., Broida, J. and Elgee, L. (2001) An investigation of coaches' perceptions of the causes of home advantage. *Perceptual and Motor Skills*, 92 (3), 933–936.

Lehman, D.R. and Reifman, A. (1987) Spectator influence on basketball officiating. *Journal of Social Psychology*, 127, 673–675.

Madrigal, R. and James, J. (1999) Team quality and home advantage. *Journal of Sport Behavior*, 22 (3), 381–398.

Neave, N. and Wolfson, S. (2003) Testosterone, territoriality, and the 'home advantage'. *Physiology and Behavior*, 78, 269–275.

Nevill, A.M., Balmer, N.J. and Williams, A.M. (2002) The influence of crowd noise and experience upon refereeing decisions in football. *Psychology of Sport and Exercise*, 3, 261–272.

Nevill, A.M. and Holder, R. (1999) Home advantage in sport: An overview of studies on the advantage of playing at home. *Sports Medicine*, 28, 221–236.

Nevill, A.M., Newell, S.M. and Gale, S. (1996) Factors associated with home advantage in English and Scottish football. *Journal of Sports Sciences*, 14, 181–186.

Page, L. and Page, K. (2007) The second leg home advantage: Evidence from European football cup competitions. *Journal of Sports Sciences*, 25 (14), 1547–1556.

Pollard, R. (1986) Home advantage in football: A retrospective analysis. *Journal of Sports Sciences*, 4, 237–248.

Schwartz, B. and Barsky, S.F. (1977) The home advantage. *Social Forces*, 55, 641–661.

Sutter, M. and Kocher, M.G. (2004) Favoritism of agents – the case of referees' home bias. *Journal of Economic Psychology*, 25, 461–469.

Thomas, S., Reeves, C. and Bell, A. (2008) Home advantage in the Six Nations Rugby Union Tournament. *Perceptual and Motor Skills*, 106, 113–116.

Wilkinson, T. and Pollard, R. (2006) A temporary decline in home advantage when moving to a new stadium. *Journal of Sport Behavior*, 29 (2), 190–197.

5.28: Aggression

One of the most infamous descriptions of sport was provided by George Orwell (1945), who is quoted as saying, 'Serious sport has nothing to do with fair play. It is bound up with hatred, jealousy, boastfulness, disregard of all rules and sadistic pleasure in witnessing violence. In other words: it is war minus the shooting.' Orwell's statement is provocative as it cuts to a key paradox in sport. Fair play is something lauded in sport, yet when one reaches the highest level, ruthlessness and the will to win at all costs are often encouraged. This begs the question, where is the line between fair play and winning at all costs, and when is the line crossed? No aspect of sport illustrates this paradox more vividly than the role played by aggression. In many sports aggression, even to the point of physical violence, is encouraged (Russell, 1993). Indeed, an aggressive approach to sport may, in the eyes of some, be associated with passion, or a hunger for success. But what precisely is meant by aggression? Where does it come from? Should it be encouraged in sport? And finally, what can be done to appropriately manage aggression?

Aggression is an element of everyday life that is brought into sharp focus by the lens of sport but in its many guises has received attention throughout the history of psychological literature. In global terms, aggression has been defined as 'any form of behaviour directed toward the goal of harming or injuring another living being who is motivated to avoid such treatment' (Baron and Richardson, 1994, p. 7). This definition warrants closer examination for a number of reasons. First, it is not restricted to physical aggression as it may also be verbal. Second, aggression cannot be directed to an inanimate object. This precludes acts such as racket abuse in tennis or squash being defined as aggression; rather, they are indicators of frustration (Maxwell, 2004). Third, there is also the implication that aggressive behaviour carries with it a certain degree of intent. However, while this definition captures much of what is meant by aggression in sport, as with many concepts brought from outside the sport psychology literature, there are sport-specific considerations. For example, how does one characterise the behaviour in boxing (Maxwell, 2004)? Clearly, outside of a sporting context, boxing is aggressive. However, when entering a boxing ring, can it accurately be said that the other individual is 'motivated to avoid such treatment'? After all, they have purposefully put themselves in this situation. Having said this, there are clearly behaviours in boxing that must be described as aggressive. Take for example Mike Tyson deliberately spitting out his mouthguard before biting a piece out of Evander Holyfield's ear. This is aggressive behaviour as it goes beyond what Holyfield may have reasonably expected when he entered the ring. The question in this instance is one of acceptability. This leads us to a key distinction in the understanding of sport aggression. In the sport psychology literature, two types of aggression are normally described, reactive and instrumental (e.g. Bredemeir, 1985), often along with a distinction between sanctioned and unsanctioned aggression (Kerr, 2006).

Given the acceptance of aggression in some sports, the need to clarify the difference between *reactive* and *instrumental* aggression is vital. Reactive aggression is akin to many lay definitions of aggression. It occurs solely with the aim of harming the other and is typically associated with anger or retaliation (Wann, 2005). Instrumental aggression, on the other hand, is motivated by a higher strategic purpose rather than designed only to harm (Donahue et al., 2009). In practice, the archetypal example of instrumental aggressive behaviour is the professional foul. The act may hurt the opponent but its purpose is to prevent a goal-scoring opportunity. However, this distinction may not be as clear-cut as it first appears. A professional foul, by its definition, implies a certain degree of necessity, that it is part of the job and, ultimately, understandable. Yet other acts of instrumental aggression may not be seen in the same light. For example, a spear tackle in rugby may be an instrumental act to take out a threatening player, yet it is judged much more harshly than a professional foul. This leads on to a further important distinction, the difference between *sanctioned* and *unsanctioned* aggression. This distinction becomes particularly important when considering acts of violence, whether they be physical or verbal. So, for example, throwing punches in boxing is sanctioned physical violence, in much the same way that sledging in cricket is sanctioned verbal aggression. While much of what is meant by sanctioned aggression is incorporated into the understanding of what is legal, the term is broader than this, expanding to incorporate the unwritten conventions of each particular sport (Kerr, 2006). So while official abuse is aggressive, and considered illegal in most sports, each sport has its own conventions as to what is acceptable. While it may be argued that the focus for psychologists should be on controlling unsanctioned aggression, the difficulty lies in the fact that the line between sanctioned and unsanctioned aggression is often ill-defined. For example, in ice hockey, a sport where fist fighting has historically been sanctioned, these fights have been governed by unwritten conventions (Colburn, 1989). The danger is that, in an aggressive mindset, a player may violate these unwritten conventions, leading them to commit acts that are viewed as unsanctioned (see for example Kerr's [2006] analysis of the Bertuzzi-Moore incident). In view of this, the central consideration when dealing with aggression would appear to be the ability to control and direct aggression into instrumental, and sanctioned, behaviours. This leads on to the next issue to be considered: where does aggression come from and how can it be managed?

Historically, the major theories to have dominated the aggression literature have been the psychodynamic, or Freudian, Frustration Aggression (Revised) Theory (e.g. Berkowitz, 1989) and Social Learning Theory (e.g. Bandura, 1973). According to Freud, human aggression is linked to a basic instinct, *thanatos*, and is unavoidable; we are 'hard wired' to be aggressive. Sport provides a socially acceptable release valve for this basic instinct and, according to this perspective, those who take part in sport (both players and spectators) will be less aggressive having 'let off steam' (i.e. sport has a cathartic effect). Suffice it to say, there is little evidence to suggest that this is true (see **5.29**) and so the theory now enjoys little support.

As an alternative approach, Frustration Aggression Theory proposed that aggression was the inevitable behavioural outcome of frustration. However, this account has been criticised for its sense of inevitability. While on occasion frustration may lead to aggression, this account fails to explain why frustration does not always lead to aggression. For this reason the theory was later revised to take into account the influence of cognitive factors, situational cues and learned responses. Particularly in this final regard, there is an overlap between Frustration Aggression Theory and Social Learning Theory. While Bandura's theory does recognise the importance of physiological and motivational factors, it is best known for highlighting the importance of observation/experience of aggression and the perceived/actual approval of aggression. This was famously illustrated by the Bobo Doll study that reported that children will imitate the aggressive behaviour of adults. Sport-specific studies have reported evidence that watching aggressive role models may lead to a more aggressive approach to sport (Smith, 1988). While these theories each contribute valuable elements to understanding aggressive behaviour, recent models have sought to accommodate and explain the numerous interacting factors (cognitive, affective, behavioural and emotional) that may underlie aggression (Geen, 2001).

This brings us to the discussion of the specific antecedents of aggressive behaviour in sport. These may be divided into two main categories: situational factors and cognitive factors. Historically, research has tended to focus on situational factors. For example, it has been reported that increased temperatures are associated with more aggressive pitching in baseball (Reifman et al., 1991). Additionally, it has been reported that aggressive behaviour by opposing teams is associated with increased aggression in the team playing at home (Harrell, 1980). While such findings are undoubtedly interesting, there now appears to be a move towards examining cognitive antecedents of aggression. This makes practical sense. While an athlete may not be able to control situational variables, he or she should be able to control cognitive reactions to them. The idea of the importance of the cognitive interpretation of events is illustrated by the finding that anger rumination increases the likelihood of aggressive behaviour, a finding reported both in the general aggression literature and the sport psychology literature (Maxwell, 2004). So while an athlete may be angered by an event during competition (e.g. a bad tackle), it is the propensity to dwell on this anger that ultimately leads to an increased possibility of retaliation. It is possible to call to mind examples of professional soccer players who have dwelt on perceived injustices for months before responding with physical aggression at a later date. Another topic explored by recent research has been the role of passion in aggression. This is an interesting subject as media accounts of athlete aggression often cite aggression as an inevitable companion of passion. However, the research would only partially support this assertion. It is reported that a high level of passion need not necessarily lead to an increased incidence of aggression. However, when an athlete derives a high degree of social acceptance and self-esteem through their sport, passion may be associated with a higher incidence of aggressive behaviour (Donahue et al., 2009). In terms of a potential role for psychologists in managing aggression, the implication of cognitive factors such as rumination and the role of self-esteem appear important as they point to potential avenues of intervention, such as cognitive behavioural models (Maxwell, 2004).

However, any conception of aggression management intervention must be balanced against the possibility that aggression may bring with it benefits. Unfortunately the literature remains inconclusive on this vital issue (e.g. Gill, 1986; Wann, 1997). While it would appear that certain sports require some degree of instrumental, sanctioned aggression, what would appear crucial is the idea of *control*. Whether aggression is beneficial or not, any loss of control ultimately may lead to suspensions and other disciplinary proceedings. Where control is lost, the possibility is that aggression may be misdirected into reactive, unsanctioned violence. It may have been incidents of this nature that Orwell was referring to when he dwelt on the more nefarious aspects of sport.

REFERENCES

Bandura, A. (1973) *Aggression: A Social Learning Analysis*. Englewood Cliffs, NJ: Prentice-Hall.

Baron, R.A. and Richardson, D.R. (1994) *Human Aggression*. 2nd edn. New York: Plenum Press.

Berkowitz, L. (1989) Frustration–aggression hypothesis: Examination and reformulation. *Psychological Bulletin*, 106, 59–73.

Bredemeier, B.J. (1985) Moral reasoning and the perceived legitimacy of intentionally injurious sport acts. *Journal of Sport Psychology*, 7, 110–124.

Colburn, K. (1989) Deviance and legitimacy in ice hockey: A microstructural theory of violence. In Kelly, D.H. (ed.) *Deviant Behavior*. New York: St. Martins Press.

Donahue, E.G., Rip, B. and Vallerand, R.J. (2009) When winning is everything: On passion, identity, and aggression in sport. *Psychology of Sport and Exercise*, 10, 526–534.

Geen, R.G. (2001) *Human Aggression* 2nd edn. Milton Keynes: Open University Press.

Gill, D.L. (1986) *Psychological Dynamics of Sport*. Champaign, IL: Human Kinetics.

Harrell, W.A. (1980) Aggression by high school basketball players: An observational study of the effects of opponent aggression and frustration-inducing factors. *International Journal of Sport Psychology*, 11, 290–298.

Kerr, J.H. (2006) Examining the Bertuzzi–Moore NHL ice hockey incident: Crossing the line between sanctioned and unsanctioned violence in sport. *Aggression and Violent Behavior*, 11, 313–322.

Maxwell, J.P. (2004) Anger rumination: an antecedent of athlete aggression? *Psychology of Sport and Exercise*, 5, 279–289.

Orwell, G. (1945) The Sporting Spirit, *Tribune*, 14 December 1945.

Reifman, A.S., Larrick, R.P. and Fein, S. (1991) Temper and temperature on the diamond: The heat-aggression relationship in Major League Baseball. *Personality and Social Psychology Bulletin*, 17 (5), 580–585.

Russell, G.W. (1993) *The Social Psychology of Sport*. New York: Springer-Verlag.

Smith, M.D. (1988) Interpersonal sources of violence in hockey: The influence of parents, coaches and teammates. In Smoll, F.L., Magill, R.A. and Ash, M.J. (eds) *Children in Sport*. 3rd edn. Champaign, IL: Human Kinetics. pp. 301–313.

Wann, D. L. (1997) *Sport Psychology*. Upper Saddle River, NJ: Prentice Hall.

Wann, D.L. (2005) Aggression in sport. *The Lancet*, 366, S31–S32.

5.29: Fans and Spectators

Definitions: Spectators are those who watch sport, either directly (in person) or indirectly (via the media), while fans also watch but have an affiliation in which aspects of identity, emotional significance and value are derived from group membership.

While sport psychology continues to focus more attention on those who do rather than those who watch, there has also been longstanding interest in those on the other side of the fence, whether as direct (physically present) or indirect (via the media) sport consumers (McPherson, 1976). This literature has considered many issues, not least speculation as to the psychology that drives spectators to become so engrossed in their chosen sports.

In one of the earliest examples, Patrick (1903) reflected on the US public's obsession with American Football, declaring that little had changed from Neolithic times. In his own words: 'Evidently there is some great force, psychological or sociological, at work here which science has not yet investigated' (p.115). In keeping with the dominant psychoanalytic tradition of the times, to him sport stirred our base instincts: 'The game thus acts as a sort of Aristotelian catharsis, purging our pent up feelings and enabling us to return more placidly to the slow upwards toiling' (p. 116). In a similar vein, Howard (1912) described the 'mob-mind of the athletic spectator' (p. 43). His disapproving tone leaps from the page: 'Violent shouts and epithets give notice that the cave-man is up' (p. 45).

As Chapter 28 demonstrates (see **5.28**), psychoanalytic predictions based on catharsis have not stood the test of time well. Indeed, a recent study of drinking behaviour among rugby fans showed that it was the followers of the winners rather than the losers who were more aggressive, and more likely to drink to excess (Moore et al., 2007). Catharsis would predict the opposite effect.

Today, millions of people have an extremely intense and time-consuming engagement with sport and yet they may never have kicked a ball, run on an athletics track or seen the inside of a snooker hall. According to an unpublished British Market Research Bureau (BMRB) survey (carried out for the Newspaper Marketing Agency in 2004), 54 per cent of tabloid newspaper readers turn straightaway to the sports pages, rising to an impressive 69 per cent of all readers when those who merely scanned the first page are included.

Despite the significant role that sport plays in so many people's lives, the majority of sport psychologists have only turned their attention to spectators infrequently. The majority of sport psychology texts and journals rarely feature this work, and the contrast between how much effort has been devoted to understanding participation motivation and how little has been spent on spectator motivation could not be more stark. Where spectator research does appear it is often in the guise of a contextual variable that impacts on the sportsperson, for example in relation to home advantage (see **5.27**), social facilitation (see **5.25**), causal attribution (see **5.24**) or the role of significant others with regard to sport socialisation and participation motivation (see **3.10**, **3.11**, **3.13**, **3.14**, **3.15** and **3.16**).

There are notable exceptions to this rule. In their book *Sport Fans: The Psychology and Social Impact of Spectators*, Daniel Wann and colleagues reflect on the range of factors that can impact on the decision to become a 'fan' (as opposed to a spectator), and subsequent fan behaviour, including violence, along with the functions that fan behaviour serves for both individuals, clubs and society in general (Wann et al., 2001).

Their work draws on earlier formulations and including the work of McPherson (1976) on sport consumer socialisation. McPherson considered four agents that impact on the fledgling consumer – peers, family, school and community – with peers having the greatest impact on young men and the family on young women. Sport consumption was then considered in relation not only to behaviour (attendance and buying) but also affect (including mood state and loyalty or 'fandom') and cognition (knowledge). This research highlights the distinction between those who merely watch and those who become involved as sport fans, and it is the latter that have attracted greatest interest. In reviewing various definitions and distinctions between the two terms, Jacobson (2003) concludes that the most critical difference lies in perceived interest and personal importance, hence the degree of emotional investment in the team and its performance. In other words, spectators watch but fans care. She also reminds us that the word 'fan' itself is an abbreviation of 'fanatic', implying excessive, even obsessional, enthusiasm. With this in mind, Wann et al. (2001) also argue the need to distinguish between fans in terms of the extent of their identification with the team, ranging from high to low. Not surprisingly, it is the former that are often the focus of research.

According to Wann (1995), having been socialised into a sport or sports, fans are then galvanised by one or more of eight possible motives: group affiliation, family, escape, entertainment, eustress, aesthetics, self-esteem and economics (i.e. gambling). The strength of each is typically gauged by using the Sport Fan Motivation Scale (SFMS), a 23-item self-report Likert-scale that contains eight sub-scales reflecting the eight motives. Typically, entertainment and eustress score highest, with the economic motive being the least important (Wann, 1995).

Of these motives, the one which has attracted greatest attention is group affiliation, or more correctly, team identification. Drawing on theories of social identity from within social psychology, and including social identity theory and identity theory (Stets and Burke, 2000), research has considered the degree to which fans come to adopt the team's identity as part of their self-concept, the factors that impact on the extent of identification, and how identification can manifest itself in behaviour towards both ingroup and outgroup members.

This research suggests that individual differences (e.g. gender, Dietz-Uhler et al., 2000) and events both on and off the field can influence loyalty (Wann et al., 2001) but the most important factor is team success. According to Mahony et al. (2000), our inclination to either 'bask in reflected glory' (BIRG) or 'cut off reflective failures' (CORF) will go a long way towards helping explain variations in fan support over time. Those with a high level of identification are likely to be those whose loyalty will carry them through the bad times as well as the good (Madrigal, 1995).

The dark side of fan loyalty can be revealed in crowd violence or hooliganism, a social phenomenon that, contrary to popular opinion, is far from new (Pearson, 1983). The topic has attracted considerable attention from a wide range of disciplines including sport sociology and sport psychology. While longstanding concerns with hooliganism are never far from the headlines, sometimes particular events or tragedies have acted as a catalyst for research. One prime example was the research that fed into the 1986 *Popplewell Inquiry into Crowd Safety and Control at Sports Grounds*. The inquiry was set up following the tragic events in early 1985, including the West Stand fire at Bradford City Football Club and the Heysel stadium disaster in Brussels. In their subsequent book *Football in its Place*, Canter et al. (1989) used their background in environmental psychology to offer practical insight and advice on the interaction between structural and psychological issues, including stadia design, spectator's attitudes and experiences, soccer club cultures, crowd and emergency behaviour and violence in sport. These ideas were acted on by the Popplewell Inquiry and were also taken into account during the subsequent Taylor Report (1989) into the Hillsborough Stadium disaster when 95 Liverpool supporters tragically died.

In contrast with sport psychology, sport sociology does have a long history of spectator research, with a particular emphasis on fan violence (e.g. Murphy et al., 2003). Using a combination of historical, observational, quantitative and qualitative techniques, various authors have tried to help understand why hooliganism and fan violence should have such a long and ignoble history in Europe, and in particular Britain (hence commonly known as the 'English Disease'). It is suggested that the interplay between personal, interpersonal, intergroup, cultural, socio-economic and political forces may help determine why particular anti-social behaviours manifest themselves only at certain times and only in certain sports. For example, neither rugby league nor rugby union have ever been associated with fan violence, yet soccer has. At the same time, it is argued that the media may distort perceptions of what may or may not have taken place, a classic example being the presentation of England soccer fans' behaviour during Euro 2000 (Weed, 2001).

While soccer violence may be hyped up, there is evidence that crowd disorder at other sports, including American football, may have been hidden from view for both political and economic reasons, along with other unsavoury associations (Young, 1991). One related example is a study by White (1989), which considered the incidence of murders in US cities that had American football teams through to the National Football League playoff games. In those cities where the team lost a playoff there was a subsequent increase in reported homicides in the subsequent six days, but the crime rate remained unchanged if the team was successful.

Over the years various approaches have been proposed to explain fan violence (Weed, 2001). In their figurational approach, Eric Dunning and colleagues see Murphy et al., 2003 place emphasis on the culture of violence still prevalent among young, working class men in Britain, while Kerr (2005) has adapted Reversal Theory to try to understand hooliganism, arguing that it is the switch between motivational states (telic – goal oriented; paratelic – playful) that best explains why trouble 'kicks off' at particular games. According to Simons and Taylor (1992) there is a need to accommodate a wide range of variables, and any approach that fails to account for all these variables is likely to be partial. Variables include:

- potentiating or general predisposing factors (socio-economic conditions, politics and geography, media influences and community norms);
- critical factors (social and personal identification, group solidarity, de-individuation, dehumanisation of the opposition, leadership);
- on-field contributing factors (type of sport, modeling, score configuration and competitive events);
- off-field contributing factors (alcohol, crowd density, frustration and role modelling).

This model offers a useful framework for understanding fan violence at a great many levels of analysis, and sits easily with developments across social psychology as a whole.

REFERENCES

Canter, D., Comber, M. and Uzzell, D.L. (1989) *Football in its Place: An Environmental Psychology of Football Grounds.* London: Routledge.

Dietz-Uhler, B., Harrick, E., End, C. and Jacquemotte, L. (2000) Sex differences in sport fan behavior and reasons for being a sports fan. *Journal of Sport Behavior,* 23, 219–231.

Howard, G. (1912) Social psychology of the spectator. *American Journal of Sociology,* 18, 33–50.

Jacobson, B. (2003) The social psychology of the creation of a sports fan identity: A theoretical review of the literature. *Athletic Insight,* 5 (2), 1–14.

Kerr, J.H. (2005) *Rethinking Aggression and Violence in Sport.* London: Routledge.

Madrigal, R. (1995) Cognitive and affective determinants of fan satisfaction with sporting event attendance. *Journal of Leisure Research*, 27, 205–227.

Mahony, D., Howard, D. and Madrigal, R. (2000) BIRGing and CORFing behaviors by sport spectators: High self-monitors versus low self-monitors. *International Sports Journal*, 4, 87–106.

McPherson, B.D. (1976) Socialization into the role of sport consumer: A theory and causal model. *Canadian Review of Sociology and Anthropology*, 13 (2), 165–177.

Moore, S.C., Shepherd, J.P., Eden, S. and Sivarajasingam, V. (2007) The effect of rugby match outcome on spectator aggression and intention to drink alcohol. *Criminal Behaviour and Mental Health*, 17, 118–127.

Murphy, P., Williams, J. and Dunning, E. (2003) *Football on Trial: Spectator Violence and Developments in the Football World*. London: Taylor and Francis.

Patrick, G.T.W. (1903) The psychology of football. *American Journal of Psychology*, 14, 104–117.

Pearson, G. (1983) *Hooligan: A History of Respectable Fears*. Basingstoke: MacMillan.

Popplewell, Mr Justice (1986) *Popplewell Inquiry into Crowd Safety and Control at Sports Grounds*. London: HMSO.

Simons, Y. and Taylor, J. (1992) A psychosocial model of fan violence in sports. *International Journal of Sport Psychology*, 23, 207–226.

Stets, J.E. and Burke, P.J. (2000) Identity theory and social identity theory. *Social Psychology Quarterly*, 63 (3), 224–237.

Taylor, Lord Justice (1989) *Interim Report into the Hillsborough Stadium Disaster*. London: HMSO.

Wann, D. (1995) Preliminary validation of the sport fan motivation scale. *Journal of Sports and Social Issues*, 19, 377–396.

Wann, D.L., Melnick, M.J., Russell, G.W. and Pease, D.G. (2001) *Sport Fans: The Psychology and Social Impact of Spectators*. London: Routledge.

Weed, M. (2001) Ing-ger-land at Euro 2000: How handbags at 20 paces was portrayed as a full scale riot. *International Review for the Sociology of Sport*, 36 (4), 407–424.

White, G.F. (1989) Media and violence: The case of professional football championship games. *Aggressive Behavior*, 15, 423–433.

Young, K. (1991) Sport and collective violence. *Exercise and Sport Sciences Review*, 19, 539–586.

social psychology of sport

6

Motor Skills

6.30: Motor Development

> **Definition:** Motor development is the sequential, continuous, age-related process whereby movement behaviour changes over time.

When we observe sports skills such as a golf swing, a tennis serve, a high jump or a cricket shot, we are observing highly complex motor skills. We are not born with the innate ability to swing a golf club, neither are we born with the most 'basic' of motor skills, such as locomotion (walking, running), that we often take for granted as our skill repertoire increases. Such motor skills are necessary not only in sport but for survival in everyday life. Locomotive, ballistic and manipulative motor skills are learned and continue to develop across the lifespan. This development begins in infancy and continues into older adulthood. Take for example a new born baby sucking. This is not a reflex but a co-ordinated, goal-directed and skilled action which is practiced *in utero* (i.e. thumb-sucking). Our capability to carry out skilled movements also changes across our lifetime, and this is often well reflected in the modern structure of sports competitions. Take Wimbledon for example. There is a junior tennis tournament, an adult tournament and a senior's tournament, separated according to age ranges. But does motor skill develop in parallel with age? What are the processes underlying motor development? What theoretical approaches are taken when studying motor development? This chapter will attempt to address these various questions.

Before continuing, it is necessary to define several of the terms that will appear in this and the following chapters, namely motor learning, motor development, motor behaviour and motor control. *Motor learning* is defined by Schmidt and Lee (1999) as 'the relatively permanent gains in motor skill capability associated with practice or experience'. Note that this definition refers to experience rather than age. *Motor development*, on the other hand, is defined as the sequential, continuous, age-related process whereby movement behaviour changes (Haywood and Getchell, 2005). A defining characteristic of development is that it is related to (but not dependent on) age, and this is the main difference between development and learning. The study of motor development is concerned with the developmental change in movement behaviour – both the processes that underlie the change and the resultant movement outcome. To use an example to illustrate the difference between learning and development, if a seasoned golfer tweaks his swing by altering his grip, we do not refer to this change as motor development but instead it is motor learning. *Motor behaviour* is a term that we use to include both motor learning and motor development, and, *motor control* refers to the neural, physical and behavioural aspects of movement. The remainder of this chapter will focus on theoretical perspectives which are currently used to study and account for motor development.

In terms of motor development, many skills such as locomotive (moving), ballistic (exerting force on an object in order to project it) and manipulative (catching) skills are fundamental to any sport performance. How do these skills change from childhood to adulthood? Take throwing as an example. Optimum performance in this motor skill exhibits movements that obey mechanical principles that will yield maximum force and speed. As children develop into adults and performance in throwing improves, changes in their movements are consistent with such mechanical principles. For example, a forward step transfers momentum into the direction of the throw and sequential movements of the projecting limb transfers momentum and increases speed. In catching, development from childhood to adulthood will gradually see different movements employed in order to become more proficient in catching. For example, we learn to catch with the hands and absorb the ball's force by 'giving', we are able to move to intercept the ball, and we can manipulate the fingers to aid catching (e.g. pointing up for a high ball).

Current theories that attempt to explain motor development fall under three overarching perspectives: the maturational perspective, the information processing perspective and the ecological perspective. We will first describe the fundamental differences between the perspectives and then present specific theories in more detail. The maturational perspective emphasises the importance of genetics and inheritance as the primary driving forces behind motor development, which is seen primarily as a series of maturational processes. It assumes motor development to be 'an internal or innate process driven by a biological or genetic time clock' (Haywood and Getchell, 2005). There is therefore little emphasis placed on the role of the environment as it is thought to have little effect on the biologically determined course.

The popular Information-Processing Model (often referred to as 'the cognitive approach') sees the brain akin to a computer where symbolic knowledge structures mediate the translation of sensory input to motor output. The ecological approach, on the other hand, places emphasis on the interrelationships between the individual, the environment and the task. According to this approach, all three of these systems interact, resulting in the emergence of a motor skill. The fundamental difference between these perspectives therefore relates to the role of internal processes. The information-processing approach sees perception of the world and movement production as separate processes whereby the brain receives perceptual information, performs calculations on it and then translates the information into movement of the muscles. The ecological approach, however, emphasises the role of the environment in shaping actions directly, rather than focusing on internalised knowledge structures (Handford et al., 1997). The distinction between these two perspectives and how they account for various aspects of motor behaviour will be a recurrent theme throughout chapters that follow.

The maturational approach was spearheaded by Arnold Gesell in the 1930s, who conducted co-twin control research in order to test the different effects of environment and inheritance on development. This paradigm saw one twin given special training while the other was allowed to develop naturally. This line of research allowed maturationists to begin to identify the sequence of skill development. Following this, Myrtle McGraw in 1943 began to look at changes in the nervous system that accounted for the emergence of new skills. In the 1950s, Anna Espenschade, Ruth Glasgow and Lawrence Rarick led a period of research that was focused on describing normative movement and biomechanics in school-aged children. Standardised tests were used to record scores in activities such as running, throwing and jumping. Although this approach was significant in describing naturally occurring sequences of change, the underlying mechanisms behind such changes were not addressed.

The most prominent theory that attempts to address *how* motor development comes about from an information processing perspective is that of Schema Theory (Schmidt, 1975). According to this theory, through practice, a learner develops expansive and flexible 'generalised motor programmes' that are called upon for a variety of similar activities. Each class of skills (e.g. throwing a ball) has its own general motor programme which has both invariant (e.g. relative timing) and changeable (e.g. overall force) parameters. For example, aspects of a throwing movement, such as the relative timing of joint flexion and extension, will remain the same for any throwing task; however, overall force applied would vary according to the particular throw in question. This theory could account for cases of athletes excelling in more than one sport. For example, Karmichael Hunt is an Australian multi-code footballer who has played at the top level in Rugby Union, Rugby League and Australian Rules Football. This suggests that he has a repertoire of flexible and adaptable schemata to allow him to perform effectively similar skilled movements in all three of these sports. Motor development according to this approach is as a result of practice and the formation of more flexible, adaptable schemata.

The most prominent model for studying motor development from an ecological perspective is Newell's model (1986). This model suggests that movements emerge through the dynamic, constantly changing interactions of the individual, the environment and the task. Newell refers to individual, environmental and task 'constraints' – characteristics that either facilitate or restrict movement. Individual constraints are related to the individual's physical and mental characteristics and can be structural (related to body's structure) or functional (related to behavioural function). For example, disabled limbs would be an individual constraint as this will affect the way that individuals will move. Environmental constraints are related to the world around us. They may be physical (e.g. surfaces) or sociocultural (e.g. societal constraints such as sexism, discouraging female participation in sports) and are not task specific. Task constraints are also external and refer to goals and rules we use. For example, the cricket bowling action is constrained by the fact that the arm must be straight during delivery of the ball. Motor development from this perspective is therefore a result of changing constraints across the lifespan. Throughout development, individuals become more refined at mapping perceptual information onto the dynamics of the system in a way that is consistent with constraints. Another constraint-led approach – the dynamic systems approach – introduced in the 1980s by Peter Kugler, Scott Kelso and Michael Turvey, also suggests that motor behaviour 'self-organises' according to constraints (Clark, 1995). This approach highlights the role of 'rate limiters' – systems within an individual that hold back or slows the emergence of a motor skill, for example muscular strength is a rate limiter for walking as a certain level of muscular strength must be gained in order to support the body weight.

Finally, another theory from within the ecological perspective is that of James Gibson's perception-action approach (1979). Gibson famously wrote 'we move to perceive and perceive to move', highlighting the strong link between perception and action and strongly suggesting the need to study together two systems that have evolved together. Central to this theory is the concept of affordances, which we directly perceive through our interactions with the environment. An 'affordance' is often described as an opportunity for action that a particular object affords, with the same object affording different actions (e.g. a ball may afford kicking, throwing or catching). Most importantly, what an environmental property offers in terms of action is specific to that individual. For example, a standard rugby ball might afford catching for an adult but not a 4-year-old child who has smaller hands. Gibson therefore proposed that we perceive the world relative to our own body scale (body-scaled affordances) and action capabilities (action-scaled affordances). As we develop, our bodies grow (e.g. longer legs) and our action capabilities change (e.g. can run faster), which means our opportunities for action (affordances) will also change. This is illustrated nicely in a study by Warren (1984), who demonstrated that the ratio between the height of the stair and the hip height was the body-scaled affordance that was used to determine whether or not a stair is climbable. As development continues into late adulthood, affordances continue to change. While maturationists tend to focus on infants and children, a constraint-led or affordance-based ecological approach accounts for motor development across the entire lifespan.

To summarise, this chapter has made the distinction between terminologies often used in motor skill research, defined motor development as an age-related process and gone on to discuss theoretical perspectives which offer descriptions and explanations as to what accounts for motor development.

REFERENCES

Clark, J.E. (1995) On becoming skilful: Patterns and constraints. *Research Quarterly*, 66, 173–183.

Gibson, J.J. (1979) *An Ecological Approach to Visual Perception*. Boston, MA: Houghton-Mifflin.

Handford, C., Davids, K., Bennett, S. and Button, C. (1997) Skill acquisition in sport: Some applications of an evolving practice ecology. *Journal of Sports Sciences*, 15, 621–640.

Haywood, K.M. and Getchell, N. (2005) *Life Span Motor Development*. 4th edn. Champaign, IL: Human Kinetics.

Newell, K.M. (1986) Constraints on the development of coordination. In Wade, M.G. and Whiting, H.T.A. (eds) *Motor Development in Children: Aspects of Coordination and Control*. Amsterdam: Nijhoff. pp. 341–361.

Schmidt, R.A. (1975) A schema theory of discrete motor skill learning. *Psychological Review*, 82, 225–260.

Schmidt, R. and Lee, T. (1999) *Motor Control and Learning: A Behavioural Emphasis*. 3rd edn. Champaign, IL: Human Kinetics.

Warren, W.H. (1984) Perceiving affordances: Visual guidance of stair climbing. *Journal of Experimental Psychology: Human Perception and Performance*, 10 (5), 683–703.

6.31: Expertise

Definition: Expertise is consistent and superior athletic performance displayed over an extended period of time that is based on practice and encompasses the physiological, technical, cognitive and emotional domains.

Several times a year millions of sports enthusiasts watch in awe as elite athletes compete in world class competition. Be it the Superbowl, a golf or tennis major, or the Champions League final in soccer, these events are an opportunity to watch sports men and women perform at the top of their game. But what separates Rodger Federer and Tiger Woods from the rest of us who try so hard to emulate their performances? The answer is: they are experts, we are not! Despite the millions of people around the globe playing soccer, a relatively tiny number will ever make it to the World Cup, just like a tiny number of the world's golfers will ever win a Major. Those who do make it seem to possess superior abilities than those who don't. Researchers in sport expertise have attempted to answer fundamental questions regarding these superior abilities for decades. What makes an expert an expert? How and why do we study expertise? Can anyone become an expert through training and practice?

The first question to consider is what exactly is expertise and what are its determinants? Frank Lloyd Wright, the famous American architect, once said 'An expert is a man who has stopped thinking – he knows.' This could be said of an expert in any domain, referring to what seems to onlookers like second nature performance in whatever the task. A more scientific definition, specific to expert performance in sport, was proposed by Starkes (1993) as being the consistent superior athletic performance over an extended period. Janelle and Hillman (2003) state that 'to obtain expert status, athletes must excel in no less than four domains: physiological, technical, cognitive (tactical/strategic; perceptual/decision-making), and emotional (regulation/coping; psychological)' (p. 21). In terms of physiological components of expertise, factors such as muscle fibre type and aerobic capacity, although malleable to an extent through training, are largely genetically determined (Swallow et al., 1998). Experts are often said to be 'built for' a certain sport, for example rowers with long levers and a natural high level of aerobic fitness. Emotional and psychological expertise refers to social-cognitive determinants such as the ability of experts to regulate and exert control over their emotions in competition and to maintain motivation and a positive mental attitude. Since the focus of this section is on motor skills and considering previous sections have dealt with many social-cognitive factors (e.g. anxiety and stress, cognitive processes), we will not expand further on these domains, but instead we will focus on the two that have most relevance to motor skill: the expert's superior ability to know *how* (technical) and *when* (cognitive/perceptual) to perform *what* actions. 'Technical expertise' refers to the movement patterns involved when carrying out co-ordinated actions in sport, such as pitching in baseball, the golf swing or the tennis backhand (i.e. knowing *how*). The expert performer will perform such techniques in a more refined, efficient and effective way than the non-expert performer. For example, Tiger Woods is said to have the 'perfect swing'. 'Cognitive and perceptual expertise' refers to the superior ability of expert performers to know *what* and *when* to carry out a certain action. Williams et al. (1999) note the increasing recognition of the relationship between skilful perception and skilful action in successful sport performance. Experts are able to attend to relevant information within their environment, ignore irrelevant information and use anticipatory cues, meaning they consistently seem to be doing 'the right thing at the right time'. For example, Wayne Gretzky once said, 'A good hockey player plays where the puck is. A great hockey player plays where the puck is going to be' (Gretzky, W. – http://www.brainyquote.com/quotes/authors/w/wayne_gretzky.html). This highlights the importance of perceptual and cognitive expertise in sport, an area that has received most attention in sport expertise research. In sum, there is not a single determinant of expertise but rather an interaction of several components which contribute to expert performance. The challenge for researchers is to describe and account for expertise phenomena through scientific study. Having addressed definitions and determinants of expertise, we will now consider why researchers study expertise, what theories exist that account for expert performance, and the methods used to study expertise.

Why study expert performance in sport? On top of providing a window through which to enhance the understanding of skill acquisition in sport, it allows for the identification of factors distinguishing experts from non-experts. This in turn highlights limiting factors to high-level performance and has implications for developing beneficial training programmes, practice regimes and the identification and selection of talent.

In terms of theoretical frameworks surrounding expertise research, the dominant approach in the past few decades has been the cognitive approach, underpinned by the information processing metaphor which sees the mind as being akin to a computer. According to this approach, expert performers are thought to differ from novices in the amount and type of information pertaining to specific sport situations. Paradigms used to explore these differences were imported directly from cognitive expertise research following famous work with chess players where both recall (de Groot, 1965; Chase and Simon, 1973) and recognition (Charness, 1976) tasks were used. Typically, these studies involved presenting chess players with game configurations via slides for a given time and asking them to recall the piece positions afterwards. So as not to attribute results to differences in 'hardware' of visual short-term memory, control trials were introduced where the pieces were laid out randomly and not structured. Results from these studies suggested that experts had an advanced task-specific knowledge base and were able to retrieve this information more efficiently. Using a similar paradigm to this, expertise effects have been demonstrated in various sports (e.g. soccer; Williams and Davids, 1995), although efforts have been made to present more realistic game configurations that involve dynamic film sequences presented on large screens. The notion that experts possess more sport-specific knowledge from which to draw upon was incorporated into a theory by Anderson (1982, 1990) through his Active Control of Thought model. This proposed that expert performers possess a larger reservoir of 'IF ... THEN ... DO' statements stored in their declarative memory, allowing them to initiate appropriate responses under certain conditions, for example, in rugby if a line of defenders approaches leaving space behind, then kick the ball into that space.

A related line of research into the recognition and recall paradigm is that of advanced cue utilisation. This paradigm has demonstrated the ability of an expert performer to pick up information more quickly from a dynamic sport-specific action sequence through the recognition and utilisation of advanced cues. Bruce Abernethy has carried out extensive work incorporating the popular temporal occlusion paradigm where stimuli (e.g. a film of an action sequence) are segmented and occluded according to the duration of presentation (temporal occlusion; e.g. a tennis serve is occluded before contact with the ball and the participant must guess the direction of the serve). This technique has highlighted an expertise effect in various sports where an elite athlete can successfully anticipate subsequent actions with less information than a non-expert (e.g. rugby union; Jackson et al., 2006).

More recently, based on ecological psychology, an alternative framework to the information-processing one has been proposed to account for expertise. This approach is reluctant to resort to cognitive constructs such as memory structures and internal representations to explain behaviour. James Gibson's (1979) *An Ecological Approach to Visual Perception* proposed the notion that humans and animals perceive and interact with surfaces (e.g. grass), places (e.g. pitch), objects (e.g. ball) and events (e.g. set-play). These so-called properties of the surrounding environment provide opportunities for action. This relationship between the environment and athlete and the ensuing action possibilities are known as 'affordances' (see **6.30**). Affordances are invitations to act and are defined by information that is constantly available to us via the visual system. For example, David Beckham knows exactly when the environment *affords* crossing the ball and has the action capability to execute the cross at this time. Using this conceptualisation, differences in novice and expert performance are thought to 'reflect, in part, differences in the informational variables upon which they rely' (Fajen et al., 2008, p. 85), rather than differences in task-specific knowledge structures that the cognitive approach would suggest. That is to say, novice and expert attunement to informational variables within the environment may differ. This approach to expertise has been likened to that of tuning a radio: the expert can tune in straight away to the correct frequency while the non-expert will experience noise while passing through other frequencies. Although quite different in their accounts for expertise, both the information-processing and the ecological approach recognise and demonstrate differences in expert and non-expert performance. Considering this as well as the determinants of expertise discussed, the final question to address concerns the development of expertise. Can the acquisition of sport expertise be facilitated?

It is most likely the case that expert performance is a result of some combination of genetic and environmental interactions. Is it the case that Tiger Woods was born with an innate golfing ability or is his success the result of the military-like practice regime that he underwent growing up? While a hard-lined naturist perspective would suggest that you have to be born with innate talent, this has been all but abandoned in recent times. The more popular approaches include the strict 'nurturist' perspective, which suggests that through practice anyone can achieve expertise, or the 'interactionist' approach, which suggests that the level of expertise achievable through practice is limited by innate hereditary factors. Ericsson et al. (1993) introduced the theory of deliberate practice, proposing that expertise will emerge through an extended period of deliberate practice which is structured, systematic, effortful and done often; typically ten years or 10,000 hours. The theory of deliberate practice is described in more detail in the 'Practicing motor skills' chapter (**6.33**), but here it is suffice to say that this theory recognises a relationship between practice and level of attainment. This has been demonstrated in both individual and team sports. Although criticised, the theory of deliberate practice has guided sport psychologists toward determining what type of practice will be effective for skill acquisition.

Some research exists where techniques have been employed in order to examine whether perceptual skills can be trained. This work is approached from the dominant cognitive perspective, and much of it has used video simulation methods in an attempt to train decision-making or anticipation skills (i.e. to pick up relevant cues further in advance). Although some studies provide examples of improved performance using pre- and post-tests following video simulation (e.g. for novice tennis players; Williams et al., 2002), a meaningful treatment effect is difficult to isolate as results could be attributed to greater familiarity with the test environment. Another difficulty is the lack of suitable transfer tests to determine whether improvements in lab settings transfer to the real world. While video simulation is by far the most popular tool used in this research, it lacks many of the features necessary to recreate a realistic sporting environment (e.g. a player perspective viewpoint and depth of information). The recent emergence of interactive, immersive Virtual Reality systems as a methodological tool in sport science provides exciting advantages over video presentation for this type of work, and with it there is the potential to develop such skill training environments (for a review, see Bideau et al., 2010).

REFERENCES

Anderson, J.R. (1982) Acquisition of cognitive skill. *Psychological Review*, 89 (4), 369–406.

Anderson, J.R. (1990) *Cognitive Psychology and Its Implications*. 3rd edn. New York: W.H. Freeman.

Bideau, B., Kulpa, R., Vignais, N., Brault, S., Multon, F. and Craig, C. (2010) Using virtual reality to analyze sports performance. *IEEE Computer Graphics and Applications*, 30 (2), 14–21.

Charness, N. (1976) Memory for chess positions: Resistance to interference'. *Journal of Experimental Psychology: Human Learning and Memory*, 2, 641–653.

Chase, W.G. and Simon, H.A. (1973) 'The mind's eye in chess' in W.G. Chase (ed.) *Visual Information Processing*, New York: Academic Press.

de Groot, A.D. (1965) *Thought and Choice in Chess*. The Hague, Netherlands: Mouton.

Ericsson, K.A., Krampe, R.Th. and Tesch-Römer, C. (1993) The role of deliberate practice in the acquisition of expert performance. *Psychological Review*, 100 (3), 363–406.

Fajen, B.R., Riley, M.A. and Turvey, M.T. (2008) Information, affordances and the control of action in sport. *International Journal of Sport Psychology*, 40 (1), 79–107.

Gibson, J.J. (1979) *An Ecological Approach to Visual Perception*. Boston, MA: Houghton-Mifflin.

Jackson, R.C., Warren, S. and Abernethy, B. (2006) Anticipation skill and susceptibility to deceptive movement. *Acta Psychologica*, 123, 355–371.

Janelle, C.M. and Hillman, C.H. (2003) Expert performance in sport: Current perspectives and critical issues. In Starkes, J.L. and Ericsson, K.A. (eds) *Expert Performance in Sports: Advances in Research on Sport Expertise*. Champaign, IL: Human Kinetics. 49–83.

Starkes, J.L. (1993) Motor experts: Opening thoughts. In Starkes, J.L. and Allard, F. (eds) *Cognitive Issues in Motor Expertise*. Amsterdam: Elsevier. pp. 3–16.

Swallow, J.G., Garland, T., Carter, P.A., Zhan, W.Z. and Sieck, G.C. (1998) Effects of voluntary activity and genetic selection on aerobic capacity in house mice (Mus domesticus). *Journal of Applied Physiology*, 84, 69–76.

Williams, A.M. and Davids, K. (1995) Declarative knowledge in sport: A by-product of experience or a characteristic of expertise? *Journal of Sport and Exercise Psychology*, 17 (3), 259–275.

Williams, A.M., Davids, K. and Williams, J.G. (1999) *Visual Perception and Action in Sport*. London: Spon.

Williams, A.M., Ward, P., Knowles, J.M. and Smeeton, N.J. (2002) Perceptual skill in a real-world task: Training, instruction and transfer in tennis. *Journal of Experimental Psychology: Applied*, 8, 259–270.

6.32: Decision-Making

> **Definition:** Decision-making is a dynamic process, based on previous experience, that combines visual search, recognition, recall and anticipation in choosing the most appropriate option in a given situation and including available time constraints.

'Decision-making' in sport is a term that encompasses many different scenarios. It could refer to the strategic decision-making of the golfer Lee Westwood when selecting an approach shot, or to Richie McCaw (the All Blacks rugby captain) making a decision to kick for goal when his team is awarded a penalty. It could also refer to more temporally constrained 'in-game' decisions such as Michael Jordan making the correct decision to pass, shoot or dribble the basketball, or Iker Casillas deciding to dive right when faced with a penalty kick in soccer. This chapter will focus most especially on occasions linked to the two latter examples as they both relate to the execution of motor skills under tight temporal constraints. Decision-making is as equally important an aspect of sport as physical prowess, yet is somewhat less obvious. This is probably due to the apparent ease with which great decision-makers perform under time pressure. Indeed, great decision-makers often seem to 'have all the time in the world' when executing a manoeuvre. What theories exist to account for decision-making? What methods are used to study and analyse decision-making? Can research inform practice in terms of improving decision-making through training?

To begin with, defining or classifying decisions is a challenge in itself. A 'right' decision is one that results in a favourable outcome for the performer or the performer's team. For example, in attack, a rugby player may decide to be tackled in order to take the ball to ground and set up another phase of play. Equally, he or she may decide to kick the ball and gain territory. Research has therefore concentrated on trying to identify the processes and mechanisms that underlie decisions and judgements. The dominating approach for understanding how these decisions come about is embedded within the information-processing perspective. Decision-making from this perspective is seen as a process, underpinned by the same concepts as outlined earlier (see **6.31**) (i.e. visual search, recognition, recall and anticipation). According to Tenenbaum (2003), skilled performers first search the environmental display when planning a motor response, and then eliminate irrelevant information and utilise advanced cues, thus enabling anticipation. This consists of an ongoing elaboration between the environmental information and the knowledge base which resides in memory. Finally, a course of action is taken. Wickens (1992) proposes that expert decision-makers possess three advantages that distinguish them from non-experts regarding these processes; they can:

- use perceptual chunking to select relevant information/cues from a displayed action sequence;
- calibrate their decisions to situational probabilities due to a more extensive knowledge base;
- couple cue recognition, hypothesis formation and decision outcomes more effectively (improved stimulus-response compatibility based on recognition and matching processes).

These advantages allow for faster and more accurate expert decision-making under tight time constraints. To account for the inefficient and costly nature of serial processing under extreme temporal conditions, this conceptualisation argues that under these conditions, the cognitive and motor systems operate faster and depend on motor schema and knowledge structures which are accessed automatically, that is, without relying on conscious awareness (Tenenbaum and Bar-Eli, 1993).

In terms of methodology for studying decision-making from this approach, similar techniques that were used in recognition and anticipatory judgement paradigms (see **6.31**) are often adopted. For example, static or dynamic sequences of play would be displayed and occluded or cut off before the decision would be behaviourally expressed. Participants would be asked to choose one of several decision options delivering a response verbally or by pressing a button. Response accuracy and response time would typically be recorded. Using these methods, several studies have shown that skill level affects decision-making (e.g. soccer; Helsen and Pauwels, 1988). However, this paradigm has been criticised because of the often unrealistic nature of the task constraints and stimulus presentation. Static presentations of game situations do not capture the dynamic, unfolding nature of real game patterns. Presenting dynamic video sequences also has limitations that prevent it from truly capturing an in-game situation. The video is usually captured from a fixed point (allocentric viewpoint) and not from the would-be decision-maker's viewpoint (egocentric viewpoint). This means that the visual information that the participant is using to make a decision in these cases is not the same visual information that they would have access to and use in a game scenario. Also, when displayed on small screens there is a loss of dimensionality with no depth information being present.

An alternative framework for considering decision-making and judgement is offered from within the Ecological Approach to Visual Perception (Gibson, 1979). One of the key concepts within this approach (see **6.31**) is the idea that people directly perceive meaningful information in the form of affordances within the environment (opportunities for action, e.g. a ball affords kicking), which does not require mediating cognitive processes. Perceiving affordances allows us to determine which actions are possible and which are not (Turvey, 1992) and therefore provides an appropriate framework under which to study sporting behaviour, where so many actions are possible within constantly changing environments. As Fajen et al. (2008) point out, 'to perceive an affordance, in Gibson's view, is to perceive how one can act when confronted with a particular set of environmental conditions' (p. 87). Decisions from this perspective are therefore not seen as a series of cognitive processes but rather a result of what behaviour an environment affords at a given moment combined with the action capabilities of the performer. Affordances are therefore said to be body-scaled (i.e. constrained by body dimensions) and/or action scaled (constrained by an actor's action capabilities). Another important feature of affordances, especially considered in sport, is that they allow for prospective control. That is to say, actions are adapted in advance to what the environment affords, based on information relating to a future course of events, that is, if current conditions persist. The successful attunement to the relevant information that specifies the future state is therefore one role of perception, but it also plays a role in online control of action as it unfolds. A series of recent studies carried out from this perspective have been able to identify the information that influences decisions and judgements in soccer free kicks (Craig et al., 2009) and rugby (Watson et al., 2010; Brault et al., 2010; Correia et al., 2011). This approach is popular as it can account for performance under high temporal constraints and variability in sporting situations.

Having discussed the main theoretical perspectives on decision-making in sport and the methodology used to research decision-making, we now raise the question 'Can research findings feed back into practice by offering potential methods to train decision-making skills?' Outside of research, from a practitioner's point of view, it is beneficial to provide feedback for all facets of a player's performance. Typical performance analysis will involve video sessions where athletes review and discuss their own decision-making performance, usually with a coach or member of support staff. However, for the reasons previously discussed, it may be difficult for players to take this feedback and apply it to a game situation in the future because the video capture of the game simply does not match the information that is available *to that player* for making decisions during the game. In **6.31** (Expertise) reference was made to studies that used video simulations in order to train perceptual skills such as anticipation which reported mixed results in terms of effectiveness. The methodological shortcomings that may limit the effectiveness of this type of training are the same ones that limit the realism of displays used in research protocols: a viewpoint that does not update or change over time according to the performer's movement and a loss of dimensionality in terms of depth based information. The relatively recent introduction of immersive, interactive Virtual Reality (VR) technology may provide an exciting potential both as a methodological tool and a potential decision-making training environment for players. Immersive, interactive VR allows a user to be totally immersed (360 degrees) in a virtual environment. By wearing a head-mounted display (HMD) that contains an integrated head tracker, movements in the real world can be tracked and translated into parallel movements in the virtual world. In other words, a movement to the left in the real world is detected by the tracker and is represented visually in the virtual environment as simultaneous movement to the left in the virtual environment. This technology not only allows for an egocentric perspective of an event, it also allows the experimenters to control the information presented to the participants (perception) and measure how they respond to that information (action). In other words, it is an ideal tool to study the perception/action cycle and how information influences decisions about when and how to act.

Bideau et al. (2010) highlight not only the advantages that VR offers over video playback in decision-making research, but also the importance of this technology in terms of the emerging results. For example, in a perception-only rugby based task where a real defender is confronted with a virtual attacker performing a deceptive stepping movement, results showed that there was a clear expert advantage over novices, with experts (professional rugby players) being more able to judge the correct final running direction much earlier than novices. Most interestingly, the professional players judged by the coach to play the best 'heads-up' rugby were significantly better than the other professional players tested. These results suggest that certain expert players can tune into the right information that specifies the correct final running direction and not the deceptive body-based information that is specifying the incorrect final running direction. Other studies have also shown how this technology can allow us to study how information picked up from a ball trajectory (e.g. a curved free kick in soccer) influences decisions about how and when to act. Again a clear expert advantage has been shown with experienced international goal-keepers waiting longer before responding, leading to less movement errors in the wrong direction (Dessing and Craig, 2010). These cases present examples where VR has been shown to be an effective means of presenting sport scenarios in a realistic yet controllable way. Furthermore, there are promising possibilities of using this technology for practitioners through the development of virtual decision-making training environments which could be used as an off-field training tool. This may be especially beneficial for injured players in that they could still benefit from the perceptual experience without having to carry out the physical practice.

The aim of this chapter was to not only describe theoretical and methodological approaches to studying decision-making but also to discuss recent work using new techniques. The use of such new and exciting technology will continue to expand our understanding of the mechanisms underlying decision-making and judgement by allowing the creation of more realistic environments through which to observe athletic performance.

REFERENCES

Bideau, B., Kulpa, R., Vignais, N., Brault, S., Multon, F. and Craig, C. (2010) Using virtual reality to analyze sports' performance. *IEEE Computer Graphics and Applications*, 30, 14–21.

Brault, S., Bideau, B., Craig, C. and Kulpa, R. (2010) Balancing deceit and disguise: How to successfully fool the defender in a 1 vs. 1 situation in rugby. *Human Movement Science*, 29, 412–425.

Correia, V., Araujo, D., Craig, C. and Passos, P. (2011) Prospective information for pass decisional behaviour in rugby union. *Human Movement Science*. doi:10.1016/j.humov.2010.07.008

Craig, C.M., Goulon, C., Berton, E., Rao, G., Fernandez, L. and Bootsma, R.J. (2009) Optic variables used to judge future ball arrival position in expert and novice soccer players. *Attention, Perception and Psychophysics*, 71, 515–522.

motor skills

Dessing, J.C. and Craig, C.M. (2010) Bending it like Beckham: How to visually fool the goalkeeper. *PloS ONE*, 5 (10), e13161. doi:10.1371/journal.pone.0013161

Fajen, B.R., Riley, M.A. and Turvey, M.T. (2008) Information, affordances and the control of action in sport. *International Journal of Sport Psychology*, 40 (1), 79–107.

Gibson, J.J. (1979) *An Ecological Approach to Visual Perception.* Boston, MA: Houghton-Mifflin.

Helsen, W. and Pauwels, J.M. (1988) The use of a simulator in evaluation and training of tactical skills in soccer. In Reilly, T., Lees, A., Davids, K. and Murphy, W. (ed.) *Science and Football.* London: Spon. pp. 493–497.

Tenenbaum, G. (2003) Expert athletes: An integrated approach to decision-making. In Starkes, J.L. and Ericsson, K.A. (eds) *Expert Performance in Sports: Advances in Research on Sport Expertise.* Champaign, IL: Human Kinetics. pp. 191–219.

Tenenbaum, G. and Bar-Eli, M. (1993) Decision-making in sport: A cognitive perspective. In Singer, R.N., Murphy, M. and Tennant, L.K. (eds) *Handbook of Research on Sport Psychology.* New York: Macmillan. pp. 171–192.

Turvey, M.T. (1992) Ecological foundations of cognition: Invariants of perception and action. In Pick, H.L., Jr., van den Broek, P. and Knill, D.C. (ed.) *Cognition: Conceptual and Methodological Issues.* Washington, DC: American Psychological Association. pp. 85–117.

Watson, G., Brault, S., Kulpa, R., Bideau, B., Butterfield, J. and Craig, C.M. (2010) Judging the 'passability' of dynamic gaps in a virtual rugby environment. *Human Movement Science.* doi:10.1016/j.humov.2010.08.004

Wickens, C.D. (1992) *Engineering Psychology and Human Performance.* 2nd edn. London: Harper Collins.

6.33: Practising Motor Skills

Definition: 'Practice' is the deliberate, effortful and repetitive rehearsal of transferable skills, both physical and mental, that are relevant to performance during competition itself.

Whether it be a once-a-week for the local pub team or a daily occurrence as a professional athlete, practice is an integral part of sports performance. While practice schedules can include tactical and strategic planning, rehearsal of the sport-specific motor skills tends to be the key component. Several famous sports personalities are renowned for their almost obsessive practice routines, but none more so than Jonny Wilkinson, the English rugby out-half. In his book '*Tackling Life: Striving for Perfection*', he explains that each week leading up to a big game, 'I hit about 250 to 300 practice place kicks alone. I average 200 to 250 punts using my left foot and exactly the same number using my right. A daily total of 20 dropped goals with each foot and 15 to 20 restarts, six to seven times a week, would pretty much constitute a solid preparational build-up ... That makes a total of about 1,000 kicks to prepare for just 20 (typical kicks per match) ... That's near enough 50 rehearsals for each single defining event. To me that has been a totally acceptable ratio.' (p. 80). Tiger Woods, David Beckham and the Williams sisters are also known for their gruelling practice routines, but is it the case that repetitive rehearsal of the same skills yields better performance? How should practice be designed and carried out so as to facilitate the learning process?

When discussing expertise (see **6.31**), the amount of deliberate practice was said to be related to the level of attainment. Ericsson et al. (1993) examined the activities that constituted the daily practice routines of expert musicians and suggested that although a monotonic relationship exists between hours of deliberate practice and performance improvements, it is not strictly the number of hours of practice that are important for the development of expertise but rather the actual structure and content of those practice hours. To constitute deliberate practice, practice routines must be structured, highly relevant, require high levels of effort and not be inherently enjoyable. However, deliberate practice research in sport has yielded some findings that may suggest that such a theory is not applicable to sport. Few sport studies to date have met the conditions of high ratings for relevance and effort and low ratings for enjoyment (e.g. Starkes et al., 1996; Starkes, 2000). We tend to enjoy practicing the games that we choose to play. Deliberate practice theory does however, draw on perhaps the most fundamental aim of practice: to improve performance in the competitive setting. The idea of transferability from practice to game is key to improving performance but is often hard to quantify, especially for open skills (skills that are performed in an environment that is unpredictable or in motion and that requires performers to adapt their movements in response to dynamic properties of the environment). Often drills and mini-games are incorporated into team game practice with a two-fold aim: to practice *how* to perform the skill and *when* to perform the skill, that is, the assumption that if a similar situation arises in a game, the appropriate action will be carried out at the appropriate time. There are however, some observable products of practicing motor skills. For example, in terms of control and co-ordination, research has shown that performers' movements become less stiff and rigid with increased practice (e.g. for racquetball forehand backswings; Southard and Higgins, 1987). Changes in the patterns of muscle activity also occur over practice, as shown by EMG studies, such as Moore and Martiniuk (1986) who showed that with practice 'co-contraction' (the simultaneous contraction of agonistic and antagonistic muscles) diminishes and the movement pattern shifts to sequential contraction (where agonists and antagonists contract only at the appropriate and necessary times). Such mechanisms result in more efficient movement, whereby the energy costs of the movement diminish with practice (Sparrow and Irizarry-Lopez, 1987).

The old adage 'practice makes perfect' is often rephrased by researchers as 'effectively designed practice makes perfect' (Schmidt and Wrisberg, 2004). So what constitutes effectively designed practice? What rehearsal techniques might be used in order to facilitate the learning experience and how might practice sessions be structured so as to get the best from them? In terms of motor learning, the most important contributor is the act of proper physical rehearsal. Physical rehearsal may take several forms, for example simulator practice and part practice.

Simulator practice involves practice in some sort of simulator which mimics aspects of a real-world task. Simulators may be simple mechanical devices such as an ergometer (an indoor rowing machine), or complex combinations of virtual environments and mechanical devices such as the rowing simulator in the M3 Sensory-Motor Systems laboratory at the Swiss Federal Institute of Technology in Zurich. While simple ergometers do not simulate realistically every aspect of rowing (e.g. the lateral balance challenges or the exact resistance of water), they still allow for comparable workloads without having to go out on the water every day. More advanced simulators, such as the one at the M3 lab, allow practice in the presence of other external factors such as crowd noise (e.g. hostile and supportive). Essentially, simulator practice must add value to regular practice routines in order to be worthwhile.

Part practice refers to 'a procedure involving the practice of a complex skill in a more simplified form' (Schmidt and Wrisberg, 2004) whereby complex skills can be: fractioned (e.g. practicing only the leg kick in swimming); simplified (e.g. use of an oversized ball in tennis, or performing slow motion movements); or segmented (progressive part practice, e.g. practicing the toss, followed by the toss and the racquet swing in the tennis serve). Part practice works best for serial tasks where the actions involved in one part do not influence the actions involved in the next (e.g. passing the baton in a relay race) and is least effective for rapid, discrete actions such as hitting a golf ball. As well as physical rehearsal techniques, practice can be in the form of mental rehearsal whereby people think through or imagine performing a motor skill in the absence of overt movement (see **4.17** and **4.18**). While evidence suggests that physical rehearsal alone is superior to mental rehearsal when learning movement skills (e.g. Hird et al., 1991), it also suggests that mental rehearsal is always superior to no rehearsal and so may prove useful when supplementing physical practice or when the opportunity to practice physically is unavailable. Furthermore, it is a combination of both mental and physical practice that appears to yield the best results of all.

Practice sessions can be structured in many different ways, each of which can influence the learning process. It is important to understand the pros and cons of the main features of a practice session. Should practice be blocked or random? Should it be constant or varied? How should it be balanced with rest? Imagine a practice schedule for a badminton player that devotes one session to serving, one session to forehand drives, one session to smashes and so on. This is an example of *blocked practice* – a sequence in which individuals repeatedly rehearse the same task. Compare this to a practice sequence where the badminton player would perform a number of different tasks in no particular order, thus avoiding consecutive repetitions of the same task. This is known as *random practice*. Research has shown superior learning in random practice as opposed to blocked practice (e.g. Tsutsui et al., 1998). Practically speaking, blocked practice has been shown to be more effective during initial rehearsal but does not promote lasting learning. It is thought that in blocked practice, athletes fail to practice the target skill within the target context. This is because the practice context does not approximate closely the movement and environmental conditions of the target context (i.e. the specificity of learning). In summary, repetitions are important in practice but repetitiveness is ineffective (Schmidt and Wrisberg, 2004). Similar to the notion of blocked practice is that of constant practice. This describes a practice sequence which involves an athlete rehearsing only one variation of a class of tasks in one session. For example, a cricket fielder practising only short throws for run-outs. An alternative to this would be the cricket fielder practicing not only short throws but also long throws from the boundary, thereby rehearsing a number of variations of the given class of task during one session. This is referred to as 'varied practice'. Again, according to the notion of specificity of learning, which advocates learning of specific actions to accomplish specific goals, varied practice would seem logical. It would allow the cricket fielder to use the same generalised motor programme (see **6.30**) and to parameterise dimensions of the action, for example select the velocity and force required for a particular throw. This facilitates the development of more effective schemas, namely the sets of rules relating the various outcomes of a person's actions to the parameter values the person chooses to produce those outcomes (Schmidt, 1975). In terms synonymous with a constraints-led approach to motor behaviour, random and varied practice would represent the variability present in the real-world context where movement emerges as a result of constantly changing task constraints.

Finally, with the physical and mental demands of rehearsal taking its toll, it is vitally important to balance practice and rest in any training schedule. Researchers have classified practice as being either *massed* (where the amount of rest between practice attempts or sessions is relatively shorter than the amount of time spent practicing) or *distributed* (rest time is relatively longer than practice time). The effectiveness of each approach depends on the nature of the task in question. For discrete tasks (e.g. shooting a netball), reducing rest time between performances has little or no influence on learning (Lee and Genovese, 1988). Therefore, fatigue during practice sessions is not a problem and repetitions can be increased. For continuous skills (e.g. cycling), reduced periods of rest between performances degrades performances and has a negative and relatively permanent effect on learning. Therefore, ample rest should be taken so as not to generate sloppy performances. Energy requirements of the task should be analysed and practice conditions tailored to meet these.

The role of the coach or support staff in an athlete's career is therefore pivotal to designing an effective practice schedule and guiding the athlete through it.

REFERENCES

Ericsson, K.A., Krampe, R.T. and Tesch-Römer, C. (1993) The role of deliberate practice in the acquisition of expert performance. *Psychological Review*, 100 (3), 363–406.

Hird, J.S., Landers, D.M., Thomas, J.R. and Horan, J.J. (1991) Physical practice is superior to mental practice in enhancing cognitive and motor task performance. *Journal of Sport and Exercise Psychology*, 8, 281–293.

Lee, T.D. and Genovese, E.D. (1988) Distribution of practice is motor skill acquisition: Learning and performance effects reconsidered. *Research Quarterly for Exercise and Sport*, 59, 277–287.

Moore, S.P. and Martiniuk, R.G. (1986) Kinematic and electromyographic changes that occur as a function of learning a time-constrained aiming task. *Journal of Motor Behaviour*, 18, 397–426.

Schmidt, R.A. (1975) A schema theory of discrete motor skill learning. *Psychological Review*, 82, 225–260.

Schmidt, R.A. and Wrisberg, C.A. (2004) *Motor Learning and Performance: A Problem Based Learning Approach*. 3rd edn. Champaign, IL: Human Kinetics.

Southard, D. and Higgins, T. (1987) Changing movement patterns: Effects of demonstration and practice. *Research Quarterly for Exercise and Sport*, 58, 77–80.

Sparrow, W.A. and Irizarry-Lopez, V.M. (1987) Mechanical efficiency and metabolic cost as measures of learning a novel gross motor task. *Journal of Motor Behaviour*, 19, 240–264.

Starkes, J.L, Deakin, J.M., Allard, F., Hodges, N.J. and Hayes, A. (1996) Deliberate practice in sports: what is it anyway? In K.A. Ericsson (ed). *The Road to Excellence: The Acquisition of Expert Performance in Arts and Sciences, Sports and Games* Mahwah, N.J: Lawrence Erlbaum. pp. 81–106.

Starkes, J.L. (2000) The road to expertise: Is practice the only determinant? *International Journal of Sport Psychology*, 31, 431–451.

Tsutsui, S., Lee, T.D. and Hodges, N.J. (1998) Contextual interference in learning new patterns of bimanual coordination. *Journal of Motor Behavior*, 30, 151–157.

Wilkinson, J. (2008) *Tackling Life: Striving for Perfection*. London: Headline Publishing Group.

motor skills

6.34: Analysis and Measurement of Motor Performance

> **Definition:** Procedures for measuring human movement that are objective, reliable and valid, and that yield results which are transferable from the laboratory to competition.

The analysis and measurement of motor performance is an important aspect in both motor behaviour research and sport practice. In research, the performance of motor skills is studied scientifically in order to enhance our understanding of the skill and the control of movement. In practice, motor performance is analysed for different reasons, namely performance enhancement, injury prevention or to examine the effects of athletic devices (e.g. protective equipment). Although the aims and objectives outlined above are different, the methods and measurements used in both cases are the same. Before describing such methods and measurements it is necessary to address the following questions: What exactly is meant by motor performance and how does it differ from motor learning? What are the criteria for good motor performance measurement systems? How is the analysis and measurement of motor performance approached?

Motor performance is defined by Schmidt and Wrisberg (2004) as 'the observable attempt of a person to produce a voluntary action. The level of a person's performance is susceptible to fluctuations in temporary factors such as motivation, arousal, fatigue and physical condition' (p.11). This differs from the definition of motor learning (see **6.30**), put forward by the same authors, which is described as 'Changes in internal processes that determines a person's capability for producing a motor task' (p.11). The key difference is that motor performance is observable and motor learning is not. Therefore, anytime you observe an athlete running, kicking a football, or swinging a golf club, you are observing motor skills being performed (i.e. motor performance). The fact that motor performance is observable leaves it open to subjective appraisal – we often admire a 'fluid' golf swing or a 'natural' cricket bowling action without being able to describe exactly what it is that makes it so pleasing to watch. One may then ask the question, does everyone find it pleasing to watch? For scientific study and for detailed analysis, objective, reliable and valid scientific means of measurement are required. These are the criteria that must be considered for any good measurement system, and measuring motor behaviour is no different. *Objectivity* refers to the extent that two observers evaluating the same performance arrive at the same (or very similar) measurements. For example, in sports such as gymnastics, diving and figure skating, judges often report similar scores due to the strict criteria and scoring systems that they adhere to, even though judgement of the performance appears subjective. On the other hand, measuring the club head speed during a golf swing using a highly accurate electronic measurement system will yield the same measurement regardless of who takes the reading. The measurement of motor performance must be as objective as possible. *Reliability*, refers to the repeatability of the measurement under similar conditions. In order for measurements to be reliable, sources of variability must be minimised. Using quality recording apparatus and careful procedures will limit variability due to technological error; however, intra-subject variability (variability in the same person performing the same skill repeatedly) is much more difficult to control. Maintaining experimental control in a laboratory setting minimises this variability as researchers can control variables that may be difficult to control if analysing the same motor performance in the natural setting (e.g. during a golf competition). *Validity* refers to the extent to which a test or measuring device measures what it is intended to measure and whether or not these measures reflect the underlying construct of interest (Schmidt and Lee, 2005). For example, we would not use a racquet-head velocity measurement if we wanted to measure the accuracy of a tennis serve. This relates to the different levels of analysis when considering motor performance, which we will now move on to discuss.

Consider the analysis of a tennis serve once more. As a researcher there are three ways of approaching this analysis. First, they may be interested in describing outcome measures (e.g. the accuracy of the serve in terms of number of serves 'in'). Second, they may be interested in describing the characteristics of the serving action itself (e.g. location of body parts throughout the serving action, the joint angles or the relative timing of body parts to one another). Third, they may be interested in the role of the central nervous system in movement production (e.g. electromyography (EMG) traces, which indicate the electrical activity in a muscle, or electroencephalography (EEG) traces for brain activity). The remainder of this chapter will deal with describing outcome measures and then focus on methods of capturing and characterising movement itself as this is widely used in the analysis of sports performance. Analysis of sports performance at a neural level is less common due to the intolerance of such techniques when performing large-scale movements.

Describing outcome measures quantifies the extent to which a movement achieved the goal that was intended. The achievement of such goals is often assessed through measures of accuracy or measures of time and speed. Taking measures of accuracy first, an accurate performance of a skill is one that is performed with minimum error. If a performer's target is taken to mean a particular force, distance, speed or time (e.g. an archer hitting a bulls-eye, a baseball batter connecting with the ball, a weightlifter exerting a certain force), then it is possible to measure deviations from this target (error) throughout a number of movement attempts. Scores can be combined in a number of ways in order to measure and analyse performance. For example, constant error, variable error, total variability, absolute error and absolute constant error can be calculated (for details on how to calculate and interpret these error measurements, see Schmidt and Lee, 2005). The most common measures in terms of time and speed that are used in research are *Reaction Time* (RT) and *Movement Time* (MT). RT is 'a measure of the time from the arrival of a suddenly presented and unanticipated signal to the beginning of the response to it'. MT is defined as 'the interval from the initiation of the response (end of RT) to the completion of the movement' (Schmidt and Lee, 2005). As discussed in the expertise chapter (see **6.31**), experts are often shown to react faster and to complete movements faster than novices, and the basic assumption for looking at such measures is that the performer who can complete a movement in less time or accomplish more in a given amount of time is the more skilful. Also, the goal of some, but by no means all, sports behaviours is to maximise the speed of movement. To do this they need to react fastest (e.g. sprint start) and move fastest (e.g. complete the 100 m in the shortest time), and so RT and MT measures of motor performance have high validity. Both measures of accuracy and measures of speed, however, interact in producing the troublesome 'speed-accuracy trade-off', which describes the basic observed phenomena where precision is sacrificed when attempting to perform a skill more quickly (e.g. kick a penalty in soccer too hard).

When analysing the characteristics of motor performance rather than the outcome measures associated with it, it is first necessary to capture the movement in some way. Following this, motor performance can be observed at different speeds and biomechanical analyses can be performed using kinematic measures (studying the 'pure' movement *without* taking into account the forces that produced it) and/or kinetic measures (studying motion *with* respect to the forces that produced it). Such analyses allow researchers to further understand the mechanisms which translate muscular contractions about articulating joints into functional movement such as dancing, performing a triple jump or pitching a baseball. These techniques also allow practitioners to assess technique and performance by acquiring performance markers and feeding back to the athlete.

Human motion analysis and the desire to understand and depict human motion can be traced back through history and has shaped the types of techniques used today. For instance, Aristotle (384–322 BC) described animal's bodies as mechanical systems in his book *De Motu Animalium* (On the Movement of Animals), Da Vinci's (1452–1519) anatomical drawings depicted the mechanics of jumping, while Galileo provided some of the earliest examples of attempts to analyse physiological function mathematically. Borelli (1608–1679) studied the equilibrium of forces in the joints, determined the position of the human centre of gravity, and was able to show that inspiration was muscle driven. This work was followed by that of Newton (1642–1727) with his laws of physics and others of equal fame. Two leading figures in terms of depicting motion then emerged in E.J. Marey (1830–1904) and Eadweard Muybridge (1830–1904). Through chronophotography and the use of his 'photographic gun', Marey was able to capture 12 frames of motion per second and used this to depict animal motion. At the same time, Muybridge was using multiple cameras to capture animal locomotion and could display animations through a device called the 'zoopraxiscope'. His techniques were able to prove that during galloping, all four of the horse's hooves are airborne. These figures were thought to strongly influence modern-day imaging techniques used to capture motion.

Today, motion capture techniques fall into two categories, *direct methods* and *imaging methods*. Direct methods include the use of goniometers – hinged devices that are fitted at the joints and measure the changes in angle between limb segments during movement. However, by far the most widely used methods for measuring and analysing motor performance are imaging techniques, such as video imaging and optoelectronic imaging. Video capture, a relatively inexpensive method, is widely used by sport practitioners. Coaches can video individual or team performances and use software to analyse aspects of the performance from the video footage. High-speed video capture (more frames per second) and analysis, allows a more in-depth (frame by frame) analysis of a particular technique and provides an opportunity for player and coach to analyse performance together. Optoelectronic methods are used widely in both research and practice due to the level of analysis that can be performed. This technique involves fitting markers to limbs and joints in the body. These markers are either reflective (passive) or light-emitting (active). Passive marker systems use infrared cameras and reflective markers. Full body motion capture for one person will usually involve somewhere in the region of 40 markers and 12 cameras. Rich data relating to the change of position over time for each individual marker is fed to a computer. From there, detailed analysis of the movement can be performed and outputs produced, such as displacement plots for the elbow during throwing. For kinetic analysis of a movement, this system is often integrated with force plates that can measure the ground reaction force, the centre of pressure and the vertical moment of force generated by standing on or moving across them. The data collected from this motion-capture technique can then be used to analyse the kinematics of movement performance or reconstruct human movement to produce realistic motion for computer simulations. This technique is used extensively in animated films and computer game development.

In conclusion, it is evident that the measurement and analysis of motor performance draws on a wide range of techniques that can be applied to an equally wide range of disciplines. As technology and measurement systems advance, the future will only bring more exciting ways of analysing motor performance, all of which will provide more insight and understanding of complex motor performance.

REFERENCES

Schmidt, R. and Lee, T. (2005) *Motor Control and Learning: A Behavioural Emphasis.* 3rd edn. Champaign, IL: Human Kinetics.

Schmidt, R.A. and Wrisberg, C.A. (2004) *Motor Learning and Performance: A Problem-Based Learning Approach.* 3rd edn. Champaign, IL: Human Kinetics.

7

Sport and Well-being

7.35: Gender Issues

> **Definition:** The impact of sex (biological and physiological characteristics) and gender (socially constructed roles, behaviours and attributes) on motivation towards, and engagement with, sport and physical exercise.

Historically, it would be no exaggeration to say that the world of sport was a man's world – run by men, for men. It is widely accepted that androcentrism (i.e. a world view centred on men) has airbrushed the role played by women out of sport's history, despite the reality that both sexes have played an active role in competition from the time of the Ancient Greek games onwards (Miller, 2004). In fact, it was only during the mid to late Victorian era (1850s onwards) that today's gendered world of sport first truly emerged (Anderson, 2010). At that time women's so-called 'fragility' and femininity were protected by ensuring that women and girls only engaged in 'lady-like' activities that did not involve undue exertion or challenge. In this way, it was argued, their reproductive capacity was safeguarded.

The net result was the development of gender-specific activities and the gendered world of sport that we are now familiar with (Allender et al., 2006). For example, while many sports were simply off-limits for Victorian girls and women, many other sports were 'adapted' or made safe by limiting either space, speed and contact (e.g. men's basketball v. women's netball) or physical contact through use of an implement (women's hockey and lacrosse) (Hargreaves, 1994).

Today's participation rates still continue to reflect significant gender differences (Sport England, 2003). For example, while female participation has risen, the largest increases have occurred in 'aesthetic', non-competitive activities such as keep-fit and aerobics. In addition, women remain under-represented in sports' infrastructure, including positions such as coaches, referees, administrators, journalists and leisure managers, and women's sport continues to receive less sponsorship and less media coverage. Coleman and Brooks (2009) found that adolescent boys are still more likely to engage in organised sport and physical activity than girls, and the gap in participation between the sexes grows over the teenage years.

As to why, recent research (Sport England, 2006) continues to show that young women find more barriers to participation than young men, with embarrassment regarding body shape and evaluation of appearance by peers (and especially boys) of particular concern during adolescence (Cockburn and Clarke, 2002; Biddle et al., 2005). Hence, while traditional gender stereotypes may be increasingly challenged, there is still evidence to suggest that subtle stereotypical gender roles operate to discourage girls from entering the world of sport.

Most early academic reviews of sex/gender in sport and exercise attributed differences to innate biological distinctions between men and women. 'Sex' is typically defined by genetically predetermined physiological characteristics, while 'gender' refers to cultural customs, roles and expectations associated with being male or female. In turn, gender will comprise many elements of personality, including the extent to which the person displays both masculinity and femininity as independent psychological characteristics. Recent research would argue that definitions of sex and gender must be sufficiently flexible to accommodate considerable variation within and between each category, with categorical discriminations often quite arbitrary. This has been revealed most starkly in the recent controversy surrounding the South African 800 m runner Caster Semenya, whose private life and dignity have been exposed to the full glare of the world's media in a futile attempt to 'officially' determine her sex. The gender verification test is supposedly sensitive to the presence of the male Y chromosome, with an XX reading signifying female and an XY reading being indicative of a male chromosomal make up. However, Oglesby and Hill (1993) report on female athletes who have been disqualified because they show cell chromosomal structures of XOY or XXY. Other tests rely on testosterone levels, but again any line of demarcation between male and female is likely to be arbitrary. For this reason it seems prudent to accept a more tolerant notion of both sex and gender categorisation, where each individual is seen as comprising a mosaic of male and female biological and socio-cultural components.

By constantly focusing attention on innate sex differences, there is also a danger that gender similarities will be disregarded. As Diane Gill (2007) remarks, 'Today, most psychologists look beyond the male–female and masculine–feminine dichotomies to developmental and social cognitive models. That is, how people *think* males and females differ is more important than how they actually differ' (p. 828).

While the search for sex/gender differences in sport may persist, the study of gender issues within sport and exercise psychology has shifted considerably over recent years (Knoppers and McDonald, 2010). Birrell (2000) argues that the history of sport science, including sport psychology, can be represented in three stages. Up until the late 1970s, the field is best described as 'atheoretical'. Sport was a man's world, and where gender was researched it tended to be work directed towards understanding sex or gender roles in sport, differences in traits and motives between men and women, and the role conflict experienced by women who took part in sport. In particular, the idea that men almost literally ran towards or embraced their sex role stereotype (based on masculinity) through sport, while women ran away from their stereotype (based on femininity).

In the late 1970s and 1980s, and influenced by the liberal feminist movement, there was a move away from considering gender as just a variable or category and towards understanding gender relations and how personal agency and culture impact on these relations. This was a time when liberal feminism led the way in opening new dialogues as to how sport perpetuated masculine values and excluded women, and this was a time when real change was achieved through civil action. For example, in the US, Title IX of the Education Amendments legislation of 1972 established that no person should be denied access to sports within state-funded schools on grounds of sex.

From this period emerged the third stage, characterised by more critical approaches and more diverse methodologies. According to Birrell (1988) four key agenda issues dominate this final phase:

- the production of an ideology of male power through sport;
- the media practices through which dominant images of women are reproduced;
- physicality, sexuality, the body sites for defining gender relations;
- the resistance of women to dominant male practices.

While sport studies may have witnessed this sea change over the last 30–40 years, within sport psychology it would be fair to say that the agenda has moved more slowly (Knoppers and McDonald, 2010). However, the emphasis on studying biological differences between men and women has given way to a broader consideration of gender roles and relationships, and it is only much more recently that greater prominence has been afforded to social psychological perspectives which emphasise social constructionist and feminist analyses of gender and sport.

For example, Diane Gill (1994) suggested that attention should focus on gender-schematic processing by significant others and how this comes to influence young people's views of sport and exercise (Giuliano et al., 2000). Parents and physical education (PE) teachers, in particular, will often reinforce stereotypes of boys as being more dominant and as possessing greater physical prowess in comparison with girls, who tend to be described in terms of their appearance and presentation rather than their ability. Over time, such influences will inevitably shape perceptions of the appropriateness of particular activities for boys and girls.

The gendered nature of physical activity throughout life is revealed in many ways, not least in psychological responses to sport participation. Scully et al. (1998) describe a tendency for women to have greater concern with their body as an aesthetic statement, while men traditionally have focused more on kinaesthetics (co-ordination, strength and speed). At the same time evidence grows that body dysmorphic disorder (BDD), or obsessive preoccupation with bodily defects, is a problem equally common among both men and women (see **7.36**), with women showing greater concern for reducing their size while men seek to increase their bulk.

Among women, it has been argued that a greater emphasis on the female form may go on to foster feelings of social-physique anxiety (SPA), often exacerbated by revealing sportswear (Frederick and Shaw, 1995). Among young men, there is growing evidence of similar concerns (Pope et al., 2002). Also, previous research has suggested that body image in general tends to be less positive among women, and is more closely linked to women's overall self-esteem. More recently it has been shown that for both men and women, significant investment and concern with the 'gender ideal' body often reflects in poorer health and well-being (Sanchez and Crocker, 2005).

Equally, earlier work considered differences in masculinity or androgyny between those who took part in sport, both men and women, and those who did not. Unsurprisingly, it was found that masculinity and sport often go hand in hand, but the construct that appears to overlap both is competitiveness. While men do tend to score higher than women on measures of competitiveness, the gender effect is strongest and most consistent for competitive sport behaviour rather than general achievement or sport goal orientation. Also, gender differences are less pronounced than differences between athletes and non-athletes of either gender (Gill, 2007).

A second psychological variable that reveals gender differences is self-confidence. In general terms, women tend to have lower expectations of success and to make fewer achievement-oriented attributions than men, but a meta-analysis has suggested that gender differences in self-confidence may be not be as large as originally thought, with a key mediating variable being the sex-linked nature of the task (Lirgg, 1991).

Finally, looking to gender-specific issues, and in some respects echoing much earlier Victorian concerns, there continues to be research dealing with how exercise may impact on women's well-being, including the stability of the menstrual cycle. Menstrual irregularities including amenorrhoea (fewer than one period in the previous six months) and oligomenorrhoea (a cycle lasting longer than 35 days) have been associated with sports that combine low body fat with rigorous training regimes, including long-distance running, gymnastics and dance. In a more positive vein, other research has shown the benefits of physical exercise for alleviating menstrual cycle disorders (see Cockerill et al., 1995), with moderate physical exercise in particular having been shown to be effective in the reduction of various physical and psychological symptoms commonly associated with pre-menstrual syndrome (PMS).

Since the 1970s there has been a plethora of work linking exercise with eating disorders, including anorexia and bulimia (Meyer et al., 2008). This work suggests that female athletes may be more likely to develop eating disorders than non-athletes due to an emphasis in certain sports on low body fat and the drive for perfection. This is especially true in 'thinness-demand sports' such as gymnastics, ice-skating, running, dancing and diving. Taken together, the evidence suggests that many women in these sports present with pathological weight control behaviours, display attitudes towards food and dieting which are similar to clinically diagnosed eating disorders, and have coaches who may unwittingly encourage pathogenic weight loss due to their own relatively negative attitudes toward, and limited knowledge about, weight and weight control. The need to raise awareness of these issues remains critical as available evidence would suggest that in the absence of professional interventions, the risk remains high and is unacceptable.

7.35: gender issues

REFERENCES

Allender, S., Cowburn, G. and Foster, C. (2006) Understanding participation in sport and physical activity among children and adults: a review of qualitative studies. *Health Education Research*, 21 (6), 826–835.

Anderson, N.F. (2010) *The Sporting Life: Victorian Sports and Games*. Westport, CO; Praeger.

Biddle, S.J.H., Whitehead, S.H., O'Donovan, T.M. and Nevill, M.E. (2005) Correlates of participation in physical activity for adolescent girls: A systematic review of recent literature. *Journal of Physical Activity and Health*, 2, 423–434.

Birrell, S. (1988) Discourses on the gender/sport relationship: from women in sport to gender relations. In Pandolph, K. (ed.) *Exercise and Sport Science Reviews*. Vol. 16. New York: Macmillan. pp. 459–502.

Birrell, S. (2000) Feminist theories for sport. In Coakley, J. and Dunning, E. (eds) *Handbook of Sports Studies*. Sage: London. pp. 61–76.

Cockburn, C. and Clarke, G. (2002) 'Everybody's looking at you!': Girls negotiating the 'femininity deficit' they incur in physical education. *Women's Studies International Forum*, 25, 651–665.

Cockerill, I.M., Lawson, S.L. and Nevill, A.M. (1995) Mood states, menstrual cycle and exercise-to-music. In Annett, J., Cripps, B. and Steinberg, H. (eds) *Exercise Addiction*. Leicester: British Psychological Society. pp. 61–69.

Coleman, J. and Brooks, F. (2009) *Key Data on Adolescence 2009*. 7th edn. Brighton: Young People in Focus.

Frederick, C.J. and Shaw, S.M. (1995) Body image as a leisure constraint: Examining the experience of aerobic exercise classes for young women, *Leisure Science*, 17, 57–73.

Gill, D. (1994) Psychological perspectives on women in sport and exercise. In Costa, D.M. and Guthrie, S.R. (eds) *Women and Sport: Interdisciplinary Perspectives*. Champaign, IL: Human Kinetics. pp. 253–284.

Gill, D. (2007) Gender and cultural diversity. In Tenenbaum, G. and Eklund, R.C. (eds) *Handbook of Sport Psychology*. 3rd edn. Hoboken, NJ: Wiley. pp. 823–844.

Giuliano, T., Popp, K. and Knight, J. (2000) Football versus Barbies: Childhood play activities as predictors of sport participation by women. *Sex Roles*, 42, 159–181.

Hargreaves, J.A. (1994) *Sporting Females: Critical Issues in the History and the Sociology of Women's Sport*. London: Routledge.

Knoppers, A. and McDonald, M. (2010) Scholarship on gender and sport in sex roles and beyond. *Sex Roles*, 63, 311–323.

Lirgg, C.D. (1991) Gender differences in self-confidence in physical activity: A meta-analysis of recent studies. *Journal of Sport and Exercise Psychology*, 8, 294–310.

Meyer, C., Taranis, L. and Touyz, C. (2008) Excessive exercise in the eating disorders: A need for less activity from patients and more from researchers. *European Eating Disorders Review*, 16 (2), 81–83.

Miller, S.G. (2004) *Ancient Greek Athletics*. Yale, NJ: Yale University Press.

Oglesby, C.A. and Hill, K.L. (1993) Gender and sport. In Singer, R.N., Murphey, M. and Tennant, L.K. (eds) *Handbook of Research on Sport Psychology*. New York: Macmillan. pp. 718–728.

Pope, H.G., Phillips, K.A. and Olivardia, R. (2002) *The Adonis Complex: How to Identify, Treat, and Prevent Body Obsession in Men and Boys*. New York: The Free Press.

Sanchez, D.T. and Crocker, J. (2005) How investment in gender ideals affects well-being: The role of external contingencies of self-worth. *Psychology of Women Quarterly*, 29, 63–77.

Scully, D., Reilly, J. and Clarke, J. (1998) Perspectives on gender in sport and exercise. *Irish Journal of Psychology*, 19, 424–438.

Sport England (2003) *Driving Up Participation in Sport – The Social Context, The Trends, The Prospects and The Challenges*. London: Sport England.

Sport England (2006) *Understanding Participation in Sport: What Determines Sports Participation among 15–19 year old Women?* London: Sport England.

7.36: Overtraining and Exercise Addiction

> **Definitions:** Overtraining involves progressively increasing training to a level that is inappropriate for performance management. Exercise addiction is an excessive and unhealthy dependence on an exercise regime that may lead to physical, psychological and emotional damage.

Sport has been normally presented as a 'good news story', promoting healthy competition along with a healthy lifestyle. While this may be true in the majority of cases, there can be a downside to physical activity which should not be ignored. This may happen where the reasons for taking part in sport and exercise have become unhealthy, and the individual begins to show symptoms that the line has been crossed – what was once a recreation or pastime now increasingly resembles an obsession or compulsion, often with dangerous consequences (Adams and Kirkby, 2001, 2002; Jones and Tenenbaum, 2009).

As one example, overtraining can easily lead to a situation where the body is unable to replenish itself before the next bout of exercise, and the result can be catastrophic, both physically and psychologically. Along with overtraining, related phenomena have been identified including overreaching. While overtraining may have serious long-term consequences, overreaching may lead to short-term but usually more easily recoverable decrements in performance. Symptoms of overtraining include a deterioration in performance, difficulties in training and an absence of motivation, behavioural disorders (irritability, melancholy), sleeping disorders, difficult in recovery, an increased occurrence of muscular accidents, and higher sensitivity to infections (Lac and Maso, 2004).

With increasing pressures on top-level athletes to continue to peak for a number of consecutive competitions, with shorter breaks between competitions and with longer playing seasons, it is likely that the incidence of overtraining will continue to increase over coming years. Halson and Jeukendrup (2004) suggest this is the case, although they also report that further investigation of the condition is necessary to truly understand the nature of the phenomenon. Despite this relative lack of research, studies have reported that one of the most revealing symptoms of overtraining is psychological staleness, accompanied by mood disturbance. Staleness can reflect in a raft of symptoms that together conspire to detract from optimal performance and which can have long-term consequences unless appropriate action is taken.

Overtraining is routinely reported by both elite and non-elite athletes, with figures as high as 64 per cent reported among elite athletes, and also evidence that a history of staleness may increase susceptibility to future risk. As to the remedy, according to Berger and Tobar (2007), the answer is simple: 'The only proven treatment for staleness is rest' (p. 608). In reality, this solution may be rather simplistic as for many athletes the core of the problem may lie deeper, for example where the 'pure' motive for taking part in the sport may have become lost over time as extrinsic factors come to dominate over-intrinsic factors and especially fun and enjoyment (Kremer and Moran, 2008).

Beyond overtraining, a wider literature has focused on exercise dependence as a problem area in sport. This condition may involve competitive sport but could extend to physical activity of any type. Debate still rages as to whether the term exercise 'adherence', 'addiction' or 'dependence' is most appropriate (Hausenblas and Downs, 2002).

According to clinical definitions of substance addiction, at least three of the following must be evident to qualify as a genuine addiction: growing tolerance over time, withdrawal effects, an intention to over-exercise, loss of control, increased time, conflict with other life domains, and continuance despite signs of harm. For many dedicated exercisers a good number of these boxes would easily be ticked, and so the term 'addiction' may not be a misnomer. Also, the dependence or addiction may be either primary (an end in itself) or secondary (a means to an end, e.g. weight loss, health). In keeping with other research, Bamber et al. (2000) found that among both men and women who exercised to excess, those whose exercise was best characterised as 'primary' (i.e. exercise for its own sake) did not show greater signs of morbidity in comparison with a control group, while those whose exercise was seen as motivated by secondary factors reported higher levels of 'psychological morbidity, neuroticism, dispositional addictiveness, and impulsiveness, lower self esteem, greater concern with body shape and weight, as well as with the social, psychological, and aesthetic costs of not exercising' (p. 131). In many ways the psychological profile of these individuals mirrored that which would be characteristic of those with eating disorders.

According to several authors (e.g. Garman et al., 2004), the prevalence of exercise dependence among both men and women could be as high as one-third among regular exercisers. Originally, the literature would have paid greatest attention to those who obviously appear to have suffered through loss of weight, and in particular young women. Since the 1970s there has been accumulating evidence to support the existence of a connection between exercise addiction or dependence and conditions including bulimia nervosa and anorexia nervosa. For example, Caroline Davis has found a significant relationship between exercise dependence, weight preoccupation and obsessive-compulsive personality traits among eating-disordered women (Davis et al., 1998). Furthermore, the same author revealed a significant relationship between the extent of physical activity and obsessive-compulsiveness in high-exercising women without eating disorders. It is often reported that exercise can act as an analogue for disordered eating where there is a pre-occupation with body weight, and when, for example, an athlete is injured or not training for some reason, then eating disorders can quickly appear.

Certain sports that value leanness or low body weight have been linked with disordered eating, including gymnastics, middle/long-distance running, ice skating and dance (Scully et al., 1998). Further, these have also been associated with what is now referred to as the Female Athlete

Triad (FAT), a syndrome in which eating disorders, amenorrhoea/ oligomenorrhoea (i.e. delay or interruption of the menstrual cycle for at least three months) and decreased bone mineral density (osteoporosis and osteopenia) are often linked through the combination of too much exercise and too little weight (see 7.35).

More recently, attention has turned to another population where exercise may be serving a different yet equally unhealthy secondary function. Among young men there is a growing evidence of a type of body dysmorphic disorder (BDD) which is distinct from that found among women (Phillips and Diaz, 1997). Whereas women may use aerobic exercise to limit their body size and weight, growing evidence suggests that men use anaerobic exercise, including gym work and weight lifting, to increase the size of their bodies, otherwise known as 'reverse anorexia', 'bigorexia' or 'muscle dysmorphia' (Pope et al., 2000; Tod and Lavallee, 2010). Disturbingly, exercise is often combined with use of illegal substances, including anabolic steroids, to help attain and maintain the required shape.

The recent phenomenon of super-adherers refers to those people who simply cannot give it up, who seek out ever more demanding challenges or exertions, and whose lives can become dominated by their quest for the next physical challenge. Clingman and Hilliard (1987) found that certain personality types were more prevalent among these super-adherers where the motivation to achieve and succeed often bordered on the obsessive.

While super-adherers may be at the end of the exercise spectrum, the reasons why any type of exercise dependence may develop are still not fully understood. In the 1980s and 1990s, the 'runners high' first attracted considerable attention as a potential explanation (Battista, 2004). The mood-enhancing and analgesic properties associated with exercise were found to be linked to naturally occurring chemicals in the brain (endorphins) which exerted an effect similar to opiates. Hence it was suggested that the craving for this endogenous drug drove athletes to continue to 'work out'. Evidence supporting this association was however weak, and instead it is now generally accepted that a combination of perspectives based on social (e.g. lifestyle, social identity), psychological (e.g. personality type, personal identity) and physiological mechanisms (e.g. endorphins, thermogenics) mechanisms may act in combination to make a dependence on exercise less than wholesome (Scully et al., 1998).

Where the individual has developed a dependence on exercise that is unhealthy, it is not surprising that when the person is deprived of that stimulation for some reason (e.g. through illness, injury or retirement), the effects can be traumatic. Research has confirmed this fact, although typically studies are based on short-term deprivation experiments and not longitudinal natural fieldwork. Those who run competitively, for example, have been shown to exhibit disturbed mood states (e.g. increased anxiety, depression, restlessness, guilt) and withdrawal symptoms after no more than one day without exercise (Aidman and Woollard, 2003), and that complete cessation can be linked to even more serious disturbances. This is especially true where the person's sense of identity is closely linked to their activity and where the removal of that significant aspect of their being requires a major re-evaluation and cognitive reframing.

REFERENCES

Adams, J. and Kirkby, R. (2001) Exercise dependence and overtraining: The physiological and psychological consequences of excessive exercise. *Research in Sports Medicine*, 10, 199–222.

Adams, J. and Kirkby, R. (2002) Excessive exercise as an addiction: A review. *Addiction Research and Theory*, 10, 415–437.

Aidman, E. and Woollard, S. (2003) The influence of self-reported exercise addiction on acute emotional and physiological responses to brief exercise deprivation. *Psychology of Sport and Exercise*, 4 (3), 225–236.

Bamber, D., Cockerill, I. and Carroll, D. (2000) The pathological status of exercise dependence. *British Journal of Sports Medicine*, 34, 125–132.

Battista, G. (ed.) (2004) *The Runner's High: Illuminations and Ecstasy in Motion.* Halcottsville, NY: Breakaway Books.

Berger, B.G. and Tobar, D.A. (2007) Physical activity and quality of life. In Tenenbaum, G. and Eklund, R.C. (eds) *Handbook of Sport Psychology*. 3rd edn. Hoboken, NJ: Wiley. pp. 598–620.

Clingman, G.R. and Hilliard, D.V. (1987) Some personality characteristics of the super-adherer: Following those who go beyond fitness. *Journal of Sport Behavior*, 10 (3), 123–136.

Davis, C., Kaptein, S., Kaplan, A.S., Olmsted, M.P. and Woodside, D.B. (1998) Obsessionality in anorexia nervosa: The moderating influence of exercise. *Psychosomatic Medicine*, 60 (2), 192–197.

Garman, J.F., Hayduk, D.M., Crider, D.A. and Hodel, M.M. (2004) Occurrence of exercise dependence in a college-aged population. *Journal of American College Health*, 52 (5), 221–227.

Halson, S.L. and Jeukendrup, A.E. (2004) Does overtraining exist? An analysis of overreaching and overtraining research. *Sports Medicine*, 34 (14), 967–981.

Hausenblas, H.A. and Downs, D.S. (2002) Exercise dependence: A systematic review. *Psychology of Sport and Exercise*, 3, 89–123.

Jones, C.M. and Tenenbaum, G. (2009) Adjustment disorder: A new way of conceptualising the overtraining syndrome. *International Review of Sport Psychology*, 2 (2), 181–197.

Kremer, J. and Moran, A. (2008) *Pure Sport*. Hove: Routledge.

Lac, G. and Maso, F. (2004) Biological markers for the follow-up of athletes throughout the training season. *Pathologie-Biologie*, 52 (1), 43–49.

Phillips, K.A. and Diaz, S.F. (1997) Gender differences in body dysmorphic disorder. *Journal of Nervous and Mental Disease*, 185 (9), 570–577.

Pope, H.G., Phillips, K.A. and Olivardia, R. (2000) *The Adonis Complex: The Secret Crisis of Male Body Obsession*. New York: Free Press.

Scully, D., Kremer, J., Meade, M.M., Graham, R. and Dudgeon, K. (1998) Physical exercise and psychological well-being: A critical review. *British Journal of Sports Medicine*, 32, 111–120.

Tod, D. and Lavallee, D. (2010) Towards a conceptual understanding of muscle dysmorphia development and sustainment. *International Review of Sport Psychology*, 3 (2), 111–131.

7.37: Injury and Retirement

Definition: Those occasions where an athlete is either compelled to give up sport through physical injury on a permanent and temporary basis, or chooses to disengage from sport through voluntary retirement.

Recent years have seen a rapid acceleration in the globalised marketing of sport. It was reported that David Beckham's departure from Real Madrid cost the Spanish soccer giants between £24 and £30 million in shirt and ticket sales alone. Increasingly, it would appear that sports stars are now brands, but when one considers the apparent increase in the incidence of serious injury in elite level sport (Orchard and Seward, 2002), it becomes obvious just how fragile and transitory these brands actually can be. It is a truism that any athlete is one misstep away from a career-threatening injury. How then do athletes cope with the spectre of injury? What can psychologists do to overcome the difficulties associated with it? In light of these questions it is important to consider the psychological effects of failing to return from injury, that is, those injuries that ultimately lead to athlete retirement.

The first issue to be addressed is the psychological effects of experiencing an injury. Initially, this area was influenced by one of the seminal psychological theories, Kubler-Ross's Stage Theory of Grief (1969). This model describes the five stages associated with the grieving process. In particular, Kubler-Ross examined responses to the diagnosis of terminal illness. The five proposed stages of grief are: denial, anger, bargaining, depression and acceptance. This theory was widely applied throughout the 1980s and 1990s as a means to understand the psychological effects of injury as a response to a traumatic loss of functioning. However, empirical evidence has cast doubt on the notion of a universal and sequential psychological response to injury. Indeed, some have questioned the presence of denial and bargaining in typical athlete responses to injury. It certainly would appear quite a leap to uniformly apply a theory associated with terminal illness to every possible injury an athlete may experience, no matter the severity. Cognitive Appraisal Models provide a mechanism for considering the role of injury severity; they outline the process by which an individual assesses their ability to cope with a situation, in this instance, injury. The first step, Primary Appraisal, involves the individual coming to an understanding of the possible implications of the situation they find themselves in. It is reasonable at this point to suggest that an athlete experiencing a groin strain will experience different emotions from one with a serious knee ligament injury. What follows, Secondary Appraisal, is the process by which the individual assesses the viability of the coping strategies available to them. The net result of these appraisals will inform how the individual feels about the situation and, ultimately, the behaviours they will exhibit. Wiese-Bjornstal et al. (1998) have outlined a sport-specific model that seeks to accommodate elements of the Grief Stages and Cognitive Appraisal Models. In their Integrated Stress Process Model they suggest that while cognitive appraisal may influence emotional response, which in turn may influence behaviour, these relationships are better characterised as bi-directional and circular, for example, behaviour may influence cognition just as much as cognitions may influence behaviour. The role of grief in this model is related to the loss of identity that may accompany a negative appraisal, leading to the emotions associated with grief. Additional to this, the suggestion is also made that personal and situational factors must be taken into account when understanding cognitive appraisals. This model has helped facilitate research into the responses associated with injury (e.g. Walker et al., 2007). In their comprehensive review of the literature, Wiese-Bjornstal et al. (1998) cite numerous studies pointing to emotional responses including tension, anger, depression, frustration and boredom. They also point to the importance of behavioural responses, including adherence to rehabilitation programmes and their subsequent impact on recovery. However, as Walker et al. (2007) report, exact processes still remain unclear, for example, outlining which emotions lead to which behaviours. In truth this is unsurprising when the myriad of factors that may influence an athlete's reaction to injury are taken into account.

The undoubted strength of the models proposed thus far lies in the structure they provide for practitioners assessing and treating athletes experiencing injury. In a similar vein, Anderson's (2001) biopsychosocial model provides a comprehensive framework within which five sets of factors are seen to affect 'intermediate biological outcomes', which in turn impact on rehabilitation outcomes. The five categories are: Injury Type; Socio-demographic Factors (including age); Biological Factors (including sleep, tissue repair etc); Psychological Factors (including affect and behaviour); and Social Factors (including social support and rehabilitation support). The relationships between these factors are complex and interactive, that is, no factor stands alone, each affects the other and the net result of these interactions will affect rehabilitation outcomes. The strength of this model for practitioners is that it provides a comprehensive framework for assessing various life domains, their relationships and, ultimately, particular responses to injury by the athlete that may require specific types of tailored intervention.

This leads naturally to the question 'What actually can be done to help athletes experiencing injury?' The answer very much depends on which factors are of primary concern. In terms of managing the social factors associated with injury, Podlog and Eklund (2007) highlight the danger of athletes losing the sense of relatedness or identity they may have previously derived from their sport. This may come in terms of isolation from others involved in their sport, a perceived lack of attention from managers, and feelings of isolation associated with missing familiar routines. The implications of these findings are clear. Coaches, physiotherapists and psychologists are well placed to provide the injured athlete with social support. Additionally, it has been suggested that isolation may lead to a premature return, which may ultimately lead to re-injury. In such cases, social support as well as appropriate goal-setting and realistic expectations appear important.

These findings relate to another important area of injury management as highlighted by Podlog and Eklund (2007): the pressure to return from injury. It is the case that athletes may not always feel psychologically prepared to return from injury at the time of their physical recovery. However, it is reported that often athletes experience feelings of pressure leading to premature return. One reason that an athlete may succumb to the temptation to return early from injury is that they have invested heavily in their athletic identity, to the point they view a prompt return from injury as a duty. Podlog and Eklund document numerous counterproductive outcomes from a premature return from injury, including poor motivation, tentative play, lowered confidence and re-injury. Again, powerful implications for intervention may be drawn. Structured goal-setting programmes (see **3.12**), incorporating techniques such as successive approximation, should assist the athlete in gradually building confidence while, at the same time, ensuring that the return to sport is not rushed (Cox, 2002). A common theme in much of the intervention literature highlights the danger of athletes developing negative cognitions associated with their injuries, particularly in terms of a fear of re-injury or a loss of confidence. Again, there are interventions available to practitioners dealing with such difficulties. These include systematic desensitisation and the use of visualisation techniques. Such approaches would appear to sit well within cognitive behavioural therapy approaches to managing negative cognitions, an area of potential future research. A further suggestion to be made is that the accumulation of this knowledge should lead to a more preventative approach as to how the injury process is managed. Coach and athlete education regarding the common pitfalls associated with injury will hopefully lead to proactive injury management strategies designed to ensure that negative outcomes are avoided. One major shortcoming of the literature as it stands is the relative reliance on anecdotal and case-study evidence. The development of large-scale empirical studies is a challenge that still faces the field.

Recent years have seen an increasing focus on the management of the return to competition. It would appear that there is much overlap between successful management of the rehabilitation process and the psychological readiness to return to competition. However, there are specific concerns that should be addressed post-rehabilitation. Taylor and Taylor (1997) suggest a stage-based approach to understanding return to competition. The five stages they suggest are: initial return; recovery confirmation; return of physical and technical abilities; high intensity training; and the return to competition. Although this model does provide a structure for the athlete returning from injury, as well as a vehicle for exploring fears surrounding the return, it is perhaps too linear to take account of individual differences. Instead, Podlog and Eklund (2007) suggest a checklist that could be used to ensure athletes are ready for return. This checklist consists of discussion of prospective return dates, approval from sports medicine, assessment of injury related cognitions, and deciding who will make the final decision that the athlete is ready to return to competition.

While the return to sport may be a difficult transition, it appears that the failure to return can be even more traumatic. It is reported that an involuntary retirement can lead to feelings of depression, as well as anger and anxiety. These difficulties may be further compounded by a lack of preparedness for retirement (Wylleman et al., 2004). This is not to say that all retirements are traumatic – research suggests that around 13–15 per cent are (Alfermann, 1995). However, it is worth noting the particular difficulties that retirement due to injury brings. While early research tended to highlight the negative outcomes that may be associated with retirement, it is now viewed as a transitional process that, if well managed, can be a positive experience (Lavallee et al., 2004). A trend in recent years is for elite-level athletes to relocate in their sport, whether this is through coaching, youth development or work in the media (Torregrosa et al., 2004). One reason for this may be the growth of retirement preparation programmes (see Wylleman et al., 2004 for a review) and the recognition that athletic retirement should not be viewed in isolation, but rather placed in the context of other life domains (Wylleman and Lavallee, 2003). Murphy (1995) highlights the key areas of self-identity, social and emotional support, coping skills and a sense of control as the main concerns facing the retiring athlete. Similar to the injured athlete, a retiring athlete with an overly prevalent athletic identity appears more likely to experience difficulties (Cecic Erpic et al., 2004). Perhaps unsurprisingly, it is also reported that athletes who achieve their career goals are likely to adapt better to retirement (Cecic Erpic et al., 2004). The implications for athletes experiencing a career-ending injury appear clear. They may lack a sense of control, they may not have achieved their career goals, they have not made a voluntary decision and may be totally unprepared for a life beyond sport. When one also considers the previously discussed difficulties that may be associated with the initial injury, it becomes apparent that this set of circumstances brings challenges to the athlete. In these circumstances, there is likely to be a need for psychological intervention, for example through cognitive restructuring, or for the sport itself to take responsibility for long-term career planning of its retired athletes (Lavallee et al., 2004).

While elite-level sport may be increasingly viewed as big business, the potentially negative reactions to injury and retirement suggest that sport continues to be extremely meaningful for those engaged in it. Inappropriately managed injuries and retirements may bring negative psychological effects. However, much progress has been made in understanding these difficulties, and in highlighting the positive management steps that can be taken to assist athletes through these challenging transitions.

REFERENCES

Alfermann, D. (1995) Career transitions of elite athletes: Drop-out and retirement. In Vanfraechem-Raway, R. and Vanden Auweele, Y. (eds) *Proceedings of the Ninth European Congress of Sport Psychology*. Brussels: European Federation of Sports Psychology FEPSAC. pp. 828–833.

Anderson, M.B. (2001) Returning to action and the prevention of future injury. In Crossman, J. (ed.) *Coping with Sports Injuries: Psychological Strategies for Rehabilitation*. Oxford: Oxford University Press. pp. 162–173.

Cecic Erpic, S., Wylleman, P. and Zupancic, M. (2004) The effect of athletic and non-athletic factors on the sports career termination process. *Psychology of Sport and Exercise*, 5, 45–59.

Cox, R. (2002) The psychological rehabilitation of a severely injured rugby player. In Cockerill, I. (ed.) *Solutions in Sport Psychology*. London: Thomson. pp. 159–172.

Kubler-Ross, E. (1969) *On Death & Dying*, London: Tavistock.

Lavallee, D., Kremer, J., Moran, A.P. and Williams, M. (2004) *Sport Psychology: Contemporary Themes*. London: Palgrave Macmillan. pp. 209–232.

Murphy, S.M. (ed.) (1995) *Sport Psychology Interventions*. Champaign, IL: Human Kinetics.

Orchard, J. and Seward, H. (2002) Epidemiology of injuries in the Australian Football League, seasons 1997–2000. *British Journal of Sports Medicine*, 36, 39–44.

Podlog, L. and Eklund, R.C. (2007) The psychosocial aspects of a return to sport following serious injury: A review of the literature from a self-determination perspective. *Psychology of Sport and Exercise*, 8, 535–566.

Taylor, J. and Taylor, S. (1997) *Psychological Approaches to Sports Injury Rehabilitation*. Gaithenburg, MD: Aspen Publications.

Torregrosa, M., Boixados, M., Valiente, L. and Cruz, J. (2004) Elite athletes' image of retirement: The way to relocation in sport. *Psychology of Sport and Exercise*, 5, 35–43.

Walker, N., Thatcher, J. and Lavallee, D. (2007) Psychological responses to injury in competitive sport: a critical review, *Royal Society for the Promotion of Health*, 127 (4), 174–180.

Wiese-Bjornstal, D.M., Smith, A.M., Shaffer, S.M. and Morrey, M.A. (1998) An integrated model of response to sport injury: Psychological and sociological dynamics. *Journal of Applied Sport Psychology*, 10, 46–69.

Wylleman, P. and Lavallee, D. (2003) A developmental perspective on transitions faced by athletes. In Weiss, M. (ed.) *Developmental Sport Psychology*. Morgantown, WV: Fitness Information Technology. pp. 503–524.

Wylleman, P., Alfermann, D. and Lavallee, D. (2004) Career transitions in sport: European perspectives. *Psychology of Sport and Exercise*, 5, 7–20.

Index

key concepts in sport psychology

index

key concepts in
sport psychology

index

key concepts in
sport psychology